DEFENDING
YOUR FAITH

JOHN ANKERBERG
& DILLON BURROUGHS

Advancing the Ministries of the Gospel

AMG Publishers

God's Word to you is our highest calling.

Following God
DEFENDING YOUR FAITH

© 2007 by John Ankerberg and Dillon Burroughs

Published by AMG Publishers. All Rights Reserved.

First Printing, October 2007

ISBN 10: 0-89957-245-6
ISBN 13: 978-0-89957-245-1

Editing by Rick Steele
Layout by Rick Steele
Cover design by ImageWright Marketing and Design, Chattanooga, Tennessee

Printed in Canada
11 10 09 08 07 06 –T– 6 5 4 3 2 1

DEFENDING
YOUR FAITH

This book is dedicated to:

Those who want to equip themselves with God's truth and stand up for Jesus Christ

Acknowledgments

This work would not be possible without the countless individuals who have prayed for and financially supported the Ankerberg Theological Research Institute throughout the years. We appreciate your investment to this resource and the lives it changes. We also thank the many scholars who have shared their knowledge over the years on *The John Ankerberg Show,* especially Dr. Norman Geisler, Dr. Gary Habermas, Dr. Darrell Bock, and Dr. John Weldon. Thanks to our friends at AMG, especially Dan Penwell, Dale Anderson, and Rick Steele.

From John:
A special thanks to the staff members of *The John Ankerberg Show* and the Ankerberg Theological Research Institute, especially to my wife Darlene and daughter Michelle Ankerberg, as well as Alan Weathers, Jack Borders, Beth Lamberson, Marlene Alley, Ben Bronsink, Steve Humble, Ruth Wilson, and Esther Wilson.

From Dillon:
A special thanks to my wife Deborah and my children, Benjamin and Natalie. Also, my eternal gratitude goes out to my prayer supporters, especially Dorothy Martin. A special note of appreciation also goes to Tim Brock and my friends at White River Christian Church in Noblesville, Indiana, who provided great encouragement during the time of writing this resource.

Most of all, we give thanks to our Lord Jesus Christ, who continues to teach and lead us in what it means to follow Him with a whole heart.

JOHN ANKERBERG & DILLON BURROUGHS

About the Authors

Dr. John Ankerberg is host of the award-winning international apologetics TV and radio program *The John Ankerberg Show*. He holds three earned degrees: a Master of Arts in Church History and the Philosophy of Christian Thought, a Master of Divinity from Trinity International University, and a Doctor of Ministry from Luther Rice Seminary. Founder and president of the Ankerberg Theological Research Institute, John has authored more than 60 books, including the bestselling **Facts On** apologetics series with over 1.5 million copies in print.

Dillon Burroughs, serves at the Ankerberg Theological Research Institute, where he writes for the international TV and radio program *The John Ankerberg Show*. He is the author and coauthor of numerous books, including *What's the Big Deal About Jesus?* and is an adjunct professor at Tennessee Temple University. Dillon is a graduate of Dallas Theological Seminary and lives in Tennessee with his wife, Deborah, and two children.

More information about the authors can be found at the following web address:

http://www.ankerberg.com

About the Following God Series

Three authors and fellow ministers, Wayne Barber, Eddie Rasnake, and Rick Shepherd, teamed up in 1998 to write a character-based Bible study for AMG Publishers. Their collaboration developed into the title, *Life Principles from the Old Testament.* Since 1998 these same authors and AMG Publishers have produced six more **character-based** studies—each consisting of twelve lessons geared around a five-day study of a particular Bible personality. In 2001, AMG Publishers launched a series of topical studies called the **Following God™ Discipleship Series**. This release of *Defending Your Faith* becomes the sixth title released in the Following God™ **Christian Living Series,** which is also topical in nature. Though new studies and authors are being introduced, the interactive study format that readers have come to love remains constant with each new Following God™ release. As new titles and categories are being planned, our focus remains the same: to provide excellent Bible study materials that point people to God's Word in ways that allow them to apply truths to their own lives. More information on this groundbreaking series can be found on the following web page:

www.amgpublishers.com

Preface

"In your hearts set apart Christ as Lord. Always be prepared to give an answer to everyone who asks you to give the reason for the hope that you have. But do this with gentleness and respect, keeping a clear conscience, so that those who speak maliciously against your good behavior in Christ may be ashamed of their slander." (1 Peter 3:15–16)

Peter wrote to believers long ago that we are to be prepared to answer those with questions regarding our faith. Yet many of us find ourselves without a response when issues emerge in our conversations on a daily basis. For instance, what would you say to someone who asked...

How do we know Jesus rose from the dead?

Don't the Bible and science conflict?

What happens after we die?

Don't all religions lead to heaven?

How could a loving God allow evil?

Often, we are at a loss on how to handle the questions people offer regarding Christianity. *Following God—Defending Your Faith* is designed to assist you in both knowing and communicating what the Bible teaches regarding some of the major issues in our culture today.

In the Book of Jude, Jude originally began to write a letter about their common faith. However, because of outside influences on the early church, he wrote, *"I felt I had to write and urge you to contend for the faith that was once for all entrusted to the saints"* (Jude 3). This is our hope for you. While these pages provide the tools you will need to discuss Christian issues with others, we also desire to help you contend for the faith and stand up for Jesus Christ in a world that often opposes His message.

Now more than ever we read about conspiracies against Jesus, the Bible, and the message of Christianity. How should we respond? We need to equip ourselves with God's truth. We hope these lessons will help you to do just that—to defend your faith.

Following Him,

Dr. John Ankerberg

Dillon Burroughs

Table of Contents

How Do We Know
the Bible Is God's Word? 1

Is the Bible We Have
Now What They Had Then? 17

How Do We Know
God Exists? 33

How Do We Know
Jesus Is God? 45

How Is Christianity Different
from Other Religions? 57

What Does the Bible Say
about Evolution and Creation? 69

What Evidence Exists
for the Resurrection? 91

How Can God Allow
Suffering and Evil? 109

What Happens after We Die? 127

Does the Bible Accurately
Predict Future Events? 145

Do Miracles Really
Happen Today? 163

How Can We Share
the Truth with Others 179

Appendix 199

How Do We Know the Bible Is God's Word?

Our answer to this question will not only determine how we view the Bible, but will also ultimately have an eternal impact on our lives. If the Bible is really God's Word, then we should honor, study, apply, and trust it. If the Bible is the Word of God, then to dismiss it is to dismiss the God who authored it.

The fact that God gave us the Bible is an evidence and illustration of His love for us. The term "revelation" simply means that God communicated to humanity what He is like and how we can have a right relationship with Him. These are things that we could not have known had not God divinely revealed them to us in the Bible. God's revelation of Himself in the Bible was progressively shared over a period of approximately fifteen hundred years. It has always contained everything people have needed to know about God in order to have a right relationship with Him. If the Bible is truly the Word of God, then it is the final authority for all matters of faith and spiritual practice.

The question we must ask ourselves is how can we know that the Bible is the Word of God and not just a good book? What is unique about the Bible that sets it apart from all other religious books? These are the types of questions that must be looked at if we are to seriously examine the claim that the Bible is the very

The fact that God gave us the Bible is an evidence and illustration of His love for us.

Word of God, divinely inspired, and completely sufficient for all matters of faith and practice.

Quick Facts about the Bible

	CHAPTERS	VERSES	WORDS
Old Testament	929	23,138	602,582
New Testament	260	7,957	169,751

*These statistics based on the King James Version of the Bible[1]

LESSON ONE

DAY ONE

Did You Know?

CHAPTER/VERSE

Chapter divisions were not added to the Bible until the 1200s. The verse divisions we use today were added for the New Testament in 1551 and for the Old Testament in 1661.

THE BIBLE IS INSPIRED BY GOD

First, there can be no doubt that the Bible itself claims to be the very Word of God. It must claim this before we can consider it. This claim is clearly seen in verses like 2 Timothy 3:15–17, which say,

"From infancy you have known the holy Scriptures, which are able to make you wise for salvation through faith in Christ Jesus. <u>All Scripture is God-breathed</u> and is useful for teaching, rebuking, correcting and training in righteousness, so that the man of God may be thoroughly equipped for every good work." (emphasis added)

In 2 Timothy 3:15–17, we find several aspects regarding all Scripture. What four specific uses are given?

1. _____
2. _____
3. _____
4. _____

Scripture is also called "God-breathed," translated from a unique word in the Greek New Testament—literally meaning that the words are of God and therefore an extension of God Himself. The result of learning God's Word is so we can be properly trained for the lifestyle and actions for which God has designed for us in Christ.

Some implications of this translation of 2 Timothy 3:16 can be drawn:

1) Inspiration deals with the objective text of Scripture, not the subjective intention of the writer.

2) The doctrine of Scripture applies to *all* or *every* Scripture, that is, the Bible in part or in whole is the Word of God.

The Scriptures *are* the very breathed-out Word of God. The *form and content* of Scripture are the very words of God. This does not mean that each individual word is inspired *as such* but only *as part of a whole* sentence or unit of meaning. There is no implication in Scripture of an *atomistic* inspiration of each word but only of a *holistic* inspiration of all words used. Just as an individual word has no meaning apart from its use in a given context, so individual words of Scripture are not inspired apart from their use in a whole sentence.[2]

📖 Psalm 19:7–14 also provides several characteristics of God's Word. Look at these verses together and describe some of the results Scripture says will bring about in our lives if we listen and follow it.

_____

_____

_____

God makes it very clear in the Bible that He uses both human and divine means to communicate His revealed truth. In 2 Peter 1:20–21, we find that the prophets wrote as the Holy Spirit enabled them. Further, we are told that the meaning of the words were not from the writer but rather from the ultimate author, God.

📖 Look at 2 Peter 1:20–21 and describe in your own words the process God used to communicate His revelation.

_____

_____

_____

_____

What biblical process did God use to communicate His Word to us? First, God spoke to the prophets according to these verses. This was done in many and various ways (Hebrews 1:1). These various ways included:

Did You Know?
PSALM 119

Psalm 119, the longest chapter in the Bible with 176 verses, focuses primarily on the issue of the truth of God's Word? It is structured as an alphabetic acrostic in which each stanza of eight verses is devoted to successive letters of the Hebrew alphabet, each verse of a particular stanza beginning with the same letter.

Ways God Spoke to the Prophets in the Old Testament

METHODS	SCRIPTURE PASSAGES
By angels	Genesis 18–19
In dreams	Daniel 7:1ff; Numbers 12:6
In visions	Isaiah 1:1; Ezekiel 1:1; 8:3; 11:24; Hosea 12:10
Through nature	Psalm 19:1
An audible voice	1 Samuel 3:4
Inner voice	Many times, using the formula of *"And the word of the Lord came to me."*
By *urim* and *thummim*	Exodus 28:30; Numbers 27:21
Casting lots	Proverbs 16:33
Through other prophetic writings	Daniel 9:1–2

God did not only speak in various ways; He spoke in their words. To put it another way, the prophets' messages were God's messages (Jeremiah 1:9).

Our ultimate authority regarding whether the Bible is inspired Scripture or not comes directly from the teachings of Jesus. In Matthew 5:17, He notes that He came not to end the Law but rather to fulfill it. In the very next verse, He teaches that even the smallest letter of the Law would not pass until all is accomplished. Later, in John 10:35, Jesus stated that the Scripture cannot be broken, which means Jesus testified to the complete authority and reliability of Scripture.

Jesus often directly compared Old Testament events with important spiritual truths. He related His death and resurrection to Jonah and the great fish (Matthew 12:40), his second coming to Noah and the flood (Matthew 24:37–39). Both the occasion and the manner of comparison make it clear that Jesus was affirming the historicity of those Old Testament events. Jesus asserted to Nicodemus, *"If I told you earthly things and you do not believe, how shall you believe if I tell you heavenly things?"* (John 3:12). If the Bible does not speak truthfully about the physical world, it cannot be trusted when it speaks about the spiritual world. The two are intimately related.

📖 Looking at Matthew 5:17–19 and John 10:35, why should we give total commitment to the Bible rather than mere external acknowledgment and obedience?

_____

_____

_____

_____

In addition to the Matthew and John passages, we observe other occurrences in the Bible where God directly commands others to write down His words. For example, in Exodus 17:4, Moses is instructed to have God's words recorded in writing. Similar statements are recorded in the prophets, including Jeremiah 30:2 and Isaiah 30:8.

In terms of practical application, we realize that: **a)** God's Word is true; **b)** the words in the Bible are God's truth; **c)** learning this truth is vital to our spiritual maturity; and **d)** the Bible's teachings provide our ultimate basis for living a life that honors God. The person who observes and practices the truth of God found in the Bible will be the blessed man or woman He desires (Psalm 1).

APPLY How does our view of the Bible influence our attitude toward reading it? What are some of your desires in studying God's Word? What is something you can do to begin today?

_____

_____

_____

_____

_____

_____

WHO WROTE THE BIBLE?

Is the Bible really the Word of God or nothing more than another collection of human words? If it is the Word of God, how do we know that this information came from God? Some people say certain parts of the Bible came from God, but then add that there are also a lot of errors in it. In an interview with Dr. Norman Geisler, founder of Southern Evangelical Seminary and author of over fifty books, I (John) asked him to answer the question, "Does it matter whether or not there are errors in the Bible?"

He responded by saying, "Is it dangerous to live downstream from a cracked dam? Ask the people in Toccoa Falls, Georgia. There's a little college nestled in the valley there near beautiful waterfalls. Years ago, an earthen dam existed behind the falls overlooking the campus. Over a period of time, a crack began to form in this dam. The Army Corp of Engineers assured people repeatedly that the dam was safe and that the crack was nothing to worry about. One night in 1977, the dam burst and the waters swept down the valley. Dozens of people were killed. The students and citizens of this quaint little college community have learned that it's dangerous to live downstream from a cracked dam."

You might be thinking, *"What's this 'cracked dam' illustration have to do with biblical inerrancy?"* Well, there are people telling us there are errors in the Bible, just little, insignificant ones, just like the crack in the dam. Little errors don't seem like a big deal, but even if there are small errors, our dependence upon God's Word comes crashing down. The issue is whether this allegation is accurate. Are there errors in the Bible or is the Bible the inerrant Word of God?

Psalm 11:3 says, *"If the foundation be destroyed, what shall the righteous do?"* The Bible claims to be the Word of God, and the Bible proves to be the Word of God.

📖 In Psalm 19:7–10, we find David praising God for His perfect word. What do David's words say about the possibility of errors in the Bible?

_____

_____

_____

_____

_____

_____

Another way we know the Bible is God's Word is by how the Bible uses statements regarding what God said and what Scripture says. The chart on the next page discussed by Dr. Geisler in our interview reveals that Scripture is clearly God's Word:

Did You Know?

BIBLICAL HARMONY

Thirty-two percent of the New Testament's verses include quotes or allusions from the Old Testament.

What the Bible Says...God Says (and Vice Versa)

God Says	Scripture Says
Genesis 12:3	Galatians 3:8
Exodus 9:6	Romans 9:17

Scripture Says	God Says
Genesis 2:24	Matthew 19:4–5
Psalms 95:7	Hebrews 3:7
Psalms 2:1	Acts 4:24–25
Isaiah 55:3	Acts 13:34
Psalms 16:10	Acts 13:35
Psalms 2:7	Hebrews 1:5
Psalms 97:7	Hebrews 1:6
Psalms 104:4	Hebrews 1:7

Word Study
SWORD OF THE SPIRIT

The Word of God is called a sword more than once in the New Testament. In addition to Hebrews 4:12, we find the Word of God called the sword of the Spirit (Ephesians 6:17). In Revelation, the words from the mouth of Christ are also referred to as a sword (1:16; 2:12, 16; 19:15, 21). In total, God's Word or the words of Jesus are referred to as a sword seven times in the New Testament.

Comparing some of the verses above, write in your own words how the Scriptures support the view that the Bible is God's Word.

_____

_____

_____

_____

But what about the New Testament? Is it the inspired Word of God? Many of the verses we just quoted refer to the Old Testament because the New Testament wasn't written when Jesus was speaking. In 2 Peter 3:16, Peter places Paul's letters on the same level of authority as the inspired writings of the Old Testament. Paul quotes a verse found in Luke as Scripture (see 1 Timothy 5:18).

The Word of God is inspired. The New Testament is also the Word of God. Hebrews 4:12 mentions that the Word of God is *alive and powerful.* Therefore, the New Testament is inspired as well. It's not just the Old Testament that claims to be the truth of God, but every book in the New Testament claims to come from an apostle of God or those who were companions of the apostles (like Mark and Luke). Jesus revealed God's truth (the incarnation, John 1:1–4), but also presented truth verbally as the Word referred to here in Hebrews. So the entire Bible, Old and New Testaments, can be trusted to be the Word of God.

Read Hebrews 4:12. What five characteristics are described about God's Word? How do they relate to you personally?

1. _____

2. _____

3. _____

4. _____

5. _____

Ephesians 6:10–20 describes the armor of God. The one offensive weapon it mentions in its list is the Word of God, which it calls the sword of the Spirit (verse 17).

In what ways can the Bible be used to prepare for upcoming spiritual battles rather than being used merely for defense against existing problems? In the following space, write a prayer to God asking for His guidance and assistance in using His sword of the Spirit to fight the spiritual battles in your life.

_____

_____

_____

_____

_____

WHERE DID WE GET THE BIBLE?

The Bible is certainly unique among all the ancient books of the world. Forty authors were involved in writing this masterpiece over a period of fifteen hundred years. One could expect errors and inaccuracies with any other book credited to so many authors and so much time involved in writing. However, God's supernatural intervention produced a book without error and a collection of writings in agreement in its essentials. Only God in His infinite wisdom and divine providence could produce such a flawless work.

Let's talk about the New Testament for a moment. How were the 27 New Testament books made available to us? Everything starts with Jesus. Most scholars hold that Jesus taught and ministered from the late 20s to the early 30s AD. He chose twelve apostles, eleven who lived and spread His message, following Him for a three-year period. The New Testament books were based on a connection with the apostles and the teachings of Jesus.

The 27 books have nine basic sources:

❏ Two apostles, **Matthew** and **John,** wrote gospels. John also wrote three letters and Revelation. **Peter** authored two letters and was the source for **Mark's gospel.** Peter also recognized **Paul's writings** as Scripture (see 2 Peter 3:16).

❏ **Luke** based his gospel on the eyewitness testimony of the apostles. He was also a traveling companion of the apostle Paul. Paul later quotes Luke's gospel as Scripture in 1 Timothy 5:18.

❏ **James and Jude** were human brothers (step-brothers) of Jesus. James did not recognize Christ as Messiah until Jesus appeared to him after the resurrection. James later became bishop of the Jerusalem Church and wrote the New Testament book bearing his name. Jude believed after the resurrection as well, writing the book that bears his name.

❏ The **author of Hebrews** was well known to his recipients but not to everyone in the church. This delayed its acceptance to some. The apostle Paul has often been suggested as the author. Others claim the author

"Voltaire expected that within fifty years of his lifetime there would not be one Bible in the world. His house is now a distribution center for Bibles in many languages."

—Corrie Ten Boom

was Barnabas, a fellow missionary with Paul. Still others suggest Apollos wrote it during his early years with Paul in Corinth. Regardless, this author was or had direct contact with an apostle.

Nine individuals wrote the 27 books received by the churches and recognized as Scripture. All were written and received before AD 95. Within approximately one generation of the New Testament's completion, every book had been cited by a church father. It was in AD 367 that Athanasius wrote an authoritative list of these 27 books.

📖 Look at 1 John 1:1–4. Why is it important that eyewitnesses or those who had personal contact with eyewitnesses wrote the New Testament books?

_____

_____

_____

_____

Where does Luke say he got the information about Jesus that he used in his book according to Luke 1:1–4?

_____

Sir Frederick Kenyon, formerly director and principle librarian of the British Museum, once wrote concerning the Bible:

> In no other case is the interval of time between the composition of the book and the date of the earliest extant [existing] manuscripts so short as in that of the New Testament. The interval, then, between the dates of original composition and the earliest extant evidence [existing copies] become so small as to be in fact negligible, and the last foundation for any doubt that the Scriptures have come down to us substantially as they were written, has now been removed. Both the authenticity and the general integrity of the books of the New Testament may be regarded as finally established.[3]

How do we know that the books of the Bible we have today are accurate copies of what the New Testament authors actually wrote? When researching the New Testament, we find that the number of the earliest manuscripts far exceed any other work in history. The earliest fragments of the Gospel of John range from within one generation of the Apostle John's life (approximately AD 125). If John wrote it in AD 95, then the first copies that still exist were produced thirty years from the time of the original.

In total, over 5,300 Greek copies of the texts (the original New Testament language), 10,000 Latin texts, and 9,300 other versions exist from the early church era. In comparison, of sixteen well-known classical Greek authors, the typical number of early copies that still exist is *less than ten*, with the earliest copies dating from 750 to 1,600 years *after* the originals were written. This means if you reject the accuracy of the New Testament, you would first have to reject all of the writings in ancient history. The copies of the New Testament came down to us earlier and with more copies to compare.

Outside of the New Testament, several additional early writings connect with the events of historic Christianity. The second generation of Christianity includes eight clear sources supporting its authority. New Testament Greek scholar Dr. Kurt Aland comments that the New Testament, "…was not imposed from the top, be it by bishops or synods, and then accepted by the communities. . . . The organized church did not create the canon [New Testament]; it recognized the canon that had been created."[4]

📖 Read John 20:30–31. What does the apostle John say was the purpose of writing his Gospel?

_____

_____

But just how were the New Testament books selected? The basic historical rules that guided recognition of the canon are as follows, listed in question format:

1. Was the book written or supported by a prophet or apostle of God? This was the single most important factor. The reasoning here is that the Word of God which is inspired by the Spirit of God for the people of God must be communicated through a person of God. If an apostle cast out demons, healed the sick, and raised the dead, you would quickly recognize that you should listen to this person.

2. Is the book authoritative? In other words, can it be said of the book as it was said of Jesus, *"The people were amazed at his teaching, because he taught them as one who had authority, not as the teachers of the law"* (Mark 1:22). Put another way, does this book ring with the sense of, "The Lord says…"?

3. Does the book tell the truth about God consistent with previous revelation? The Bereans were considered more noble because they searched the Old Testament Scriptures to determine whether Paul's teaching was true (Acts 17:11). They knew that if Paul's teaching did not resonate with the Old Testament writings, it could not be of God. Agreement with all earlier revelation was essential (Galatians 1:8).

4. Does the book give evidence of having the power of God? Any writing that does not exhibit the transforming power of God in the lives of its readers could not have come from God. Scripture says that the Word of God is "living and active" (Hebrews 4:12). If the book in question did not have the power to change a life, then the book could not have come from God.

5. Was the book accepted by the people of God? In Old Testament times, Moses' scrolls were immediately placed into the Ark of the Covenant (Deuteronomy 31:24–26), as were Joshua's (Joshua 24:26). In the New Testament, Paul thanked the Thessalonians for receiving his message as the Word of God (1 Thessalonians 2:13). Paul's letters were also circulated among the churches (Colossians 4:16; 1 Thessalonians 5:27). It was common that the majority of God's people would initially accept God's Word.

In the above list of questions, which do you find the most important in understanding the Bible to be God's Word? If you were to explain to a skeptic why the Bible truly came from God, how would you go about it? Use the space below to write some of your ideas:

_____

_____

_____

"The Bible is not an end in itself, but a means to bring men to an intimate and satisfying knowledge of God, that they may enter into Him, that they may delight in His Presence, may taste and know the inner sweetness of the very God Himself in the core and center of their hearts."

—A. W. Tozer

_____

_____

_____

But what about the development of the Old Testament? Dr. Geisler presents the case about the facts of the Old Testament this way:

> Jesus taught definitely that God was the originator of the Hebrew Old Testament. He taught as authoritative or authentic most of the books of the Hebrew canon. . . . he asserted that the Old Testament as a whole was unbreakable scripture (John 10:35); that it would never perish (Matthew 5:18); and that it must be fulfilled (Luke 24:44). . . . Jesus not only defined the limits . . . but he laid down principle of canonicity.[5]

📖 Read Luke 24:44. How did Jesus define which books in the Old Testament were to be considered Scripture?

_____

_____

_____

Jesus categorized the books of the Old Testament in this verse, referring to the Law, the Prophets, and the Writings. These represented the three major classifications of the Hebrew Old Testament.

How do we know the Bible is God's Word? Because Jesus told us. He is the One who claimed to be God and proved His claim by rising from the dead. It is on His authority as God of the universe that we are sure the Bible is the Word of God. Jesus confirmed the Old Testament's authority, as well as an authoritative New Testament through His disciples. Jesus affirmed to the Old Testament to be the Word of God and promised to guide His disciples to know all truth. Jesus claimed for the Bible:

Divine authority	(Matthew 3:3, 7, 10)
Indestructibility	(Matthew 5:17–18)
Infallibility	(John 10:35)
Ultimate supremacy	(Matthew 15:3, 6)
Factual inerrancy	(Matthew 22:29; John 17:17)
Historical reliability	(Matthew 12:40, 24:37–38)
Scientific accuracy	(Matthew 19:4–5; John 3:12)[6]

If Jesus is God's Son, then His authority affirms that the Bible is the Word of God.

APPLY If the Bible is God's Word, how does this impact your life today?

_____

_____

_____

_____

_____

_____

_____

"Bible reading is an education in itself."

—Alfred Lord Tennyson

What verse from today's material could you write out to meditate on throughout the day today? Choose one and focus on it throughout the day:

_____

_____

_____

How Do We Understand the Bible?

A proper understanding of the Bible can be found in two important concepts: illumination and inspiration. Illumination means that to understand God's Word, we must have God's Spirit living within us. Without it, we are limited in our understanding. Paul discusses this issue in 1 Corinthians 2:14.

📖 In 1 Corinthians 2:12–16, what does Paul say is the importance of God's Spirit in understanding spiritual truth?

_____

_____

Further, Jesus also promised us that those who know God will have the capability to understand His Word. Look at John 16:12–15 and discover:

Who is the teacher (verse 13)?

_____

What does the teacher speak (verse 13b)?

_____

What is the purpose of the teaching (verse 14)?

_____

The other aspect is interpretation. While God offers believers an understanding of truth, this does not mean diligent study is unimportant. On the contrary, since God's Word is literally "God-breathed," an extension of Himself, a continuous encounter with Scripture is vital to a healthy spiritual walk.

📖 What do the following passages say to you about studying the Bible?

Psalms 1:2

_____

_____

2 Timothy 2:15

_____

_____

Deuteronomy 6:1–9

_____

_____

Revelation 22:18–19

_____

_____

Acts 17 shows an example of people who studied Scripture in their effort to seek the truth. There, Paul, a well-known teacher, provides teaching to a group of people called the Bereans. In response, they checked the Scriptures before accepting Paul's teaching as true. They were determined to understand for themselves what God had spoken on the subject.

However, the Bereans were far different from the Thessalonians. In Acts 17:1–9, we read that:

> "When they had passed through Amphipolis and Apollonia, they came to Thessalonica, where there was a Jewish synagogue. As his custom was, Paul went into the synagogue, and on three Sabbath days he reasoned with them from the Scriptures, explaining and proving that the Christ had to suffer and rise from the dead. "This Jesus I am proclaiming to you is the Christ," he said. Some of the Jews were persuaded and joined Paul and Silas, as did a large number of God-fearing Greeks and not a few prominent women.

> "But the Jews were jealous; so they rounded up some bad characters from the marketplace, formed a mob and started a riot in the city. They rushed to Jason's house in search of Paul and Silas in order to bring them out to the crowd. But when they did not find them, they dragged Jason and some other brothers before the city officials, shouting: 'These men who have caused trouble all over the world have now come here, and Jason has welcomed them into his house. They are all defying Caesar's decrees, saying that there is another king, one called Jesus.' When they heard this, the crowd and the city officials were thrown into turmoil. Then they made Jason and the others post bond and let them go."

The Thessalonians heard God's truth, yet *rejected* it. The Bereans *investigated* it.

📖 Read Acts 17:10–12 and share what Luke stated about the Bereans:

Their character

_____

_____

Their attitude

_____

_____

Their work ethic

_____

_____

Did You Know?

THE BEREANS

During the time of Paul, Berea was an area that included a significant community of Jewish immigrants. They already believed in God, the Old Testament, and the coming of a future Messiah. Paul's work was to help them understand that Jesus was the Messiah, something that the Bereans were eager to discover. Their desire to check the Scriptures to see if Paul's teaching was accurate is an excellent model we can use both for ourselves and in challenging others to investigate the Christian faith today

Their response:

_____

_____

 Is their attitude true of you? Why is it important to analyze what others teach regarding the Bible, even if they are well-known teachers?

_____

_____

_____

_____

Ultimately, illumination, interpretation, and application must converge together for the best spiritual growth. We accept God's divinely inspired Word, study the Scriptures for wisdom, and live it out in our daily lives. This pattern has marked people of God from the earliest times and continues to mark those who draw near to God today. Our hope is that this will include you as you decide to regularly spend time learning from God's Word.

FOR ME TO FOLLOW GOD

LESSON ONE · DAY FIVE

In Mark 13:31, Jesus tells us, *"Heaven and earth will pass away, but my words will never pass away."* Why will His words never pass away? Because they are of God, and God is eternal. Yet the daily implications of these sacred words are often difficult for us to process today. We find ourselves asking, "How does this apply to me today?"

The Bible was written to reveal God's instructions for life. As we interact and study it, we find power for our daily lives from the God of eternity who assures us He is with us now and of our future with Him in heaven. In some ways, the Bible serves as a lifeline between us and God. Jesus said it best when He responded to temptation with the words, *"Man does not live on bread alone, but on every word that comes from the mouth of God"* (Matthew 4:4).

 As you think about your own life, take a few minutes to evaluate how you are doing at integrating Scripture into your own life.

Regular Reading or Meditation upon Scripture...

1	2	3	4	5
Rarely or never				Daily/Nearly every day

Applying what I learn from the Bible...

←————————————————————————————→

1   2   3   4   5

Rarely or never   Daily/Nearly every day

Sharing God's Word with others...

←————————————————————————————→

1   2   3   4   5

Rarely or never   Daily/Nearly every day

How much time would you think is appropriate for you to spend reading God's Word? Five minutes? Fifteen minutes? God's Word teaches us that if we draw near to Him, He will draw near to us (James 4:8). What are some ways that you could better draw near to God this week?

_____

_____

_____

_____

Often our best intentions fall short in studying God's Word. What are some of the distractions that hinder you from spending time in Scripture?

_____

_____

_____

Bible reading is often better when it is a shared experience.

APPLY Bible study is often better when it is a shared experience. What are some of the ways you could help study and live out the Bible with others to help in your spiritual growth and knowledge of the Scriptures?

_____

_____

_____

_____

We have seen that the Bible has more historical evidence that it came from God than any other book ever written, yet many continue to disregard the evidence. What are some ways you have seen this in your life experiences? How could you help inform others in such situations in the future?

_____

_____

_____

_____

If you could have a conversation with Jesus, what would you ask Him? What do you want to know? In many ways, reading God's Word is like communicating directly with God Himself and allowing Him to speak to you. To close this section, spend some time in prayer with God right now, using the following prayer adapted from Psalms 19:7–14 as a guide:

The law of the LORD is perfect, reviving the soul. The statutes of the LORD are trustworthy, making wise the simple.

The precepts of the LORD are right giving joy to the heart. The commands of the LORD are radiant, giving light to the eyes.

The fear of the LORD is pure, enduring forever. The ordinances of the LORD are sure and altogether righteous.

They are more precious than gold, than much pure gold; they are sweeter than honey, than honey from the comb.

By them is your servant warned; in keeping them there is great reward.

Who can discern his errors? Forgive my hidden faults.

Keep your servant also from willful sins; may they not rule over me. Then will I be blameless, innocent of great transgression.

May the words of my mouth and the meditation of my heart be pleasing in your sight, O LORD, my Rock and my Redeemer.

Take a few moments to write down a prayer of application from what you have learned this week:

_____

_____

_____

_____

_____

_____

_____

_____

_____

Notes

IS THE BIBLE WE HAVE NOW WHAT THEY HAD THEN?

The 27 books of the New Testament include over 5,686 Greek manuscripts in existence from the earliest period. In total, over 24,000 ancient citations exist. If we compare these statistics to the number of copies in existence for other ancient literature, we see that no other work of writing compares in quantity.

On the next page is a chart illustrating the New Testament manuscripts compared to other early writings, such as those authored by Plato and Euripides. We notice that the next closest document in terms of the time between the original writing and its earliest existing copy is Homer's *Iliad*, with 500 years separating the two. When we look at the materials from this perspective, the New Testament stands as the best-documented book in history. As New Testament scholar F. F. Bruce, Rylands Professor of Biblical Criticism and Exegesis at Manchester University states, "There is no body of ancient literature in the world which enjoys such a wealth of good textual attestation as the New Testament."[7]

The New Testament stands as the best documented book in history.

Author[8]	Date Written	Earliest Existing Copy	Approx. Time Span Between Original & Copy	Number of Copies
Lucretius	Died in 55 or 53 BC	"...is perfect"	1100 years	2
Pliny	AD 61–113	AD 850	750 years	7
Plato	427–347 BC	AD 900	1200 years	7
Demosthenes	4th Century BC	AD 1100	800 years	8
Herodotus	480–425 BC	AD 900	1300 years	8
Suetonius	AD 75–160	AD 950	800 years	8
Thucydides	460–400 BC	AD 900	1300 years	8
Euripides	480–406 BC	AD 1100	1300 years	9
Aristophanes	450–385 BC	AD 900	1200 years	10
Caesar	100–44 BC	AD 900	1000 years	10
Livy	59 BC–AD 17	???	????	20
Tacitus	circa AD 100	AD 1100	1000 years	20
Aristotle	384–322 BC	AD 1100	1400 years	49
Sophocles	496–406 BC	AD 1000	1400 years	193
Homer (Iliad)	900 BC	400 BC	500 years	643
New Testament	AD 50–100	ca. AD 130	less than 100 years	5600

CAN THE BIBLE BE WRONG?

Critics claim the Bible is filled with errors. Some even speak of thousands of mistakes. However, Christians through the ages have claimed that the Bible is without error in the original text. Not one error that extends to the original text of the Bible has ever been demonstrated.

The argument for an errorless (inerrant) Bible can be put in this logical form:

God cannot be wrong.

The Bible is the Word of God.

Therefore, the Bible cannot be wrong.

An infinitely perfect, all-knowing God cannot make a mistake. The Scriptures testify to this, declaring emphatically that *"it is impossible for God to lie"* (Hebrews 6:18). Of course, this argument only works for those who accept that there is a God. We will discuss the issue of God's existence in detail in the next chapter.

What do the following verses state about God?

Titus 1:2

_____

_____

2 Timothy 2:13

_____

_____

John 14:6

_____

_____

Psalm 119:160

_____

_____

Jesus said, *"Until heaven and earth disappear, not the smallest letter, not the least stroke of a pen, will by any means disappear from the Law until everything is accomplished"* (Matthew 5:18 NIV). Paul added, *"All Scripture is God-breathed"* (2 Timothy 3:16). Although human authors recorded the messages, *"prophecy never had its origin in the will of man, but men spoke from God as they were carried along by the Holy Spirit"* (2 Peter 1:20–21).

If God cannot be wrong and if the Bible is the Word of God, then the Bible cannot be wrong. God has spoken, and He has not stuttered. The God of truth has given us the Word of truth, and it does not contain any untruth. This is not to say that there are not *difficulties* in reading and understanding the Bible. But God's people can approach difficult texts with confidence, knowing that they do not possess errors.

Did You Know?
MATTHEW 5:18

Matthew 5:18 (NIV) says, *"Until heaven and earth disappear, not the smallest letter, not the least stroke of a pen, will by any means disappear from the Law until everything is accomplished."* The smallest letter in the Hebrew alphabet is yodh, which looks like an apostrophe. A stroke is an extremely small extension on certain Hebrew letters to distinguish similar letters from one another (like P and R in English).

📖 Look at Mark 7:13. What did Jesus call the Scriptures?

_____

Some have suggested that Scripture can always be trusted on for matters of faith and life, but it is not always historically reliable. If true, this would make the Bible ineffective as a divine authority, since the historical and scientific is inextricably interwoven with the spiritual.

A close examination of Scripture reveals that the factual and spiritual truths of Scripture are often inseparable. We cannot separate the spiritual truth of Christ's resurrection from the fact that his body permanently and physically vacated the tomb and walked among people (Matthew 28:6; 1 Corinthians 15:13–19). If Jesus was not born of a biological virgin, then he is no different from the rest of the human race. Likewise, the death of Christ for our sins cannot be detached from the literal shedding of his blood on the cross (Hebrews 9:22). Adam's existence and fall cannot be a myth. If there were no literal Adam and no actual fall, then the spiritual teaching about inherited sin and physical and spiritual death are wrong (Romans 5:12). Historical reality and the theological doctrine stand or fall together.

📖 Jesus often directly compared Old Testament events with important spiritual truths. Note the spiritual connections between the historical and spiritual lessons in the following accounts:

Matthew 12:40:

_____

_____

Matthew 24:37–39

_____

_____

John 3:12:

_____

_____

If the Bible does not speak truthfully about the physical world, it cannot be trusted when it speaks about the spiritual world. The two are intimately related.

Inspiration includes not only all that the Bible explicitly _teaches,_ but everything the Bible _touches._ The Bible is God's Word, and God does not deviate from the truth. All the parts are as true as the whole they comprise.

But what do we mean when we talk about the Bible's inerrancy?

What Inerrancy Does Claim:
Inerrancy proclaims that our Bibles come from an absolutely perfect original text. Inerrancy means that what the Bible teaches is true without a single error in the original manuscripts. Dr. Paul Feinberg defines inerrancy as follows: "Inerrancy means that when all facts are known, the Scriptures in their original autographs and properly interpreted will be shown to be wholly true in everything that they affirm, whether that has to do with doctrine or morality or with the social, physical, or life sciences."[9]

> **Other books were given for our information; the Bible was given for our transformation.**

A more concise definition would be, "What Scripture says, God says—through human agents and without error."[10]

To apply equally to all parts of Scripture, inerrancy must apply equally to all parts of Scripture as it was originally written. A belief in limited inerrancy (some parts are true and others aren't) demands the impossible—that a fallible interpreter becomes an infallible discerner and interpreter of the "Word of God" within the Scriptures. This only opens the door for confusion and uncertainty directed by either subjectivism or personal bias.

To be limited to the proper application of hermeneutics, higher critical interpretive methods first assume errors in the Bible and then have little trouble finding them (from their perspective). However, the proper way to interpret the Bible involves a respect for the text as given until proven otherwise. In other words, due attention is given to claims for biblical authority. Also, interpretation must involve an objective and impartial methodology. If one does not first determine the authority of Scripture and second the correct meaning of a text, one is incapable of saying whether or not it is true or false. Here, we must also understand that inerrancy is related to the intent of Scripture. For example, when the intent of the writer is to record a lie or error by someone (such as a false prophet or the Devil), the fact of a lie or error can hardly deny inerrancy, for inerrancy only affirms that what is recorded is recorded accurately. What the Bible records must be distinguished from what the Bible approves.

What Inerrancy Does Not Claim:

Inerrancy does not claim to be absolutely proven. The doctrine of inerrancy cannot guarantee the final solution to every alleged problem passage. Given the present limited state of human knowledge, no one can logically expect proof when the means of proof are absent. Proof of inerrancy is therefore limited by our present state of knowledge. Nevertheless, such realities in no way deny or disprove inerrancy, especially when the weight of the evidence so strongly supports inerrancy. The fact that so many opportunities exist within the biblical record to disprove inerrancy and yet it remains capable of rational defense after nearly two thousand years is certainly impressive. The fact that historically, alleged errors are routinely proven later to be truths when more knowledge becomes available is equally impressive.

Inerrancy does not refer to manuscript copies or translations, but only to the original manuscripts. Copies and translations may be considered inerrant only to the degree they reproduce the originals. An accurate translation, based upon a 99+ percent original text, virtually reproduces the originals and the remaining 1% is present in the variant readings. We can confidently state without being proven wrong that we have "inerrant originals and virtually inerrant copies."

Inerrancy does not claim absolute precision. Approximations are not errors. To illustrate, no one would argue it was an error to say the following:

❏ I earned $40,000 last year (it was really $40,200).

❏ In 1995 I received my college degree (it was June of 1995).

❏ What a lovely sunset (the earth's rotation appears as the sun setting).

❏ Look! There just ain't no free lunch! (breaking the rules of grammar to emphasize a point).

❏ Steve went to the store (he also stopped by the pool on the way back).

"There is no body of ancient literature in the world which enjoys such a wealth of good textual attestation as the New Testament."

—F. F. Bruce

In the interest of improved communication we often use approximations, or statements that are technically incorrect in grammar, number, science, history, etc. This is also true of the biblical writers: their purpose was to communicate, not to write in technicalities. Inerrancy does not demand that the Bible be written in the technical language or knowledge of modern twenty-first century science, which would certainly keep it a book closed to all but the specialist. Also, precision may become so precise as to be awkward or useless sometimes during communication. To speak of a setting sun is not error in spite of its scientific imprecision.[11]

APPLY How should the inerrancy of God's perfect Word influence how we view the Bible? How we study and apply it in our lives?

_____

_____

_____

_____

_____

_____

LESSON TWO   DAY TWO

WHAT ABOUT SUPPOSED CONFLICTS IN THE BIBLE?

Allegations of error in the Bible are based on errors of the interpreter or interpretation. No informed person would claim to be able to fully explain all Bible difficulties. However, it is a mistake for the skeptic to assume that the explained cannot and will not be explained. When a scientist comes upon an anomaly in nature, he does not give up further scientific exploration. Rather, the unexplained motivates further study. Scientists once could not explain meteors, eclipses, tornadoes, hurricanes, and earthquakes, yet the unexplained only motivated further research into the unknown.

The Bible should be researched with the same presumption that there are answers to the unexplained. Critics once proposed that Moses could not have written the first five books of the Bible, because Moses' culture was preliterate. Now we know that writing had existed thousands of years before Moses.

Critics once believed that Bible references to the Hittite people were fictional because the group had never been discovered. Now that the Hittites' national library has been found in Turkey, the accusations fall flat. Liberal scholars once argued that certain Old Testament books could not have been written before the first century BC The discovery of the Dead Sea Scrolls proved that the prophecies from the Old Testament had existed long earlier than had been claimed. These and many more examples inspire confidence that the biblical difficulties that have not been fully explained are not mistakes in the Bible.

How would you respond to someone who claims the Bible is full of contradictions?

_____

_____

_____

_____

_____

Other critics assume the Bible is guilty until proven innocent. However, like an American citizen charged with a crime, the Bible should be read with at least the same presumption of accuracy given to other literature that claims to be nonfiction. This is the way we approach all human communications. If we did not, life would not be possible. What if we assumed that road signs and traffic signals were not telling the truth? Such an assumption would lead to chaos. If we assumed food packages were mislabeled, we would have to open up all cans and packages before buying.

The Bible, like any other book, should be presumed to be telling us what the authors said, experienced, and heard. Negative critics begin with just the opposite presumption. Little wonder they conclude the Bible is riddled with error.

📖 Read Romans 3:4. What does it mean to say, *"let God be true and every man a liar?"*

_____

_____

_____

_____

The Bible, like any other book, should be presumed to be telling us what the authors said, experienced, and heard.

Jesus affirmed that the "Scripture cannot be broken" (John 10:35). Let's take a look at what Jesus said about the inspiration of the Bible.

Jesus' Teachings on the Old Testament
If God verified Jesus' message by raising Him from the dead, then perhaps the chief issue concerns whether Jesus taught the inspiration of Scripture. And certainly the Gospels agree on a variety of fronts that Jesus had total confidence in the text of the Old Testament. Assuming the reliability of the texts, as we just mentioned, we are told that Jesus made many statements regarding the trustworthiness and even the inspiration of Scripture. An inductive examination of Jesus' teachings provides a clear indication of this.

One of Jesus' strongest statements concerning the Old Testament Law was His affirmation that heaven and earth would pass away before even the smallest portion of a letter (Matthew 5:17–18). Jesus also taught that these fractions of letters would never fail (Luke 16:17). Further, after citing a particular text in Psalm 82:6, Jesus stated that Scripture could not be nullified (John 10:35). These comments are striking reminders regarding the extent to which Jesus thought Scripture spoke the truth.

Regularly, Jesus also demonstrated His trust in the Old Testament by utilizing it as His source for solving theological disputes. On more than one occasion, His argument turned chiefly on the significance of a single word in the

On many occasions, Jesus cited Scripture as a "proof text" while debating His adversaries.

text. In Mark 12:35–37, Jesus based an important theological point on the second usage of the word "Lord," arguing that the Messiah was more than just the son of David. In Matthew 22:31–32, Jesus builds His case against the Sadducees on the word translated in English as "am," in order to teach the doctrine of the resurrection of the body, which they rejected. Such confidence in the very words of Scripture is a crucial indication of Jesus' high view of their truth.[6]

On many other occasions, Jesus cited Scripture as a "proof text" while debating His adversaries. During the wilderness temptation, Jesus quoted Old Testament texts in opposition to Satan (Matthew 4:4, 7, 10). Elsewhere, Jesus responded to His detractors by asking them, *"Have you not read. . . ?"* or a similar comment, also served to refute an opposing view. In Matthew 22:29, Jesus remarked that an ignorance of Scripture caused the Sadducees to make a theological error. It seems clear from these uses of Scripture that Jesus considered its contents to be the definitive authority in solving theological issues.

In yet another debate with Jewish leaders, after citing portions of the Law and prophets, Jesus appears to refer to the entire Old Testament as the *"commandment of God"* and *"the word of God"* (Mark 7:8–13). Such descriptions indicate that Jesus knew that God was the Authority behind Scripture. The Bible indeed is an inspired text, written for our edification. As such, its writings must be fulfilled (see Matthew 26:54; Luke 4:21; John 7:38). Jesus used the Old Testament as a proof text that serves as God's blueprint for correct theology and behavior. It disproves contrary positions. Jesus did not doubt the authority of His Word.

Jesus referred to the entire Old Testament both as the Law and the prophets (Matthew 5:17), as well as adding the Psalms (Luke 24:44). By either designation, Jesus indicated that each section was the Word of God. Moses, the author of the Law (Luke 16:31; 24:44), spoke God's words in Exodus 3:6 (see also Mark 12:26). David wrote by the inspiration of the Holy Spirit in Psalm 110:1 (see Mark 12:36). The prophets also spoke God's words because their prophecies of the Christ had to be fulfilled (see Luke 24:27, 44).

Jesus' Teaching on the New Testament
A case for the inspiration of the New Testament must be made differently than that of the Old Testament, since the former was not written until after Jesus' death. Whereas Jesus approved the already-written Old Testament, He provided for the as yet unwritten New Testament.

First, Jesus taught His disciples that they were His designated witnesses and spokesmen (Luke 24:48; Acts 1:8; John 15:27). As His students, they learned His teachings so that they, in turn, might impart these principles to others. This was even true to the extent that those who believed and obeyed the disciples' words would actually be receiving Jesus Christ Himself (Matthew 10:14–15, 40; John 13:20).

Second, Jesus also promised His disciples the inspiration and guidance of the Holy Spirit. He would teach them additional matters (John 16:12–13), causing them to remember His earlier statements (John 14:26) and revealing to them the future (John 16:13b). Perhaps the key item is that, in all these matters, the Holy Spirit would lead the disciples to truth (John 16:13).

Third, as the New Testament writers penned their words, they recognized that they were inspired. They claimed Jesus' twofold promise. The apostles' teachings were based on the foundation that Jesus provided (see Ephesians 2:20; Hebrews 2:3–4; 2 Peter. 3:2). They believed their words were inspired. First Peter l:12 contains one example of apostolic confidence in the words they wrote, and such confidence is especially evident in Paul's epistles. These men were convinced that the Holy Spirit empowered both their teaching and their writing.

Fourth, the New Testament writers recognized that Jesus' promise of inspiration also extended to other writers, as well. For instance, 1 Timothy 5:18 notes two citations, referring to both as Scripture. The first is obviously drawn from Deuteronomy 25:4. Although the second may be in reference to certain Old Testament texts, it is much more similar in wording to statements Jesus made in Matthew 10:10 and Luke 10:7. Comparing a quote from the Law to one found in the teachings of Jesus, and calling them both Scripture, is certainly significant, and for more than one reason. It shows some conviction that the existing canon of inspired texts of Paul's day, consisting only of Old Testament writings, was not the end of the matter. After all, if any writings are considered to be inspired, the words of Jesus should be included! Moreover, Jesus' saying is even placed on a par with the Law itself.

Another example is found in 2 Peter 3:15–16, where Paul's epistles are placed alongside other Scripture, thereby being given the same status. Additionally, Jude 17–18 seems to cite 2 Peter 3:3 (or a common text) as the words of an apostle.

It is true that we cannot move from a few examples to an entire theory. But by recognizing the sayings of Jesus and the words and writings of apostles as being on a par with Old Testament scriptures, we do glimpse a growing conceptualization that the Old Testament is not the end of God's revelation. Inspiration actually extended to other writings! The main reason for believing in the inspiration of New Testament texts rests on the approved teachings of Jesus. He promised His disciples that they were His special witnesses and that they would be inspired and guided to all truth by the leading of the Holy Spirit. We also have many instances where New Testament authors claimed this promise personally for their own writings, as well as a few examples where they extended this promise to other qualified authors. Lastly, although we cannot pursue the issue here, we also have a plethora of New Testament texts that recognize the inspiration of various Old Testament figures and passages.

But, while the Bible is infallible, human interpretations are not. Even though God's word is perfect (Psalms 19:7), as long as imperfect human beings exist, there will be misinterpretations of God's Word.

In John 10:35, what did Jesus mean when he said that, *"Scripture cannot be broken"*?

_____

_____

APPLY How can you live out the words of Jesus in a specific area of your life today?

_____

_____

_____

Even though God's word is perfect (Psalms 19:7), as long as imperfect human beings exist, there will be misinterpretations of God's Word.

DOESN'T THE BIBLE CONTAIN ERRORS?

Critics of the Bible jump to the conclusion that a partial report is a wrong report. However, this is not the case. If it were, most of what has ever been said would be false, since seldom does time or space permit an absolutely complete report. Occasionally biblical writers express the same thing in different ways, stressing different things. For example, the four Gospels relate the same story—often the same incidents—in different ways to different groups of people and sometimes even quotes the same sayings with different words.

📖 Look at Peter's confession of Christ in the following three Gospels. What differences and similarities do you find?

Matthew 16:16

_____

_____

_____

Mark 8:29

_____

_____

_____

Luke 9:20

_____

_____

_____

If such important topics can be stated in different ways, then there is no reason the rest of Scripture cannot speak truth without using identical words to express meaning.

Others point to variations in the New Testament use of Old Testament Scriptures as a proof of error. They forget that every *citation* need not be an exact *quotation*. Sometimes we use indirect and sometimes direct quotations. It was a perfectly acceptable literary style to give the *essence* of a statement without using precisely the *same words*. The same meaning can be conveyed without using the same verbal expressions.

📖 Compare the following Old Testament verses with their New Testament quotations. What differences can you find?

Zechariah 12:10 with John 19:37

_____

_____

_____

> "On the basis of manuscript tradition alone, the works that made up the Christians' New Testament were the most frequently copied and widely circulated books of antiquity."
>
> —F. E. Peters

Isaiah 61:1–2 with Luke 4:18–19

_____

_____

_____

Hosea 11:1 with Matthew 2:15

_____

_____

_____

In no case does the New Testament misinterpret or misapply the Old Testament, nor draw some invalid implication from it. The New Testament makes no mistakes in citing the Old Testament.

Some claim that because two or more accounts of the same event differ, that the description is inaccurate. For example, Matthew 28:5 says there was one angel at the tomb after the resurrection, while John informs us there were two (20:12). But these are not contradictory reports. An infallible mathematical rule easily explains this problem:

📖 Compare Matthew 27:5 with Acts 1:18. How do these accounts seem to differ?

_____

_____

_____

Matthew informs us that Judas hanged himself. But Luke says that he burst open in the middle and all his entrails gushed out (Acts 1:18). Once more, these accounts are not mutually exclusive. If Judas hanged himself from a tree over the edge of a cliff or gully in this rocky area, and his body fell on sharp rocks below, then his entrails would gush out just as Luke vividly describes.

The Bible was written for the common person rather than as a scientific manual. Because of this, some claim that the Bible contains errors because it speaks of the sun rising, for instance, even though the sun does not move, but rather the earth. However, the Scriptures were written in *ancient* times by ancient standards, and it would be unfair to require such scientific standards. Even today, people continue to speak of the sunrise and sunset.

📖 Read Psalms 104:18–23. How does using poetic language speak highly of God without speaking error?

_____

_____

_____

God spoke through His Word in ways humans could connect with both in accuracy and with their emotions in worship to God.

> *In no case does the New Testament misinterpret or misapply the Old Testament, nor draw some invalid implication from it.*

CAN THE BIBLE BE ACCURATE IN ALL ITS DETAILS?

Can the Bible really be accurate in all of its details? Some argue that Scripture is inaccurate regarding the use of numbers. For instance, the Bible often uses rounded numbers (e.g., Joshua 3:4; 4:13). It refers to the diameter as being about one-third of the circumference of something (1 Chronicles 19:18; 21:5). While this technically is only an approximation, it is not incorrect. Such measurements are sufficient for the large metal basins or bowls (2 Chronicles 4:2) in an ancient Hebrew temple, even though they would not suffice for a computer in a modern rocket. One should not expect to see people in a pre-scientific age to always use precise numbers when recounting an event.

In addition to numbers, critics often neglect the importance of literary figures of speech. There is no reason to suppose that only one literary genre was used in a divinely inspired book. Whole books are written as *poetry* (Job, Psalms, Proverbs). The Synoptic Gospels feature *parables*.

What figures of speech do you find in each of the following verses?

James 3:6

_____

John 21:25

_____

Psalm 36:7

_____

Matthew 19:24

_____

It is not a mistake for a biblical writer to use a figure of speech, but it is a mistake for a reader to take a figure of speech literally. Obviously when the Bible speaks of the believer resting under the shadow of God's wings (Psalms 36:7) it does not mean that God is a feathered bird.

Some argue that the text of the Bible is flawed because of certain manuscripts that contain mistakes. Yet God only inspired the original text of Scripture, not the copies. Therefore, only the original text is without error. Inspiration does not guarantee that every copy and translation are without error, especially in copies made from copies made from copies made from copies. Therefore, we are to expect minor errors in the manuscripts available to us.

For example, in the King James Version, 2 Kings 8:26 gives the age of King Ahaziah as 22 while 2 Chronicles 22:2 says 42. The latter number cannot be correct, or he would have been older than his father. This is obviously a copyist error, but it does not alter the inerrancy of the original.

So, yes, there are errors in the copies but not in the originals. Yet these errors are minor, are relatively few in number, and do not affect any teaching. When scripture passages relating the same event or circumstance vary in consistency, we usually can tell by the context which statement is in error. In spite of an occasional copyist error, the entire message of God's Word still comes through.

📖 Read the account of Josiah's discovery of the Book of the Law in 2 Kings 22:8–13. How did he respond to hearing a copy of God's Word after a period of its neglect?

_____

_____

_____

Critics often jump to the conclusion that unqualified statements leave no room for exceptions. The Book of Proverbs has many of these. Proverbial sayings, by their very nature, offer general guidance, not universal assurance. They are rules for life, but rules that allow for exceptions. Proverbs 16:7 affirms that, *"When a man's ways are pleasing to the Lord, he makes even his enemies to be at peace with him."* This obviously was not intended to be a universal truth. Paul pleased to the Lord and his enemies stoned him (Acts 14:19). Jesus pleased His Father, and his enemies crucified him. Nonetheless, it is a general truth that one who acts in a way pleasing to God can minimize his enemies' antagonism. Wisdom literature applies God's universal truths to life's changing circumstances. The results will not always be the same. Nonetheless, they are helpful guides.

📖 Read Proverbs 22:6. In what ways is this a general statement that includes room for exception?

_____

_____

_____

_____

Another important factor is the issue of progressive revelation. God does not reveal everything at once, nor does He lay down the same conditions for every period of history. Some of His later revelations will further explain his earlier statements. For instance, the book of Hebrews shares many of the Old Testament laws and prophecies, and then explains how these teachings coincide with the teachings of Jesus. Bible critics sometimes confuse a *furthering* in revelation with a *mistake*.

There was a period under the Mosaic Law when God commanded that animals be sacrificed for people's sin. However, since Christ offered the perfect sacrifice for sin (Hebrews 10:11–14), this Old Testament command is no longer in effect. There is no contradiction between the later teaching regarding Christ's redeeming sacrifice and the earlier Old Testament teaching concerning animal sacrifice. The earlier animal sacrifices ultimately point to Christ.

📖 Compare Genesis 1:29 with Genesis 9:3. What new revelation did God give to His people? How can this be viewed as a progression rather than as a contradiction?

_____

_____

_____

_____

LESSON TWO

FOR ME TO FOLLOW GOD

God's Word is the foundation upon which our Christian faith is built. It is essential to understand the integrity and accuracy of Scripture as we begin our task of defending Christianity from attack. As we look at an example of the apostle Paul, we find that the Word of God has been under assault even since the earliest days of the faith. For instance, in Galatians 1:6–7, he wrote, *"I am astonished that you are so quickly deserting the one who called you by the grace of Christ and are turning to a different gospel—which is really no gospel at all. Evidently some people are throwing you into confusion and are trying to pervert the gospel of Christ."*

How did Paul respond to those who opposed the truth about Jesus? In the following verse, he teaches, *"But even if we or an angel from heaven should preach a gospel other than the one we preached to you, let him be eternally condemned!"* According to his teachings, we are not to allow anyone to deceive us into believing the Gospel is anything less than the revealed Word of God.

APPLY In what ways are you tempted to compromise regarding your Christian beliefs? (For example, in a work or family relationship.)

_____

_____

_____

_____

_____

Acts 18:24–28 shares about the life of Apollos, a man who became an early leader in the Christian church. What were the characteristics that mark his lifestyle?

_____

_____

_____

_____

Acts tells us Apollos was an educated man with a thorough knowledge of Scripture. Even though he had limited knowledge about Jesus, he spoke accurately regarding everything he did know. He showed himself to be very teachable (18:26) and was a tremendous help to other believers as a missionary to Achaia. His effectiveness can be measured by the way he was able to refute opponents with the facts of the Bible that Jesus is the Christ.

 APPLY List some situations in your life right now in which you feel the need for guidance from God's Word.

_____

_____

_____

_____

Using a study Bible, concordance, or online search at www.biblegateway.com, look up some of the related verses regarding one of the issues you noted in the last question. What are some principles provided in Scripture that relate to the issue you face?

_____

_____

_____

_____

In a recent survey, an estimated seventy-five million adults (42%) said that reading the Bible is very important to them, but less than fifty percent of Americans can name the first book of the Bible. Among Bible readers, the average amount of time spent reading the Bible is less than seven minutes a day. And yet, the average person spends almost five hours a day watching TV.[12]

Did you know that you can read the entire New Testament in a year by only reading it for five minutes a day? The entire Bible can be read in a year by reading only about three-to-four chapters per day. It has been observed that the entire Bible can be read in only ninety days by reading twelve pages per day, approximately the same length of text as four pages of the *USA Today*.[13]

If you are a Christian, have you ever read your Bible through from cover to cover? If not, why not?

- ❏ It tells us where we came from, and why
- ❏ It tells us what our purpose for life is
- ❏ It tells us who God is
- ❏ It tells us how and why Jesus came to earth
- ❏ It offers comfort for hard times
- ❏ It has examples to follow
- ❏ It provides words to use when words fail us
- ❏ It is the set of instructions God asks His children to live by
- ❏ It is God's "love letter" to you
- ❏ Why not start today?

Several options exist to begin, including a chronological journey through the Bible available at www.oneyearbibleonline.com.

Remember that God's Word is designed to inspire, instruct, and assist in your times of need. When we come to His truth, we not only find words of wisdom, but words of life.

Spend some time with the Lord in prayer right now.

 Lord, I praise You for Your perfect truth found in God's Word. You have provided the answers to so many of my questions. Yet I often

> "I have found that my spiritual growth is directly proportionate to the amount of time and effort I put into the study of Scripture."
>
> —Dr. John MacArthur

struggle in my pursuit to find and apply Your ways. Lord, I ask now for Your strength and discipline to focus on Your will as found in Your Scriptures. Help me to understand Your Word and live it out in my daily decisions and within my relationships with others. I look to You alone for my source of help and refuge. Amen.

Take a few moments to write down some of the applications you desire to implement this week as a result of your learning:

_____

_____

_____

_____

_____

_____

_____

_____

How Do We Know God Exists?

The existence of a personal, moral God is fundamental to all that Christians believe. If there is no moral God, there is no moral being against whom we have sinned. Therefore, salvation is not needed. Furthermore, if there is no God, there could be no acts of God (miracles), and the stories of Jesus can only be understood as fiction or myth. In understanding, defending, and sharing our faith, one of the first questions that must be addressed is, "How do we know God exists?"

There have traditionally been four basic arguments used to prove God's existence. They are called the cosmological, teleological, axiological, and ontological arguments. Of course, these are big, technical names for what we could more simply call the argument from creation (*cosmos* means creation), design (*telos* means purpose), moral law (*axios* means judgment), and being (*ontos* means being).

> *"Without God, God cannot be known."*
>
> *—Irenaeus about 175 A.D.*

ATHEISM	AGNOSTICISM	THEISM	POLYTHEISM	PANTHEISM
There is no God	I don't know if there is a God	There is a God	Multiple Gods	Everything is God

THE ARGUMENT FROM CREATION

The basic idea of this argument is that since there is a universe, it must have an initial cause beyond itself. It is based on the law of causality, which says that every limited thing is caused by something other than itself. There are two different forms of this argument, so we will show them to you separately. The first form says that the universe needed a cause at its beginning. The second form argues that it needs a cause right now to continue existing.

The Universe Was Caused at the Beginning

This argument says that the universe is limited in that it had a beginning and that its beginning was caused by something beyond the universe. It can be stated this way:

1. The universe had a beginning.

2. Anything that has a beginning must have been caused by something else.

3. Therefore, the universe was caused by something else, and this cause was God.

In order to avoid this conclusion, some people say that the universe is eternal; it never had a beginning—it just always existed. However, this assumption has largely been abandoned as a result of the scientific evidence for the Big Bang, which states that the universe (all energy, matter, space, and time) had a beginning. Further, scientists say that a transcendent causal agent (outside of space and time) brought our universe into existence. That transcendent causal agent is the personal God of the Bible.

📖 What does Genesis 1:1–2 claim about the creation of the universe?

_____

_____

Another way of demonstrating that the universe must have a cause is from the second law of thermodynamics. This law states that the universe is running out of usable energy. But if it is running down, and will eventually reach bottom, then it could not be eternal. It had to have a start.

📖 Read Isaiah 40:25–26. What does it claim about the power of God and the origin of the stars (like the sun) in the heavens?

_____

_____

_____

_____

📖 Read Hebrews 11:3. Why might this verse capture the attention of astronomers and astrophysicists?

_____

_____

_____

"Were we able to extract from any man a complete answer to the question, 'What comes into your mind when you think about God?' we might predict with certainty the spiritual future of that man."

—A. W. Tozer

The Universe Needs a Cause for its Continuing Existence

Something is keeping us in existence right now so we don't simply disappear. Something has not only caused the world to come into being, but is also continuing to provide its existence in the present (Colossians 1:17). The world needs both an originating cause and a sustaining cause. In a sense, this question is the most basic question that can be asked, "Why is there something rather than nothing?" It can be put this way:

1. Finite, changing things exist. For example, I am not self-existing, because I had a start and will come to an end. It was the same with my parents. But who caused them? What caused the existence of the first human on the earth? That first cause, of course, was God.

2. Every finite, changing thing must be caused by something else. If it is limited and it changes, then it cannot be something that exists independently. If it existed independently, or necessarily, then it would have always existed without any kind of change. God is such a being.

3. There cannot be an infinite number of past causes. Somewhere you need a start or first cause, especially in light of the Big Bang and the law of thermodynamics. You cannot have an infinite number of limited, changing beings without a start. To simply state that the universe has always existed does not explain why I am existing right now.

4. Therefore, there must be a first uncaused cause of every finite, changing thing that exists. This argument shows why there must be a present, sustaining cause of the world, but it doesn't tell us very much about what kind of God exists. How do we know that this is really the God of the Bible? God claims this for Himself.

Read John 1:2 and Colossians 1:16–17. What do these verses say about God's creating power?

_____

_____

_____

_____

Read Psalm 14:1 and 53:1. What do these verses say about those who deny God's existence?

_____

_____

_____

_____

Biblically, philosophically, and scientifically, there is overwhelming evidence that there must be a First Cause behind the ongoing presence of the known universe.

But what do atheists believe about a First Cause? Though a recent poll indicates that only about five percent of Americans do not believe in God, the influence of atheistic thinkers in our time is certainly widespread. While a skeptic doubts that God exists, and an agnostic says that he doesn't know if

God is out there, the atheist claims to know that there is no God. According to them, there is only the world and the natural forces that operate it.

What Do Atheists Believe about God?

There are different forms of atheism, but the classic view holds that there never was and never will be a God either in the world or beyond it. Those who hold this view claim that the arguments used to prove God's existence are faulty. They assert that God is simply a creation of human imagination.

What Do Atheists Believe about the World?

Many atheists believe the world is uncreated and eternal. Others say it came into existence out of nothing and by nothing. It is self-sustaining and self-perpetuating. They argue that if everything needs a cause, then one can ask, "What caused the first cause?" Atheists claim that the universe is not caused; it is just there.

What Do Atheists Believe about Evil?

While atheists deny God's existence, they affirm the reality of evil. They think the existence of evil is one of the primary evidences that there is no God. Some argue that it is absurd to believe in God since God made all things, and evil is a thing, so God must have made evil.

What Do Atheists Believe about Values?

To atheists, if there is no God, and humans are merely a collection of chemicals, then there is no reason to believe that anything has eternal value. Atheists believe that morals are relative and situational. In other words, there may be some enduring ethical principles, but these were created by man—not revealed by God. Goodness is defined as whatever works to achieve the desired results.

Atheist philosophers have asked some questions which challenge us to think about our faith. However, atheism fails to answer the larger issues of life in a satisfying manner. Only the existence of God as revealed through Jesus Christ in the Bible provides the answers for these issues.

APPLY How would you answer someone who asked you to explain why you believe God exists?

_____

_____

_____

_____

LESSON THREE — DAY TWO

THE ARGUMENT FROM DESIGN

This argument reasons from some specific aspect of creation to a Creator who put it there. It argues from design to an Intelligent Designer. For example, if you are walking along the beach and come across the words in the sand, "I love you. Hope to see you soon," you assume an intelligent being wrote that message. It just didn't organize itself by the water swirling around the sand. If you see a beautiful watch on the floor, you immediately realize that an intelligent designer designed and created it. This line of thought includes three parts:

1. All designs imply a designer.
2. There is great design in this universe.
3. Therefore, there must be a Great Designer of the universe.

Again, any time we see a complex design, we know by previous experience that it came from the mind and hands of the designer. A work of art requires an artist who created it. A high-quality film does not create itself. It involves the work of a director and many filmmakers who apply great effort toward its development.

📖 Look at Isaiah 51:13. What does this verse note about God's design?

_____

_____

The second part of this argument is that the design we see in the universe is complex. The universe is a very intricate system of forces that work together for the mutual benefit of the whole. A single DNA molecule, the building block of life, carries the same amount of information as one volume of an encyclopedia. No one seeing an encyclopedia lying in the forest would hesitate to think that it had an intelligent cause. So when we find a living creature composed of millions of DNA-based cells, we should think that it likewise was the result of an intelligent cause.

📖 Read Job 38:11. What does God claim regarding the order of the earth's complexity?

_____

_____

Some have objected to this argument of intelligent design, preferring the process of chance. Blindfolding a monkey and allowing him to type on a computer keyboard will produce random letters by chance, but we would not expect a message. We would certainly not expect the typing to result in a Shakespearian sonnet. Chance does not produce complex specific information. Only an intelligent agent does. The only reasonable conclusion is that there is a great Designer behind the design in the world.

📖 What phrase do the following verses in Psalms have in common: 115:15; 121:2; 124:8; 134:3; 146:6?

_____

_____

📖 What does Ecclesiastes 11:5 reveal about our ability to understand our Designer?

_____

_____

_____

Scientists have uncovered a little of how God has designed the universe and life, but have a hard time understanding how it all was brought into being.

"That you have forgotten the LORD your Maker,

Who stretched out the heavens

And laid the foundations of the earth,

That you fear continually all day long because of the fury of the oppressor,

As he makes ready to destroy?

But where is the fury of the oppressor?"

Isaiah 51:13

It is similar to seeing a complex building. We can understand portions of it simply through observation. However, to understand it more fully, we need to talk with the architect who designed the building. We need him to speak.

THE ARGUMENT FROM MORAL LAW

The argument from moral law claims that the cause of the universe must be moral, in addition to being powerful and intelligent. The process includes that:

1. All people are conscious of an objective moral law in their minds.
2. Moral laws imply a moral lawgiver.
3. Therefore, there must be a supreme moral lawgiver.

Moral laws are different from natural laws. Moral laws don't describe what is; they prescribe what ought to be. They are not simply a description of the way people behave, but how they intuitively believe others should act. When somebody cuts you off in your car and you think, "He shouldn't do that. That's not fair," where did that standard originate? Moral laws tell us what people ought to do, whether they are doing it or not. Therefore, any moral "ought" comes from beyond ourselves and the natural universe. You can't explain it by anything that happens in the universe, and it can't be reduced to the things people do in the universe. It transcends the natural order and requires a supernatural cause, a moral lawgiver.

📖 Read Romans 1:18–23. What does it claim about a transcendent moral law?

_____

_____

_____

_____

Some suggest that this moral law is not really objective; it is nothing but a subjective judgment that comes from social surroundings. However, this view fails to account for the fact that most people hold certain shared things as wrong (like murder, rape, theft, and lying). I bet you believe that it is not right for people to steal your belongings, that murder is wrong, and that a person lying to you is a wrongful act. But if there are no objective moral laws, then there can be no right or wrong value judgments, and you should not get mad at someone who cuts you off in your car.

📖 In Revelation 20:11–15, on what basis does God say He will judge those who do not believe in Christ, but live by their own moral system?

_____

_____

_____

We find that even those who say that there is no moral order expect to be treated with fairness, courtesy, and dignity. If one of them raised this objection and we replied with, "Who cares what you think?" we might find that this person does believe there are some moral rights and wrongs, because the person has been offended. Everyone expects others to follow some moral codes, even those who try to deny them. But moral law is an undeniable fact.

 **APPLY** When you think about what you believe deep in your own heart, have you broken your own moral standards? Have you ever told a lie, stolen something, or cheated? How will you explain it to God? Will He accept you with that kind of track record? What does God's Word advise us to do in John 3:16–17 and Romans 4:5–8?

_____

_____

_____

_____

_____

_____

_____

THE ARGUMENT FROM BEING

A fourth argument attempts to prove that God must exist by the very fact that we can think of an idea of a perfect God. In other words, once we get an idea of who God is, that idea necessarily involves existence. There are several forms of this argument, but let's talk about the idea of God as a perfect being.

1. Whatever perfection can be attributed to the most perfect being possible must be attributed to it (otherwise it would not be the most perfect being possible).
2. Necessary existence is a perfection that can be attributed to the most perfect being.
3. Therefore, necessary existence must be attributed to the most perfect being.

The very idea of a perfect God states it is impossible for Him not to exist. Eternal existence must be the perfect kind of existence because it can't go away. This argument succeeds in showing that our idea of God must include necessary existence of a creator; but it fails to show that God *actually* exists. It shows that we *think* of God as existing, but does not prove that He does.

📖 Read Ecclesiastes 3:11. What does it mean that God has placed *eternity in our hearts*?

_____

_____

_____

The "argument from being" never answers the big question that it claims to address. God does not necessarily exist just because we can think of an almighty God. It can be useful, though, because it shows that, if there is a

"ETERNITY IN THEIR HEART"

God has given every person an eternal perspective that extends beyond the routines of daily life. However, this does not mean that God has revealed all of life's mysteries to us, since Ecclesiastes 3:11 tells us that "man will not find out the work which God has done from the beginning to the end."

God, it would be necessary for Him to exist and exist eternally. If all these arguments have some validity but rely on the principle of causality, what is the best way to prove that God exists? If you answer, the argument from creation, you are on the right track.

📖 Review Romans 1:20. What does it say about God's power and nature being revealed to humanity?

_____

_____

_____

But the best way to prove that God exists is if He came to this planet Himself, lived among people, and revealed Himself.

📖 Read John 1:1–4 and 1:10–14. What do you think the apostle John was saying about God Himself coming into this world and living among us?

_____

_____

_____

_____

What did Jesus say to Philip in John 14:8–9 about God coming to live among people?

_____

_____

What do you believe is the best evidence to prove that God exists?

_____

_____

_____

_____

LESSON THREE

DAY FIVE

FOR ME TO FOLLOW GOD

Belief in the existence of God does not get a person to heaven, but is a foundational starting point for our other beliefs. Throughout Scripture, we repeatedly find that it is assumed God exists and that He is perfect in every way. As David wrote in the Psalms, only _"the fool says in his heart there is no God"_ (Psalm 14:1).

Yet there is often a great disparity between what we claim to believe about God and how we live our lives. Some have called the lifestyle of living as if God does not exist "practical atheism." In other words, we live as if God is not there, watching, listening, and will not someday hold us accountable. Yet according to 1 Samuel 16:7 God says: _"Do not consider his appearance or his height, for I have rejected him. The LORD does not look at the things man looks at. Man looks at the outward appearance, but the LORD looks at the heart."_

APPLY Name some areas in your life where you tend to live as if God is not watching?

_____

_____

_____

_____

God not only created us; He sees our hearts. According to 1 Samuel 16:7, the Lord does not view us as people do. He can peer directly into our thoughts and desires. Think of an area in your life where others typically do not see that God may be convicting you toward change?

_____

_____

_____

_____

Remember, in David's situation, the attitude of His heart was the difference between him becoming king or one of his brothers taking the position. God desires purity in every part of our lives.

📖 In Matthew 5:21–22 and 5:27–28, Jesus spoke about two areas of purity—anger and lust. Read these verses and write why you think these two areas cause so much impurity in the lives of people.

_____

_____

_____

_____

APPLY How does your belief that God exists impact how you live your life? What do you think God wants you to do to live more like He wishes?

_____

_____

_____

_____

Some have called the lifestyle of living as if God does not exist "practical atheism." In other words, we live as if God is not there, watching, listening, and will not some-day hold us accountable.

Reasons for Defending the Faith[14]

God Commands the Use of Reason

The most important reason for doing apologetics is that God told us to do it. Over and over the New Testament exhorts us to defend the Faith.

First Peter 3:15 says, *"But in your hearts acknowledge Christ as the holy Lord. Always be prepared to give an answer to every one who asks you to give the reason for the hope that you have."* This verse addresses several important concepts. First, it says that we should be ready. Being ready is not just a matter of having the right information available, it is also an attitude of readiness and eagerness to share with others the truth of what we believe. Second, we are to give a reason to those who ask the questions. Everyone has questions; we must be prepared to address them. Finally, it links evangelism with our own spiritual growth. Why? Because we are making Christ Lord in our hearts. If

He is really Lord, then we should be obedient to Him by *"destroying speculations and every lofty thing raised up against the knowledge of God, and . . . taking every thought captive to the obedience of Christ"* (2 Corinthians 10:5). In other words we should be confronting issues in our own minds and in the expressed thoughts of others that are preventing them from knowing God.

In Philippians 1:7 speaks of his mission as one of the *defense and confirmation of the gospel."* He added in verse 16, *"I am put here for the defense of the gospel* (NIV).*"* We are put where we are to defend it as well.

📖 What does Jude 3 share about addressing questions regarding Christ?

_____

_____

_____

_____

False teachers had assaulted the people Jude was reaching with this letter, and he needed to encourage them to protect the faith as it had been revealed through Christ. Jude makes a significant statement about our attitude in verse 22 when he says, *"have mercy on some, who are doubting."* Defending our faith is seen as a form of compassion.

Titus 1:9 even makes a knowledge of Christian evidences a requirement for church leadership. An elder in the church should be *"holding fast the faithful word which is in accordance with the teaching, that he may be able both to exhort in sound doctrine and to refute those who contradict."*

📖 Read 2 Timothy 2:24–25. What does Paul say about the reason for using God's truth to speak out regarding our faith?

_____

_____

_____

Reason Demands It
God created us with human reason. It is part of His image in us (Genesis 1:27; Colossians 3:10). A fundamental principle of reason is that we should have sufficient grounds for what we believe. Socrates said, "The unexamined life is not worth living." It is vital for Christians "to give a reason for their hope." This is part of the great command to love God with all our mind, as well as our heart and soul (Matthew 22:36–37).

The World Needs It
Many people refuse to believe without some evidence. Since God created us as rational beings, He doesn't expect us to live irrationally. He wants us to look before we leap. This does not mean there is no room for faith. But God wants us to take a step of faith in the light of evidence. He does not want us to leap in the dark.

We should have evidence that something is true before we place our faith in it. For example, no rational person steps in an elevator unless he has some reason to believe it will hold him up. Likewise, no reasonable person gets on an airplane that has a broken wing and smoke coming out the tail end. Evidence and reason are important to establish belief that faith in Christ is reasonable. Once this is established, a person can place his or her faith in it.

Jude makes a significant statement about our attitude in verse 22 when he says, "have mercy on some, who are doubting." Defending our faith is seen as a form of compassion.

Results Confirm It

On countless occasions, Christians who lovingly address the questions of skeptics have helped influence them to begin a relationship with Christ. This has been the case in the lives of many throughout the history of the church and continues in our time.

 In the account of Jesus and Nicodemus in John 3, his problem was not whether God existed, but how to know God and have eternal life (John 3:16). Describe in your words your own Nicodemus experience, retelling the story of how you came to realize you were a sinner in need of God's mercy and forgiveness, trusting in Jesus by faith to forgive you and change your life.

_____

_____

_____

_____

Remember that God not only exists; He desires a personal relationship with you (John 6:40). Jesus said, *"If anyone loves me, he will obey my teaching. My Father will love him, and we will come to him and make our home with him"* (John 14:23). Regardless of your current situation, He still longs to hear you turn to Him with every issue of your life.

Spend some time with the Lord in prayer right now.

 Lord, I acknowledge that You exist. Far more than merely existing, You long for a relationship with me. I admit that I have failed many times along the way, living as if You were not there to watch or to help. Help me right now to turn over my unseen flaws to You. Strengthen me to walk in Your ways, and to help others along the journey to do the same. You are the one and only God, my God, my Savior. Amen.

Take a few moments to write down the thoughts and ideas that have impacted you the most this week:

_____

_____

_____

_____

_____

_____

_____

_____

_____

> *Remember that God not only exists; He desires a personal relationship with you (John 6:40).*

Notes

HOW DO WE KNOW JESUS IS GOD?

Did Jesus ever claim to be God? If He did claim this, what are the implications for people living today? In evaluating the claims of Jesus, readers should understand that even skeptics can't logically deny that the four Gospel biographies of Christ are based on accurate historical reporting and that at least two, Matthew and John, were eyewitnesses—those who knew Christ personally and traveled closely with Him for more than three years. Luke, who traveled with the apostle Paul and knew some of the other apostles, asserts that he *"carefully investigated everything from the beginning"* in completing his biography (Luke 1:3), and it is generally agreed that Mark got the information for his biography directly from the apostle Peter. For those and other reasons, we know the Gospels constitute reliable historical reporting.

The kind of scholarly misinformation we find in skeptical endeavors like theories about the Lost Tomb of Jesus is all too common today, and, despite its consequences in the lives of the uninformed believer or unbeliever, it only serves to discredit the skeptic's own credibility and make plain his prejudices. Due to advances in textual criticism and other areas, it is now considered a historic fact that Jesus said and did what the Gospel writers claim He said and did. In other words, when we read the Gospels—Matthew, Mark, Luke, and John—we are, in fact, reading what Jesus Himself actually said, taught, and did.

"Most men are notable for one conspicuous virtue or grace. Moses for meekness, Job for patience. John for love. But in Jesus you find everything."

—J. Oswald Sanders

Was Jesus Human or Divine? Yes, He Was!
JESUS AS ONE PERSON[15]

Jesus is worshiped (Matthew 2:2, 11; 14:33; 28:9)	Jesus worshiped the Father (John 17)
Jesus is prayed to (Acts 7:59; 1 Corinthians 1:1–2)	Jesus prayed to the Father (John 17:1)
Jesus was called God (John 20:28; Hebrews 1:8)	Jesus was called man (Mark 15:39; John 19:5)
Jesus was called Son of God (Mark 1:1)	Jesus was called Son of Man (John 9:35–37)
Jesus was sinless (1 Peter 2:22; Hebrew 4:15)	Jesus was tempted (Matthew 4:1)
Jesus knew all things (John 21:17)	Jesus grew in wisdom (Luke 2:52)
Jesus gives eternal life (John 20:28)	Jesus died (Romans 5:8)
The fullness of deity dwells in Him (Colossians 2:9)	Jesus had a body of flesh and bones (Luke 24:39)

LESSON FOUR

 DAY ONE

WHAT DID JESUS CLAIM?

Read the following claims Jesus made for Himself and ask yourself, "What kind of person would say these things?" Notice the personal emphasis:

"I am the light of the world. Whoever follows **me** *will never walk in darkness, but will have the light of life."* (John 8:12)

"I am the resurrection and the life. He who believes in **Me** *will live, even though he dies."* (John 11:25)

"No one has ever gone into heaven except the one who came from heaven—the Son of Man." (John 3:13)

"For the bread of God is he who comes down from heaven and gives life to the world. . . . I am the bread of life. He who comes to **me** *will never go hungry, and he who believes in* **me** *will never be thirsty."* (John 6:33, 35)

Now, what did Jesus declare about His own bold assertions? Only that, *"My testimony is valid"* (John 8:14), and *"I am the one I claim to be"* (John 8:28).

📖 Jesus also claimed to be a king. Read John 18:37 and note why Jesus said He came into this world:

_____

_____

_____

_____

Throughout history, untold millions have believed Jesus' claims were true. Even those in the first century who either knew Him personally or critically, examined His claims, and believed what Jesus said.

📖 If someone claimed to be God, or God's Son, there would certainly be reports of this in the writings of his friends. Mark 14:60–61 records four specific titles Jesus used of Himself. Read these verses and describe the significance of each title:

"Christ"

_____

_____

_____

"Son of the Blessed One"

_____

_____

_____

"I am" (see also Exodus 3:13–15; John 8:56–59)

_____

_____

_____

"Son of Man"

_____

_____

_____

Mark wrote that Jesus claimed to the Jewish Sanhedrin during His trial that He was the Christ (the Greek word for Messiah), the Son of the Blessed One (meaning Son of God), the "I am" (a title for God's name), and calls Himself the Son of Man. The phrase "Son of Man" was nonexistent in Jewish culture before Jesus lived. Neither Jews nor Christians commonly used the term after Jesus' earthly life. There was no reason for someone who lived after Jesus to write this back into his life story. Jesus used this phrase of Himself eighty-one times in the Gospels, and the phrase is never used by anyone but Jesus. Outside of the gospels, it is used only twice, both in reference to Jesus Himself.

📖 Read Daniel 7:13–14. What kind of power and authority did Daniel predict about the Son of Man? Do you think Jesus really did claim He had that kind of authority and power over the nations that Daniel describes?

_____

_____

_____

_____

> I am trying here to prevent anyone saying the really foolish thing that people often say about Him: "I'm ready to accept Jesus as a great moral teacher, but I don't accept his claim to be God." That is the one thing we must not say. A man who was merely a man and said the sort of things Jesus said would not be a great moral teacher. He would either be a lunatic—on a level with the man who says he is a poached egg—or else he would be the Devil of Hell. You must make your choice. Either this man was, and is, the Son of God; or else a madman or something worse. You can shut Him up for a fool, you can spit at Him and kill Him as a demon, or you can fall at His feet and call Him Lord and God.

C. S. Lewis, *Mere Christianity*[16]

JESUS, THE I AM

In another passage, we experience Jesus with a different audience that led to a similar reaction. During an encounter in which Jesus sent away a demon, the crowd shouted "Who do you think you are?" In the end, the crowd picked up stones to kill Jesus because of His reaction.

📖 Read John 8:52–59. How does Jesus respond to the question of His audience?

_____

_____

_____

The Jewish audience couldn't believe what they were hearing. Jesus was not even fifty years old, yet he claimed to have seen Abraham? Then Jesus presented the final piece of his hotly contested conversation: *"before Abraham was born, I am"* (verse 58). Fury incensed the angry mob as they rushed to execute Him.

📖 Review the story of Moses and the burning bush in Exodus 3:13–15. What did Jesus mean by calling Himself "I am"?

_____

_____

_____

_____

In this historical account, Moses was told that the name of God he should use was the "I am." In John's report, Jesus claims the same name, clearly attempting to connect himself with the "I am" from the burning bush in Exodus 3. Just think if you had been standing there, listening to Jesus say this, would you have believed Him or reacted like the religious leaders of His day?

_____

_____

_____

Once again, the actions of the Jewish leaders communicated their understanding of what Jesus was saying. Here He was, standing before them, claiming to be none other than God. The leaders decided that this man must be brought to justice. Jesus slipped away, but the accusation had been made. He was considered a marked man.

📖 Jesus' claim to be the "I am" was more than just a claim to be divine. What does Exodus 3:14 claim about the "I am"?

_____

_____

_____

> "Jesus is God spelling Himself out in language that man can understand."
>
> —S. D. Gordon

Jesus' claim to be the "I am" was to identify Himself as being the Lord Yahweh, the God who created the heavens and the earth in Genesis 2:4. This also connects with John's other reports regarding Jesus' claims in John 1:1 and Revelation 1:8.

Further indication of who Jesus claimed to be is found in the Sermon on the Mount. On a hillside near the Sea of Galilee is a place where Jesus preached this famous sermon. In one place, Jesus says, *"You have heard that it was said, 'Do not commit adultery.' But I tell you that anyone who looks at a woman lustfully has already committed adultery with her in his heart"* (Matthew 5:27–28). In this instance, the people knew Jesus was quoting one of the Ten Commandments, the very words of God. Then Jesus spoke with equal authority. At the conclusion Matthew records, *"When Jesus had finished saying these things, the crowds were amazed at his teachings, for he was teaching them as one having authority and not as their scribes"* (Matthew 7:29). What kind of authority did Jesus have? He claimed that His teachings were equal in authority to God's teachings.

Dr. Darrell Bock summarized this authority when he commented,

> He forgave sin. He told the Jews what they could and could not do on the Sabbath. The Sabbath is one of the Ten Commandments. You don't mess with the Ten Commandments unless you have authority. He talked about who we should and should not be associated with. He claimed that he could sit at the right hand of the Father. There's not any person who gets to go directly into God's presence and park there. You must have a lot of authority and a lot of nerve to think that you can sit next to God.[17]

APPLY Did you realize God said these things? How does this impact your thinking about who Jesus is and your relationship with Him?

_____

_____

_____

_____

_____

_____

I AND THE FATHER ARE ONE

One of the most important and amazing statements Jesus made can be found in John 10. As Jesus walked through the Jewish Temple, some Jewish leaders demanded of him, *"If you are the Christ, tell us plainly"* (verse 24).

📖 Read John 10:25–30. How did Jesus respond to the question of the Jewish leaders?

_____

_____

_____

The Jews would have clearly had a problem with Jesus' strong language. According to the Law of Moses, anyone declaring to be God was worthy of execution. They understood that Jesus was calling God *my* Father rather than *our* Father. He also taught that he could *personally* give eternal life to people.

📖 How did the people respond to what Jesus said in verses 31–33?

_____

_____

Wouldn't you agree that Jesus claimed to be God? His audience did and planned to punish him for it. In an interview I (John) conducted on Jesus' claim to be the Messiah, I asked Dr. Claire Pfann of the University of the Holy Land and an expert on the culture of Bethlehem during the time of Jesus, her response to scholars who suggest Jesus' disciples created the idea of a divine Jesus.

According to Dr. Claire Pfann,

> I think that is laughable in the face of Jewish literature from the second temple period. We have to look at the Dead Sea Scrolls, for example, to see the messianic hope that existed among Jews before the coming of Jesus. We recognize, of course, things like Cave 4, Qumran, Manuscript 521—in which it says that when the Messiah comes, he will heal the blind, he will heal the lame, and he will raise the dead.

> We see the same claim given by Jesus himself in Luke chapter 7 when John the Baptist sends his disciples to ask Jesus, "Are you it? The real thing? Or do we wait for somebody else?" Jesus says, "Tell John what you've seen: the blind are healed, the lame walk, and the dead are raised." This is a pre-Christian, Jewish messianic expectation that finds its fulfillment in Jesus.[18] Another way of saying this is that Jesus quoted a passage from the Dead Sea scrolls that John would have known, saying my miracles I.D. Me as the coming Messiah.

📖 Read this account in Luke 7:20–23. In what ways did Jesus' response to being the Messiah also confirm His claims to being God?

_____

_____

_____

_____

_____

Another scholar in this same program, Dr. Craig Evans, shared similar concern from his experiences and evaluation of the Jesus Seminar materials,

> I think a good example of where the Jesus Seminar is inconsistent in their own criteria is the whole question of Jesus' messianic self-understanding. They assume that this is the early church reading back into the gospels. Here's the problem with this. You have multiple attestation. Everywhere in the tradition, Jesus is regarded as the Messiah—in all four Gospels, in the Epistles, everything in the New Testament. How in the world could that have emerged in the aftermath of Easter if Jesus had never claimed to be Messiah and had never allowed his following to think of that? Where does all of this come from? It's multiply attested.

> "Almost everyone who has heard of Jesus has developed an opinion about Him. That is to be expected, for He is not only the most famous person in world history, but also the most controversial."
>
> —Dr. Tim LaHaye

Another criterion is the criterion of result. How do you explain that? Or, another way of putting it is, "Where there's smoke, there's usually fire." Everybody is calling him the Messiah after Easter. Where did that come from? Probably from the 'fire' of Jesus himself in his ministry before Easter.[19]

📖 Read John 8:42–43, 54–59. Jesus calls God "my Father" thirty-nine times in the Gospels. How do such statements about Jesus as His personal Father strengthen His claims to being God's Son?

_____

_____

_____

APPLY Is there any doubt in your mind that Jesus claimed to be God? If He claimed to be God, do you think He was telling the truth? If so, how should you respond to Him?

_____

_____

_____

_____

_____

Is Jesus the Only Way to God?

Thomas said to him, "Lord, we don't know where you are going, so how can we know the way?"

Jesus answered, "I am the way and the truth and the life. No one comes to the Father except through me. If you really knew me, you would know my Father as well. From now on, you do know him and have seen him." (John 14:5–7)

With the more nurturing crowd of His loyal followers at his side, Jesus shared a meal with His closest men. During their time together, Jesus predicted that Peter, His leading follower, would soon deny Him. Then turning to Thomas, Jesus comforted him with the statement that He was, *"the way, the truth, and the life"* (John 14:6). Many people don't realize that Jesus claimed to be the only way to God.

📖 During this time, Philip asked Jesus to show them the Father. What does John 14:9–10 share about Jesus' relationship to the Father?

_____

_____

_____

Philip was an orthodox Jew. As such, he believed there was only one God. So when Jesus said *"he who has seen Me has seen the Father,"* what conclusion do you think Philip came to? He had to conclude Jesus was the one God. In this case, instead of responding with stones, his followers grappled with the mind-blowing significance of Jesus' words. Soon afterwards, Jesus led them to the Mount of Olives where He was arrested. His followers fled for safety, and abandoned him just as was predicted.

📖 In Mark 14:36, how does Jesus address God the Father? What does He say?

_____

_____

_____

What does Abba mean? The Aramaic term "Abba" was an affectionate form of our English word "father." When Jesus used this term in reference to God, He indicated that He had an intimate, personal relationship with the Father unlike the relationships others have with God. Is this evidence that Jesus thought He had a special relationship with God?

According to Dr. Ben Witherington, professor of New Testament at Asbury Seminary,

> Abba means 'father.' It's not quite like 'daddy,' but it means 'father dearest.' It implies an intimate relationship with one's heavenly parent. Jesus believed he had that unique kind of relationship" that only the Son of God could have. . . . There's plenty of evidence for [Christ being the Son of God]. . . . It's in the Synoptics, the Gospel of John, and the Pauline letters. It's all over the New Testament. It's one of the most characteristic things predicated of Jesus—that he was the Son of God.[20]

📖 The term "Abba" is used two additional times in the New Testament. Who is the one who cries "Abba" in the following verses?

Romans 8:15

_____

Galatians 4:6

_____

By God's Spirit, we as believers have the ability to pray to God in this same, intimate way Paul describes in his epistles. Why? Because we are considered God's children, heirs with Him, and have the same Spirit living in us with the Holy Spirit that Jesus had on earth in communicating with His Father.

📖 Jesus is also called the Son of God throughout the New Testament, a name closely related to His use of "Abba." The phrase "Son of God" is used forty-one times in the New Testament. Below, look up just a few of the verses that identify the way Son of God is used in each context. Write what stands out to you:

Matthew 14:33

_____

_____

_____

Matthew 26:63

_____

_____

_____

Matthew 27:54

_____

_____

_____

Mark 3:11

_____

_____

_____

Luke 1:35

_____

_____

_____

Luke 22:70

_____

_____

_____

_____

John 19:7

_____

_____

_____

_____

APPLY Do you believe Jesus is the only was to God? Why? On what evidence do you base your belief? How would explain this belief to someone else?

_____

_____

_____

_____

_____

_____

> *"The words he spoke, the works he performed, the life he led, the person he was—all disclosed the unseen Father. He is, in Paul's words, the visible 'image of the invisible God.'"*
>
> *—F. F. Bruce*

WHAT DOES IT MEAN TO FOLLOW JESUS AS GOD? HOW CAN I DO IT?

"Jesus answered them, "Is it not written in your Law, 'I have said you are gods'? If he called them 'gods,' to whom the word of God came—and the Scripture cannot be broken—what about the one whom the Father set apart as his very own and sent into the world? Why then do you accuse me of blasphemy because I said, 'I am God's Son'? Do not believe me unless I do what my Father does. But if I do it, even though you do not believe me, believe the miracles, that you may know and understand that the Father is in me, and I in the Father." (John 10:34–38)

In Jesus, we find a man who stands strong in faith, yet is not ashamed to be identified with His Father. Despite accusations, persecution, and ultimately the cross, Jesus never once wavered regarding His own identity and His relationship with God. Unlike the feel-good messages some communicate in our time, we see that Jesus was willing to speak truth in controversial ways and in unpopular situations that often led to conflict rather than avoiding it. His life offers several helpful applications in these areas from which we can learn and implement in our lives today.

Think for a moment of your own life. In what ways have you found yourself avoiding tough conversations in order to avoid conflict with others?

_____

_____

_____

_____

_____

More important than even the issue of conflict is our view of Jesus Himself. Many see Him as a good man, but nothing more. But Jesus claimed to be the only way to God. As followers of Christ, our goal is to first know Him personally, and then to share Jesus with others.

APPLY When are some of the times you have experienced the greatest closeness with God?

_____

_____

_____

_____

_____

_____

What have been a few of your most fruitful attempts in sharing your faith in Jesus with other people? What happened?

"My Lord and my God!"

—Thomas, addressing Jesus in John 20:28, (NKJV)

_____

_____

_____

_____

_____

_____

📖 Read Philippians 2:5–11. What are some of the key characteristics of humility communicated about the life of Jesus in these verses? How do they portray both His power as God's Son and His humanity as God in human form?

_____

_____

_____

_____

_____

What is the ultimate goal described in final three verses of this passage?

_____

_____

_____

APPLY Wherever you are in your relationship with God, do you believe there is still room for continued growth in your life? Then tell that to Jesus. Write some of your thoughts concerning this below. List some areas where you envision God working in and through you.

_____

_____

_____

_____

_____

In your group, select a person who can serve as your accountability partner for the week. Share your desires to be more open to the Holy Spirit's leading and how you can help encourage one another in this area.

My Partner

_____

_____

_____

_____

His/Her Goal(s)

_____

_____

_____

How I Will Help him/her

_____

_____

_____

My Goal(s)

_____

_____

_____

How he/she will help me

_____

_____

_____

Spend some time with the Lord in prayer.

Lord, I thank You that You have sent Your Son Jesus Christ to set the example for us and to die in place of our sins. Thank you for Your ongoing power through Your Holy Spirit and wisdom through Your Word. I admit that I have much room for improvement to allow Jesus to live as King in my life. Despite my failures, I come to ask for Your help as I seek specific ways to grow closer to You this week. Please continue to provide Your grace for my time of need. Guard my thoughts and my actions as I pursue knowing You and sharing You with others. I pray this in the name of Your divine Son Jesus. Amen.

Write a prayer to God in your own words, personalizing the words found in Philippians 2:5–11:

_____

_____

_____

_____

_____

_____

_____

_____

How Is Christianity Different From Other Religions?

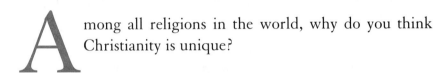mong all religions in the world, why do you think Christianity is unique?

❐ It claims the most famous teachings in history—the teachings of Jesus of Nazareth.

❐ It claims the most famous person in history—the person of Jesus of Nazareth.

❐ It claims the most famous death in history—the death of Jesus of Nazareth.

❐ It claims the only religious leader to raise from the dead.

Jesus Christ is unique in His miraculous birth and His miraculous life. He is unique in the content of His teaching and preaching. He is unique in the personal power He displayed over men and nature. He is unique in the degree of His love and compassion. He is unique in His sacrificial atoning death, physical resurrection from the dead, His ascension, and His self-predicted second coming.

Nevertheless, it is a common belief today that Christianity is not unique, because all religions are basically the same and all religious paths finally lead to the same God. But this idea flies directly in the face of the well-established facts of comparative

"Even though many religions seem to be the same on the surface, the closer one gets to the central teachings, the more apparent the differences become. It is totally incorrect to say that all religions are the same."

—Josh McDowell

religion. First, all religions are not the same; in terms of teachings and worldviews, they are as varied and discrepant as a hundred different philosophies.

Second, in terms of its claims, Christianity stands out like a lighthouse on a lonely shore. The Christian faith and the resurrection of Jesus Christ are of a singular nature:

- "The Christian claim maintains that, in the case of one whose life and teaching, whose miracles and impact were unparalleled, even death proved unable to hold him. Such a claim has never been made with any shred of credibility for any other person on this earth."
- "Christianity alone has dared to claim" the resurrection of its central figure.
- "Here is a teacher of religion, and he calmly professes to stake his entire claims upon his ability, after having been done to death, to rise again from the grave. We may safely assume that there never was, before or since, such a proposal made."
- "No founder of any world religion known to men ever dared say a thing like that."
- "There is no record or claim of Resurrection in the case of any historical founder of religion."

In essence, other religions follow the teachings and philosophies of revered but long-dead founders. These religions have never taught a literal, physical resurrection of a living Savior.

Buddha claimed to be only a man. He is still in the grave.

Muhammad claimed to be only a prophet. He is still in the grave.

Confucius claimed to be only a man. He is still in the grave.

Moses was only a man and a prophet. He is still in the grave.

Zoroaster was only a prophet. He is still in the grave.

No resurrection has ever occurred in history, neither among any Hindu, Buddhist, or Muslim prophets or leaders, nor among any other prophets or leaders in any other world religion. *No other founder of a religion actually proved that his religious claims and teachings were true in the manner Jesus Christ did.*

Jesus, by rising from the dead, proves that Christianity alone offers the way to God, and further, proves that the sincere inquirer seeking truth need not become confused or lost amid the jumble of religious claims the world offers.

LESSON FIVE **DAY ONE**

CHRISTIANITY IS BASED ON THE RESURRECTION OF JESUS CHRIST

If you can prove Jesus didn't rise from the dead, then you can prove Christianity is a false religion. If Christianity's claims are unique, so is its evidence and the manner by which it may be proven true or false. In no other religion in the world is one single event so completely tied to the truth or falsehood of that religion. In every religion but Christianity the teachings of the religious founder are secondary to the teachings. The founder can be removed and little or nothing is altered. In other words, he makes little or no difference to the continued success of his religion.

However, in Christianity, the person of Christ and His resurrection are central. Remove these and nothing credible remains of Christian faith.

📖 Read 1 Corinthians 15:14–18. What does Paul say would be true if the resurrection did not happen?

_____

_____

In addition, the truth claims of other religions do not rest upon evidence that can be objectively examined. For example, Muhammad claimed to be the last major prophet of Allah, but never gave any evidence to prove this. Hinduism claims the world is the *maya* (illusion) of Brahman, while Buddhism maintains that enlightenment can be achieved only by destroying one's personality. It offers no historical evidence to support its teachings.

But Christianity is unique in teaching that the truth of its doctrines can be determined by whether or not the resurrection occurred. If Christ rose again, His teachings and the doctrines He taught must be true. One very important example of this is that Christianity is the only religion in history that has ever taught that personal salvation is by grace through faith in Christ alone. This particular doctrine is wholly dependent on the fact that Jesus' resurrection did occur.

📖 What good news about a person's acceptance before God is found in these verses?

Ephesians 2:8–9

_____

_____

_____

John 1:12

_____

_____

_____

John 3:16

_____

_____

_____

Romans 10:9–10

_____

_____

_____

Christianity is unique in teaching that the truth of its doctrines can be determined by whether or not the resurrection occurred. If Christ rose again, His teachings and the doctrines He taught must be true.

How have you taken advantage of these promises?

_____

_____

_____

To disprove Christianity during the time period following Jesus' death would have been far easier than most people realize. For example, consider a man today who becomes a religious prophet and starts predicting he will rise from the dead on the third day. His controversial religious actions and teachings eventually cause state persecution. He is captured and charged with capital crimes. After a public trial, the man is found guilty and executed by electrocution in front of eyewitnesses, with some of his own critics among them. Further, his hundreds of followers and other eyewitnesses also see his burial in a well-known local cemetery. In addition, the military actually places a contingent of the National Guard at the tomb to prevent anyone from stealing the body to fulfill the prophecies of a resurrection.

Now, would it be difficult at all to determine whether or not this man was ever resurrected from the dead? Of course it wouldn't! Especially if he had predicted he would accomplish this event in only three days. Both the state and his enemies would be committed to making sure no one could get to the grave to steal his body.

But the same situation existed for Jesus in Jerusalem. Jesus' enemies were the most anxious of all to see Him dead and buried and for Him to stay dead. His own disciples had fearfully deserted Him before He died and struggled with the notion that He could possibly be their Messiah. So what changed everything? Why was the tomb empty three days later? What happed to the body? What emboldened the disciples?

📖 What did Jesus' enemies say happened to His body after the resurrection in Matthew 28:11–15?

_____

_____

How would the Roman soldiers have known the disciples had stolen Jesus' body if they were asleep? Their explanation doesn't make sense.

📖 What occurred after the resurrection to disprove that Jesus' body had been stolen? See Acts 1:3.

_____

_____

_____

According to 1 Corinthians 15, over 500 people saw Jesus alive during the forty days following His resurrection. Many of these leaders would later die for this belief. The only reasonable answer for this is that the resurrection did happen. (See more on this issue in Lesson 7.)

How would the Roman soldiers have known the disciples had stolen Jesus' body if they were asleep? Their explanation doesn't make sense.

CHRISTIANITY IS UNIQUE COMPARED TO OTHER RELIGIONS THEN AND NOW

The resurrection of Christ is also unique when compared to other religions. In fact, the very idea of bodily resurrection was scoffed at. For example, in Stoicism, one's personal identity continues only until death or, in some forms, possibly to the end of time but not forever. To Stoics, death is a desirable end to the sufferings of life, and some Stoics have gone so far as to recommend suicide. Stoicism is also fatalistic and pantheistic (the belief that God is all and all is God) and teaches that death is nothing more than a cyclic re-absorption into the universal world soul or deity.

For another example, Epicureanism, a materialistic philosophy, teaches that all existence consists of atoms that might temporarily be organized in a certain form but which could change forms later to become a different substance. When the body was dissolved by death, the person ceased to exist. The idea that the body can be absorbed into other elements or organisms is a strong barrier to the idea of a real bodily resurrection from the dead.

Thus it is not surprising that when the apostle Paul spoke in Athens, Greece, concerning the resurrection of the dead, the Stoics and Epicureans openly ridiculed him (Acts 17:18–32). The idea of an actual historical person being physically resurrected from the dead was thought as impossible in the minds of the Greeks as any New Testament truth could possibly be.

📖 Read about the reaction in Acts 17:18–32 to Paul's preaching of Jesus' bodily resurrection from the dead. Notice also the impact on some in verses 32–34. What were the different ways people responded to the message of Paul?

_____

_____

_____

_____

_____

_____

How were the responses to Paul similar to the responses people have today when Christians speak of the resurrection of Jesus?

_____

_____

_____

_____

What are the particular historical facts upon which Jesus' resurrection is based? First, there is the fact of the death of Jesus. No one survived crucifixion, especially after a spear pierced the heart of Jesus. Second, He was honorably buried in the tomb of Joseph of Arimathea. Third, the tomb was empty. No one argued against this fact, not even His enemies. Fourth, hundreds of people claimed to see Jesus alive again. Then, fifth, Christianity spread rapidly throughout the Roman Empire, reaching dozens of locations and the capital of Rome before the deaths of the apostles. Scholars have shown that no religion before or after Christianity has held to the concept of a three-day period prior to the resurrection.

📖 Read Matthew 12:39–41. What does it say about the death and resurrection of Jesus?

_____

_____

📖 If Jesus predicted His resurrection before it happened, what does this tell you? Note what the following verses share about His predictions:

Matthew 27:62–64

_____

_____

Mark 8:31–32

_____

_____

Mark 9:30–32

_____

_____

Mark 10:33–35

_____

_____

What is the origin of this new belief of Resurrection? The only answer is Jesus actually rose from the dead and appeared to His followers.

The Christian idea of the resurrection certainly did not derive from its cultural environment. The teaching of the New Testament came to the Greco-Roman world with a message that had not previously been proclaimed in the temples of the gods or in the halls of the philosophers. What is the origin of this new belief? The only answer is Jesus actually rose from the dead and appeared to His followers.

📖 How did Paul communicate the resurrection during his time in Athens in Acts 17:16–18?

_____

_____

_____

📖 Read Acts 17:22–23 and 17:28. What points of reference did Paul use to communicate the uniqueness of Christianity to his audience?

_____

_____

_____

APPLY What are some similar points of reference in your workplace, school, or community activities that could be used to share about the uniqueness of Christianity?

_____

_____

_____

_____

CHRISTIANITY IS UNIQUE IN ITS IMPACT

LESSON FIVE | DAY THREE

Christianity is also unique in its effect on the individual and at the social level. Many things in life can lead to or force a significant or even radical change in a person's life, such as marriage, divorce, inheriting money, or changing careers. But the change brought about by Christ, when a person decides to trust in Christ as his or her personal Savior is unique. People's lives may change in other ways, but never in the manner that Christ changes a life.

Note some of the powerful changes in the lives of those mentioned in the following passages:

Paul, in Acts 9:20–21

_____

_____

Barnabas, in Acts 4:34–36

_____

_____

Mary Magdalene, in Mark 16:9–10

_____

_____

First Corinthians 6:9–11 teaches:

> _"Do you not know that the wicked will not inherit the kingdom of God? Do not be deceived: Neither the sexually immoral nor idolaters nor adulterers nor male prostitutes nor homosexual offenders nor thieves nor the greedy nor drunkards nor slanderers nor swindlers will inherit the kingdom of God. And that is what some of you were. But you were washed, you were sanctified, you were justified in the name of the Lord Jesus Christ and by the Spirit of our God."_

It isn't just good people Jesus saves and changes. When we consider the manner of change produced by non-Christian religion, we can see that committed members of other faiths experience change produced by a combination of inner need and an outward conformity to a system of rules and ethics. It is a shift in behavior, a personal reworking of priorities, but does not compare to the radical inner alteration that Jesus performs in a person who believes in

Him by faith in Christ. This change is accompanied by the regeneration of the Holy Spirit (John 3:6–8; 6:63; 7:38–39) and leads to a radical inward change that can only be described as "eternal transformation."

📖 Look up John 3:6–8; 6:63; 7:38–39 and note the changes that result from the Holy Spirit:

_____

_____

_____

When people are converted to almost any other religion besides Christianity, they enter and then begin to earn the favor of the god. They never claim a relationship which is secure and totally a product of God's grace that has brought them into a loving, personal relationship with the God of the universe. They will never claim that their words and obedience assures them of forgiveness of sins. They will never claim their conversion guarantees them eternal life or personal immortality. Some only hope it might; others don't even have hope.

A Hindu doesn't claim to come into *a personal* relationship with Brahman, because Brahman is impersonal. A Buddhist never claims to know Buddha *personally,* because Buddha no longer exists. At best an adherent claims merely to be enlightened with the impersonal "Buddha nature." A Muslim cannot come into an eternal, loving, *personal* relationship with either Muhammad or Allah, because the Quran does not teach that Allah desires such a relationship. Of course, the prophet (Muhammad) is still in the grave. A Muslim claims only that knowledge of the prophet's writings in the Quran may enable one to enter heaven, should his or her obedience and other conditions warrant it.

But a Christian claims to have come into *a personal,* eternal relationship with Jesus Christ at the moment of faith. Why? Because Jesus, who is alive eternally, saves as a free gift when a person trusts in Him. Jesus is none other than the very God who made the universe.

📖 According to John 5:24, what happens to the person who accepts Jesus Christ by faith?

_____

_____

_____

_____

📖 What does Jesus promise the person who believes in Him in John 6:47?

_____

_____

Indeed, the kind of change produced by any other religion would simply not have been capable of generating the needed momentum to establish the early Christian church, given the conditions faced by the apostles both after the crucifixion (their dejection and depression) and in the early years of apostolic preaching (the severe persecution). We simply cannot explain the changed lives of the apostles and the founding, spread, and continuance of the church based on any supposition other than that of the resurrection.

No Comparable Force for Good

Worldwide, the message of the resurrection has had a force for good that no other faith has provided. Nations and cultures have been altered. Bedrock changes have been made in people's view of themselves, God, society, and others. For two thousand years, millions of families have been reconciled, immoral people have become godly, proud people humble, selfish individuals selfless and filled with love for other people. Around the globe, Christians have made incredible sacrifices, the nature of which is impossible to explain unless the resurrection really occurred.

Further, we need only compare the practical results of the Christian faith worldwide to that of any other faith to note the radical difference—a difference that can only be explained by the person and resurrection of Jesus Christ.

What are some of the major changes Christianity has provided the world?

_____

_____

_____

_____

People become dissatisfied with movements and causes, but not with Jesus. Why? Because Christianity has everything. Besides offering a personal relationship with God, the forgiveness of sins, and eternal life, it satisfies every aspect of the heart and mind of humanity. Its moral teachings to social good are unsurpassed. Christian philosophy and theology are unequalled in their influence.

📖 Read Colossians 1:3–6. How did the Colossian believers influence those around them? How do you see this in your church today?

_____

_____

_____

_____

Only by starting with a Christian worldview—the existence of an infinite, personal, triune God do we have satisfying explanations for the deep philosophical questions asked throughout the ages. No other philosophy explains so much of the universe while simultaneously offering so much. Without it, there would be no U.S. Constitution, and therefore, no America as we know it.

📖 Read Paul's words in Galatians 1:11–24. In what ways was his life changed?

_____

_____

_____

_____

> *Worldwide, the message of the resurrection has had a force for good that no other faith has provided.*

After Paul's life was changed, how was he able to help change the lives of others?

_____

_____

_____

_____

Only Christ's resurrection can adequately explain the tremendous impact He has had upon human history. Just as the Bible itself has had more impact on humanity than any other book, so Jesus Christ has had more impact than any other person. This is not merely the conclusion of Christian scholars, it is the general consensus of secular thought as well.

What changes does the gospel make according to 1 Thessalonians 1:4–10?

_____

_____

_____

_____

Christ changes because He is alive and has the power to do so. He is a living Savior, not a dead prophet. He is alive and powerful for every person who calls upon Him.

LESSON FIVE

DAY FIVE

FOR ME TO FOLLOW GOD

Many times we hear that all religions are basically the same and lead to the same place. However, as we have seen, this is far from true. In order to follow God, it is important to understand that Jesus is not only a way but **the way** to know God, both now and for eternity (John 14:6).

APPLY When we become outspoken about our beliefs in Jesus Christ, others will sometimes become offended or ridicule what we say. Can you think of a time when you have experienced this in your attempts to communicate your faith? What happened?

_____

_____

_____

_____

_____

When we become outspoken about our beliefs in Jesus Christ, others will sometimes become offended or ridicule what we say.

It is important to realize that negative reactions are a normal part of our Christian faith. When Paul spoke to the people of Athens (Acts 17), he encountered three responses: **1)** those who were hostile, **2)** those who were curious, **3)** and those who believed the message. Yet he continued to speak the truth about the Christian faith, despite severe persecution at times.

What are some of the times you are most likely to not speak up about your faith to non-believers? Why is that the case?

_____

_____

_____

_____

_____

Paul tells Timothy in 2 Timothy 1:7 that *"God did not give us a spirit of timidity, but a spirit of power, of love and of self-discipline."* In Romans 1:16, Paul says, *"I am not ashamed of the gospel, because it is the power of God for the salvation of everyone who believes."*

APPLY What are one or two ways you can become bolder in telling others about Jesus this week?

_____

_____

Take a couple of minutes to write down how you came to believe in Jesus. Share your response with someone in your group.

_____

_____

_____

_____

_____

_____

Using your story, how could you share about God's grace in your life with an unbeliever? Who could you plan to talk with this week about Jesus?

_____

_____

_____

_____

First Peter 1:8–9 tells us, *"Though you have not seen him, you love him; and even though you do not see him now, you believe in him and are filled with an inexpressible and glorious joy, for you are receiving the goal of your faith, the salvation of your souls."* In what ways has God provided "glorious joy" in your life? In what ways do you need to change to live with this inexpressible, glorious joy?

_____

_____

_____

_____

_____

_____

_____

As we close this week's lesson, make this prayer your own:

Lord, I believe that Your Son Jesus Christ is the way, the truth, and the life. No other religion compares with what you offer. Thank you for your grace that saves me and changes me through faith alone. Forgive me for the times when I have failed to speak up on Your behalf or for Your ways. Help me not to be timid, but bold in speaking about You with others. Help me not to be ashamed of the Gospel, but to share it through my actions and through my words with all who will listen.

What Does the Bible Say about Evolution and Creation?

The issue of creation and evolution is one of the most hotly-debated issues for Christians today, but why is it important? The issue of creation and evolution is important because the subject of origins tells us who we are. Are we the product of impersonal forces of matter, chance, and time? Or are we the result of a special creation by an infinite, personal God? Because of this issue's larger implications in areas such as science, religion, and culture, in addition to our personal meaning in life, no one can deny the relevance of this subject.

Three Theistic Views of Creation

POSITION:	YOUNG EARTH CREATION	OLD EARTH CREATION	THEISTIC EVOLUTION
DEFINITION:	Creation in six 24-hour days	Six-day creation not 24-hour days	God created through evolution
WORLDVIEW:	Theistic	Theistic	Theistic
AGE OF UNIVERSE:	Thousands of Years	Millions of Years	Millions of Years

Note: Several variations exist within each of these views

HOW DID IT ALL BEGIN?

Genesis 1:1–2 reads, "In the beginning God created the heavens and the earth. Now the earth was formless and empty, darkness was over the surface of the deep, and the Spirit of God was hovering over the waters." This is the beginning of the universe (Hebrews 11:3). God creates the universe *ex nihilo* (out of nothing). Before that there was nothing but God, and merely by means of His incredible wisdom and awesome power He brings the universe into existence.

Scientists like Stephen Hawking have said that we have proven time has a beginning, that time was created. Scientists now believe the Big Bang is the coming into existence of all matter, energy, space, and time a finite time ago by what they call a "transcendent causal agent" who from outside of space and time brought it into existence. For us, that transcendent causal agent is God, mentioned in Genesis 1:1–2.

However, even among those who believe in the authority of the Bible, there is much discussion concerning how Genesis 1—2 is to be interpreted. In a program I (John) hosted on this issue, we discussed the two major viewpoints, labeled Old Earth Creationism and Young Earth Creationism. We'll talk about these views today as we study through Genesis 1–2.

What are some of your concerns when talking about the debate regarding creation and evolution?

_____

_____

_____

_____

_____

Theology is man's attempt to interpret the words of the Bible, which are inspired and inerrant.

Science is man's attempt to interpret the record of nature.

Scripture itself tells us this is so. Psalm 19:1–4 tells us, *"The heavens declare the glory of God; the skies proclaim the work of his hands. Day after day they pour forth speech; night after night they display knowledge. There is no speech or language where their voice is not heard. Their voice goes out into all the earth, their words to the ends of the world."*

What do you believe Psalm 19:1–4 tells about the activities of the universe?

_____

_____

_____

Sometimes from God's truthful statements in Scripture, theologians will misinterpret it and teach false theological views. On the other hand, sometimes scientists will misinterpret the record of nature and posit false scientific views.

"In the beginning God created the heavens and the earth."

Genesis 1:1

So although God has spoken truthfully in Scripture (for God cannot lie) and the record of nature has also come truthfully from His hand, the interpreters can misinterpret one or the other or both areas. Thus we have differences.

Differences Between Young-Earth and Old Earth Creationism

The primary difference between young and old-earth creationists is the speculated amount of time between God's creative acts. The young-earth view insists that it was all accomplished in 144 hours–six successive 24-hour days–while old-earth (progressive) creationists allow for millions (or even billions) of years. This theory regarding the period of time that God took to create the universe is usually explained by:

1) Observing how the author Moses literally used the term "day" in four different ways in Scripture.

How Moses Used "Day"

- As part of a day, referring to twelve hours of daylight (1:14)
- To summarize the entire time of creation (2:4, KJV—*"in the day that the LORD God made the earth and the heavens."*)
- A twenty-four hour period of time (as in Genesis 7:11)
- An unspecified period of time (Psalm 90:4, authored by Moses, where a day is compared to a thousand years)

2) Placing long periods of time before Genesis 1:1 (making it a recent and local Creation)

3) Placing the long periods of time between Genesis 1:1 and 1:2 (called "gap" views)

4) Making the "days" of Genesis 1 long periods of time (similar to number one)

5) Allowing long periods of time between literal 24-hour days in Genesis 1(called alternate day-age views) or

6) Making the days of Genesis to be days of revelation of God to the writer, not days of Creation (called "revelatory day" views)

There are several variations within these perspectives, comprising a total of more than a dozen different views held by evangelical theologians on the matter. However, a majority of Christians throughout centuries has held the view that creation took place in six days of some length.

Old-earth (progressive) creationists are not to be confused with theistic evolutionists. Old-earth creationists do not teach or believe that macroevolution is a method by which God produced the originally created kinds of Genesis 1. Rather, they believe in immediate creative acts of God during each of the six days mentioned which they believe are long periods of time. Old-earth creationism was strong among nineteenth-century creationists, though this view dates from at least the fourth century (in Augustine and other church fathers).

Theistic Evolution

Broadly speaking, theistic evolution is the belief that God used evolution as His means of producing the various forms of physical life on this planet, including human life. All theistic evolutionists believe that God performed at least one supernatural act—the act of creating the physical universe form nothing.

Most theistic evolutionists hold to at least two acts of Creation:

1) the creation of matter out of nothing
2) the creation of first life.

After that, allegedly, every other living thing, including human beings, emerged by natural evolutionary processes that God had ordained from the beginning. Some theistic evolutionists do insist that God directly created the first soul in the long-evolved primate to make it truly human and in His image.

Why is theistic evolution inconsistent with the Bible's teaching on creation?

_____

_____

_____

_____

_____

Areas of Agreement Between Young- and Old-Earth Creationists
Young and old-earth creationists have much in common. This includes several basic things:

Direct Supernatural Creation of All Forms of Life
Both young- and old-earthers believe that God supernaturally, directly and immediately produced every kind of animal and human as separate and genetically distinct forms of life. Both hold that every kind produced by God was directly created *de nova* (brand-new) and did not come about by God's using natural processes over a long period of time or tinkering with previous types of life in order to make higher forms (evolution).

> **APPLY** In contrast with evolutionary views, both of these two views believe God supernaturally created plant, animal, and human forms of life. Why is it important for all Christians to believe that God is the supernatural creator of life?

_____

_____

_____

_____

Opposition to Naturalism
Both groups are also agree in their opposition to naturalism (a worldview in which everything happened as a result of chance, plus time, wholly impersonal), which they see as the philosophical presupposition of evolution. They correctly observe that without a naturalistic bias, evolution loses its credibility. Ruling out the possibility of supernatural intervention in the world begs the whole question in favor of evolution even before one begins.

Opposition to Macroevolution
Likewise, both are united in their opposition to macroevolution, either theistic (started by God) or non-theistic (evolution by chance); that is, they reject the theory of common ancestry. They both deny that all forms of life descended by completely natural processes without supernatural intervention from the outside. They deny that all living things are like a tree connected to a common trunk and root; rather, they affirm the separate ances-

try of all the basic forms of life, a picture more like a forest of different trees. *Micro*evolution, where small changes occur within the basic kinds of created things, is acknowledged, but macro (large-scale) evolution between different kinds is not accepted. For example, both old and young-earth creationists agree that all dogs are related to an original canine pair—part of the same tree. However, they deny that dogs, cats, cows, and other created kinds are related like branches from one original tree.

The Historicity of the Genesis Account
Further, both young and old-earth views that are evangelical hold to the historicity of the Genesis account: They believe that Adam and Eve were literal people, the first people of the entire human race. While some may allow for poetic form and figure of speech in the narrative, all agree that it conveys historical and literal truth about origins. This is made clear by the New Testament references to Adam and Eve, their creation and fall, as literal (Luke 3:38; Romans 5:12; 1 Timothy 2:13–14).

📖 Read 1 Timothy 2:13–14. What does it teach regarding the creation of Adam and Eve?

_____

_____

Clearly, any Christian view of origins must take into account the New Testament references regarding Adam and Eve. Here, Paul specifically writes that Adam and Eve were created supernaturally by God.

Major Differences Between Young- and Old-Earth Creationists
Of course, there are some differences between the two basic evangelical views on Creation. The primary ones include the following.

The Age of the Earth
A crucial variance between the two views, naturally, is the age of the earth. Young-earthers insist that both the Bible and science support a universe that is only 6,000-12,000 years old, while old-earthers allow that the universe was brought into existence 13.7 billion years ago, the earth approximately 4.5 billion years ago, first life (bacteria) 3.8 billion years ago, and Adam and Eve about 40,000 years ago. Young-earthers connect their view to a literal interpretation of Genesis (and Exodus 20:11), but old-earthers claim their view is a literal interpretation of Genesis and Exodus 20, based on their interpretation of the word "day." They, too, cite scientific evidence in their favor.

At a minimum, it would be wise if both sides could agree on the following:

1) The age of the earth is not a test for orthodoxy.

2) Neither view is proven with *scientific* finality, since there are unproven presuppositions associated with each. The evidence from God's creation helps us understand what God has revealed in Scripture.

3) The fact of Creation (vs. evolution theory) is more important than the time of Creation.

4) Their common enemy (naturalistic evolution without God) is a more significant focus than their intramural differences.

In spite of these points of contention, the doctrine of Creation is a cornerstone of the Christian faith. The essentials of this teaching have universal consent among orthodox theologians. They include the following:

> "[The Bible] really does talk about an absolute beginning, and the text says, 'In the beginning.' It's very, very crucial that all who believe in the inerrancy of Scripture understand this is where it all started."
>
> —Dr. Walter Kaiser

1) There is a theistic God.

2) Creation of the universe was *ex nihilo* (out of nothing).

3) Every living thing was created by God.

4) Adam and Eve were a direct and special creation of God.

5) The Genesis account of creation is historical, not mythological.

While there is lively debate about the time of Creation, all evangelicals agree on the fact of Creation. There is also agreement on the source of Creation (a theistic God) and the purpose of Creation (to glorify God). The exact method of Creation is debated. Yet increasingly the scientific evidence supports a supernatural Creation of the universe, the direct creation of first life, and the special creation of every basic life form.[21]

APPLY What issues do you face regarding evolution and creation in your school, workplace, or community relationships? How can you respond with both the love of Christ and truth of Christ in these situations?

_____

_____

_____

_____

_____

_____

THE DAYS OF CREATION

The Book of Genesis opens with a specific story regarding the creation of the universe. In six days, God created the following according to Genesis 1:

Day 1: The heavens, the earth, light and darkness.

Day 2: The water in the atmosphere and waters in the ocean below (the water cycle).

Day 3: God separates the dry ground from the oceans and then brings forth vegetation on the dry ground.

Day 4: The sun, the moon and the stars become visible on earth, marking days, seasons, and years.

Day 5: Marine creatures great and small, birds of the air.

Day 6: Land animals and Adam and Eve.

Day 7: God rested.

Yesterday we discussed the various views regarding the creation of the universe. Today, we'll look at what Genesis 1—2 teaches regarding each day of creation.

The First Day (1:1–5)
The opening words of the Bible reveal that, "In the beginning God created the heavens and the earth" (1:1). This one sentence reveals several facts about how God started the known universe.

First, it tells us *who* created the earth: God. Regardless of one's view of the process, it is clear that it was God who created it.

Second, it tells us *how* it happened. God *created it*. He did not build upon the work of anyone else. He created all of the matter in the universe.

Third, it tells us *what* was created: the heavens and the earth. God Himself originally created everything we can view in the universe.

Fourth, it tells us *when* creation happened: in the beginning. Of course, we are not told when the beginning was, but in the beginning God was alone and no one else existed. It was His power that caused creation.

Fifth, God has a purpose, a reason for creating the universe, the stars, earth, and people (Romans 1:20; Ephesians 1:4–14).

📖 Compare Genesis 1:1–3 with John 1:1–3. What similarities do you find between these two verses?

_____

_____

_____

_____

In John, we find that the word (Jesus) was God. He was involved in the creation process (Colossians 1:16). In Colossians 1:16, we see part of the why in creation—that all things were made *for* Him, in other words, for His pleasure.

📖 How did the beginning of creation look in Genesis 1:2?

_____

_____

_____

_____

In Genesis 1:1, the perspective is the entire universe. Light was created in the beginning when God created matter, energy, space, and time. Genesis 1:2 brings us down to the surface of the earth. The clue is that the Spirit of God was hovering over the surface of the waters. From there on we are to understand what God tells us from the perspective of an observer on the surface of the waters. Here it was dark on the surface of the waters. Scientists would tell us that the atmosphere of the earth and the interplanetary debris of the early solar system would have prevented the passage of sunlight and starlight to the surface of the earth, creating this darkness.

📖 What does James 1:17 tell us about creation?

_____

_____

James points out that everything that is good comes from God, which would include His creation.

The Second Day (1:6–8)

On the second day, God said let there be a firmament (an expanse) to separate the water in the atmosphere above from the waters in the oceans below. This is the establishment of the very fine-tuned water cycle that is enhanced by what takes place on the third day.

The only way to get water dispersed relatively evenly over the whole surface of the earth is if the continents are positioned just right relative to the oceans; the moon has to be in just the right position as well. God deals with the land on the third day.

The Third Day (1:9–13)

On the third day, God separated the seas from the dry land. The current ratio of land to water surface is twenty-nine to seventy-one percent, which scientists say is perfect for life. Also, the continental landmasses are oriented north/south rather than east/west, an ideal orientation for distributing water, which makes the maximum surface of the planet available for human habitation.

📖 Read Job 38:8–11. How does Job describe this third day of creation from God's point of view?

_____

_____

Here again, God, in successive miraculous steps, creates advanced plant vegetation and trees bearing fruits on the continents.

The Fourth Day (1:14–19)

On the fourth day in Genesis 1:14–19:

> *"And God said, 'Let there be lights in the expanse of the sky to separate the day from the night, and let them serve as signs to mark seasons and days and years, and let them be lights in the expanse of the sky to give light on the earth.' And it was so. God made two great lights—the greater light to govern the day and the lesser light to govern the night. He also made the stars. God set them in the expanse of the sky to give light on the earth, to govern the day and the night, and to separate light from darkness. And God saw that it was good. And there was evening, and there was morning—the fourth day."*

Notice what the Bible says, *"Let there be lights"* and *"let them serve."* It doesn't say God created the lights at this point.

In verse 16, we are told God created the sun, moon, and stars. In the Hebrew language there are no verb tenses as there are in English. However, there are three main verb forms: one for commands, one for action not yet finished, and one for action that has been completed at some unspecified time in the past. Verse 16 is in that third form. It is telling us that the sun, moon, and stars were completed entities before the fourth day. As Genesis 1:1 records events surrounding the first day of Creation, when God created the heavens and the earth, this would have also been when the stars and galaxies were made. But their light wouldn't have become visible on the surface of the earth which was changed by God from permanently overcast, to occasionally transparent. As such, this is the time they started to serve as signs, markers of days, years, and seasons. The atmosphere was transformed for the benefit of life.[22]

📖 Read Psalm 33:6–9. What does the psalmist have to say regarding God's creation?

_____

_____

_____

Here, we find that God just said the word and created. His words were the initiator.

The Fifth Day (1:20–23)
On the fifth day, we read that God "created" the animals of the air and sea. This is God intervening and creating something that didn't exist before, and it tells us that these animals didn't exist before. Previously, God had prepared the world for these creatures, including water, food, light, and oxygen. Though dinosaurs are not mentioned here, they would have been created on this fifth day as well.

Interesting, this is the first time where we find that God creates a "living" creature. Plant life, though important in creation, was not discussed as having conscious life like animals or people.

Regarding God's creation up to this point, He did pronounce that it was very good. But in the midst of this "good" creation, and before Adam sinned, the Bible tells us that "Satan," as well as "the tree of good and evil" were present. So, "good" doesn't necessarily mean "perfect."

Romans 8 does not say that the first animal deaths were linked to Adam's sin, but only that the _"creation was subjected to frustration"_ as a result of it (verse 40). Scripture gives no reason why animals couldn't have died before Adam's sin. Nowhere does the Bible say that animals die as a consequence of human sin. The Bible does tell us that human death entered through Adam's sin, but says nothing specifically about animal or plant death. Many species of life can't survive even three hours without food, and the mere ingestion of food by animals requires the death of at least plants or plant parts.

📖 Read Genesis 1:20–23. With what characteristics were animals created according to these verses?

_____

_____

Here, God called these animals "good." From the perspective of these verses, they did not need to evolve into another form to improve. God created them good and gave them the command to multiply. They were to reproduce after their kind throughout the earth.

The Sixth Day (1:24–31)
On the sixth day, God began by creating land animals. They were created distinctly from the animals of the air and sea by the following differences:

■ Created on a different day (five and six)
■ Created in different classifications (land animals that had three divisions)

Also notice the following parallelisms in the verses concerning land animals:

Verse 24   *And God said*   *And it was so*
Verse 25   *God made*   *It was good*

What three categories of land animals did God create in Genesis 1:24–25?

_____

_____

The three categories were livestock (domesticated animals), creatures that crawl on the ground, and wild animals. Each serves a distinct purpose in God's creation and received specific mention in this section.

On the sixth day God also created human beings in His expressed image. We will spend Day Three further examining this important aspect of creation.

The Seventh Day (2:1–3)
On the seventh day, we are told that God's creation was complete. At that point, God rested or ceased from His creative work (verse 2). He then made the seventh day a holy day, a pattern He used to teach Israel that just as God worked for six of His days of creation and then rested, they were to work six of the days and rest on the seventh (Exodus 20). The pattern of one out of seven must be an analogy to our days, as the length of time for the seventh day according to Hebrews is still going on (Hebrews 4:1–4). Even today, the seven days are the division that make up our week and add up to the appropriate number of days in the year. God signature has been upon creation from the very beginning.

APPLY   What response do you feel after reading God's creation account? How does it change or enhance your worship of God as Creator?

_____

_____

_____

_____

_____

LESSON SIX   DAY THREE   THE CREATION OF HUMAN BEINGS

When God created the earth, Genesis says the crowning moment came when he created man and woman in His own image. God took one of Adam's ribs to create Eve, the first woman. Together they would become the parents of the entire human race. When God created Adam, He made him from the dust of the ground and breathed into Him life and He created a living soul (Genesis 1:26–27; 2:7, 22–23). God then created Eve from Adam's rib, completing Adam with a fitting counterpart. Before God, they were equal in importance as male and female.

The Hebrew word for Adam literally means "humanity," including both men and women, serving as an appropriate term for the first two representatives of the human race. Eve's name means "giver of life." Through her, the rest of humanity was born.

We learn from the Bible that human beings are created beings, created a little lower than the angels (Psalm 8:3–6; Hebrews 2:7–8) by God's own hands (Job 10:8–12; Isaiah 64:8). Humans are designed with complexity (Psalm 139:14) and everyone alive today descended from the same original man and woman (Acts 17:26).

Created in God's Image

Genesis offers the following words regarding the supreme importance of human beings being made in the image of God:

Genesis 1:26: *"Then God said, "Let us make man in our image, in our likeness. . . ."*

Genesis 1:27: *"So God created man in his own image, in the image of God he created him; male and female he created them."*

Genesis 9:6: *". . . the image of God has God made man."*

  In what ways are humans made in His image according to the following passages?

Genesis 1:28

_____

_____

Ephesians 4:24

_____

_____

Colossians 3:10

_____

_____

Mormonism mistakenly teaches that such verses refer to the idea that God the Father looks like a person. However, the Bible is clear that we are made in His *image,* not that we physically look the same.

Created with a Spiritual Dimension

Though some argue that humans consist of only a physical nature, the Scriptures show that humans are also composed of a spiritual nature. Bible scholars debate whether this immaterial aspect contains one part (soul) or two parts (soul and spirit), but agree that humans are created with both a physical and spiritual dimension.

In the Bible, this spiritual aspect of humanity is actually discussed using several words. What words does Scripture use to highlight the spiritual part of humans in the following verses?

1 Peter 2:11

_____

_____

Romans 8:16

_____

_____

Hebrews 4:12

_____

_____

1 Peter 2:19

_____

_____

Romans 12:2

_____

_____

Jude 23

_____

_____

In these verses, we find references to the soul, spirit, heart, conscience, mind, and flesh. Though the flesh is often used to refer to the human body, it is also sometimes used in reference to the sin within us which is a spiritual issue.

Men AND Women Created Equal in God's Image
Too often in history, the Bible has been used to dictate poor treatment regarding women. However, Genesis 1:27 notes that both men and women were created in the image of God. While each has distinctly different divine purposes, God created both with equality.

📖 Read Galatians 3:28. How is the equality of men and women described in this verse?

_____

_____

While men and women have different roles, their status is equal in the eyes of God as part of His "good" creation.

Humans Did Not Evolve
Regardless of one's view regarding the other portions of creation, the Bible is extremely clear about the creation of humans.

📖 How does Hebrews 3:4 describe God's role of creation?

_____

_____

Here, we are told that God created all things, including humans. He is our "builder" or designer, meaning there is something more at work than an evolutionary process.

In addition, according to Dr. Ron Rhodes, modern science fails to account for the following issues:

Scientist largely agree that the universe had a beginning. They may disagree regarding the process, but generally concede that something created or started it.

The complexity of the universe points to a master designer.

The fossil records favor creation more than evolution.

The theory of evolution assumes a long series of positive and upward mutations. However, in almost all known cases (over 99 percent), mutations are not beneficial but are harmful to living beings.

The first and second laws of thermodynamics do not support evolution. The first law states that matter and energy are not destroyed; they just change forms. The second law states that the natural course of a closed system (like our universe) is to degenerate. The universe is *de*volving, not *e*volving.

Scientists have never observed macroevolution. While mutations within a species do occur (microevolution), macroevolution is built on theory without sufficient evidence.[23]

Many have stated that it takes more faith to believe in evolution than creation. The historical facts seem to provide more of a basis for creation than evolution.

In Matthew 19:4 we read Jesus' response to the Pharisees regarding divorce. He said, *"Haven't you read, . . . that at the beginning the Creator 'made them male and female. . . .'"* Here, Jesus clearly notes that Adam and Eve were made at the beginning. This shows that Jesus Himself argued for a divine creation of Adam and Eve as the first humans.

APPLY How does understanding God's creation of people help us gain a deeper sense of worship of God?

_____

_____

_____

_____

_____

Questions about God's Creation

LESSON SIX   DAY FOUR

In addition to the questions addressed in our previous days, there are several common questions regarding the origin of the universe and aspects of the Bible and science. We discuss several of these in today's study, offering information from science and answers from Scripture on the subject.

What are the two major views with regard to the time involved in creation?
There are two major views with regard to the time involved in Creation: the old-earth view and the young-earth view. The latter believes the universe is no more than approximately 6,000 to 12,000 years old, while the former holds that it is probably about 13.7 billion years old.

Science in the Bible

Hydrology

Phenomenon or Process	Scripture
Hydrologic Cycle	Ecclesiastes 1:7; Isaiah 55:10
Evaporation	Psalm 135:7; Jeremiah 10:13
Condensation Nuclei	Proverbs 8:28
Condensation	Job 26:8; 37:11, 16
Precipitation	Job 36:27, 28
Run-off	Job 28:10
Oceanic Reservoir	Psalm 33:7
Snow	Job 38:22; Psalm 147:16
Hydrologic Balance	Isaiah 40:12; Job 28:24–26

Geology

Phenomenon or Process	Scripture
Principle of Isostasy	Isaiah 40:12; Psalm 104:5–9
Shape of Earth	Isaiah 40:22; Psalm 103:12
Rotation of Earth	Job 38:12, 14
Gravitation	Job 26:7; 38:6
Rock Erosion	Job 14:18, 19
Glacial Period	Job 38:29, 30
Uniformitarianism	2 Peter 3:4

Astronomy

Phenomenon or Process	Scripture
Size of Universe	Isaiah 55:9; Job 22:12; Jeremiah 31:37
Number of Stars	Jeremiah 33:22; Genesis 22:17
Variety of Stars	1 Corinthians 15:41
Precision of Orbits	Jeremiah 31:35, 36

Meteorology

Phenomenon or Process	Scripture
Circulation of Atmosphere	Ecclesiastics 1:6
Protective Effect of Atmosphere	Isaiah 40:22
Oceanic Origin of Rain	Ecclesiastics 1:7
Relation of Electricity to Rain	Jeremiah 10:13

Biology

Phenomenon or Process	Scripture
Blood Circulation	Leviticus 17:11
Psychotherapy	Proverbs 16:24; 17:22
Biogenesis and Stability	Genesis 1:11, 21, 25

Biology (Continued)

Phenomenon or Process	Scripture
Uniqueness of Man	Genesis 1:26
Chemical Nature of Flesh	Genesis 1:11, 24–27; 3:19; 1 Peter 1:24, 25

Physics

Phenomenon or Process	Scripture
Mass-Energy Equivalence	Hebrews 1:3; Colossians 1:17
Source of Energy for Earth	Genesis 1:14, 17; Psalm 19:6
Atomic Disintegration	2 Peter 3:10
Radio Waves	Job 38:35

Adapted from Mark Eastman and Chuck Missler, *The Creator Beyond Time and Space* (Costa Mesa, CA: The Word For Today, 1996), p. 156.

Young-earthers take the "days" of Creation to be six successive, literal, solar days of twenty-four hours each, totaling 144 hours of Creation. They also reject any significant time gaps between the accounts in Genesis 1 or within the genealogies in Genesis 5 and 11. In support of this view, it is noted that Jesus stated in Matthew 19:4 "*that <u>at the beginning</u> the Creator 'made them male and female.'* " Also, the language of the Psalms and Job point toward literal days, though others note that these portions of Scripture are poetic. Further, there is much debate regarding the definition of the "days" in Genesis 1, which we will address below.

Old-earthers stress the various ways the word "day" is used by Moses and in the Old Testament. Second, in response to Matthew 19:4, they suggest that the phrase "*at the beginning*" does not specify the period of the days of creation, only that God created Adam and Eve.

📖 What does God say about the creation of humans in Matthew 19:4?

_____

_____

Can a "day" be more than twenty-four hours?
It is contended that the usual meaning of the Hebrew word *yom* ("day") is twenty-four hours unless the context indicates otherwise. The context does not indicate anything but a twenty-four hour day in Genesis 1; hence, the days should be taken as solar days.

In response, some suggest that while it is true that most often the Hebrew word *yom* (day) means "twenty-four hours," that this is not definitive for its meaning in Genesis 1. First, the meaning of the term is not determined by a majority vote but by the context in which it is used. It is not important how many times it is used elsewhere but how it is used here. Second, in the Creation story itself in Genesis 1—2, "day" (*yom*) is used of more than a twenty-four hour period. Speaking of the whole six days of Creation, Genesis 2:4 refers to it as "the day" (*yom*) when all things were created (KJV). Thirdly, *yom* is elsewhere used of long periods of time as in Psalm 90:4 (written by Moses), which is cited in 2 Peter 3:8: "*A day is like a thousand years.*"

In summary, a "day" (*yom*) in the Hebrew language could literally be used to mean a period longer than a twenty-four hour day. Those holding to the young-earth view argue that creation took place in six, twenty-four hour days. Old-earth theory suggests that there is enough linguistic evidence to literally assert that each day is a long period of time, as the record of nature seems to indicate to us.

Why do you believe Christians have such difficulty understanding the age of creation?

_____

_____

_____

_____

"While there is lively debate about the time of Creation, all evangelicals agree on the fact of Creation."

—Dr. Norman Geisler

What happened to the dinosaurs?

At the time of the Flood, many of the sea creatures died, but some survived. In addition, all of the land creatures outside the Ark died, but the representatives of all the kinds that survived on the Ark lived in the new world after the Flood. Those land animals, including dinosaurs, found the new world to be much different than the one before the Flood. Several species have died out since that time. Dinosaurs just happened to die out, too. Extinction of plants and animals seems to be the rule in history rather than the formation of new types of animals as you would expect from evolution. Historically, some historians believe that the stories of dragons are based on real creatures that would be categorized as dinosaurs. Some suggest that dinosaurs are mentioned in a couple of places in the Bible, such as Job 40:15–20 (the "behemoth").[24]

How big a problem is bias among scientists and theologians when it comes to the creation and evolution questions?

At the end of the day, we all have biases that we bring to the table. No scientist or theologian is completely objective. Honest scholarship demands that these biases be clearly communicated and taken into consideration.

APPLY As you discuss creation and evolution with others, how do you see their personal biases influencing their perspectives? Your perspective?

_____

_____

_____

_____

_____

Are the Bible and science in conflict?

If God, the Creator, is responsible for the words of the Bible then nature's record, when correctly interpreted through scientific study, should never disagree with the words of the Bible. The Bible, correctly interpreted through theological study, should not disagree with science. In fact, the Christian view is that God has revealed Himself to humanity not only through special revelation (the Bible), but also through His creation (Psalm 19:1–4; Romans 1:20). When there is a disagreement between science and theology, it is due to a faulty interpretation from either one or both accounts. However, in issues specifically addressed in the Bible, all of God's revelation is truthful and is generally clearer than scientific theory. The Bible should continue to stand as our supreme guide.

Yet because it is true does not always mean we automatically understand it. God put the cookies on the bottom shelf when he gave us the Gospel so all could understand. But there are other topics and doctrines in which the cookies are not on the bottom shelf and require careful study.

📖 Read Psalm 19. Verses 1–6 describe God in creation. Verses 7–14 describe God's Word. How do these areas help us in our understanding of God?

God's Creation

_____

_____

God's Word

_____

_____

How could people live over nine hundred years before the Flood?

Astrophysicists and biologists I (John) have interviewed on my television program have shared that Genesis 6:3 states that God acted purposefully to shorten human life spans, and Genesis 6:5 and 11 imply that the shortening of human life spans at the time of the Flood served a specific spiritual purpose.

Why did God allow for long life spans in the first place? Long life expectancies early in human history reflect God's mercy and provision. Long life spans make it possible for human technology and civilization to emerge rapidly. Living nine hundred years gives people ample opportunity to make discoveries, have numerous children, develop technology, refine technological achievements, and teach all that has been learned to ensuing generations. Under these conditions, human civilization can make dramatic advances in relatively few generations.

One benefit of a *shorter* human life span is that it serves to limit the spread of wickedness. An exceptionally evil person can hurt, destroy, or limit the effectiveness of a large number of righteous people during the course of 900 years. Moreover, wicked people find it easier and safer to wreak destruction upon the righteous than they do upon other wicked people. The net result of such long life spans is that the righteous tend to be exterminated whereas the wicked tend to survive. Over time, the balance of the population tilts toward the wicked, with only a few righteous people left. By truncating human life spans to only about 120 years, God mercifully limited the spread of evil, ensuring righteousness a presence in society after the Flood.

The long life spans during the days before the Genesis Flood provide people today with a helpful object lesson. Many seem to think that "life's too short," that life would be better if people could just live a few more years. The human condition in the days just before the Flood suggests the opposite. It serves as a reminder that people are *much* better off with brief life spans. God allows most people to live on Earth long enough to recognize and choose (or reject) Him, long enough to fulfill their destiny, and long enough to receive the training they will need for the new creation. Once that work and training are accomplished, however, Christians can move on to a life far more wonderful and blessed than anything possible on Earth (see 1 Corinthians 2:9). Therefore, believers can rejoice that God has shortened humanity's race toward the heavenly prize.[25]

APPLY What are some of the questions you have regarding the earth's origins? How can you investigate these questions and still grow in your relationship with God?

_____

_____

_____

_____

_____

LESSON SIX DAY FIVE

OUR RESPONSE TO GOD'S CREATION

While a young shepherd, David would have spent many nights gazing into the stars. Scientists have stated that God created ten billion trillion stars in the universe, and that they are all needed for life to exist on earth. In Psalms 8:3–4, we read David's reflection on viewing the stars:

"When I consider your heavens, the work of your fingers, the moon and the stars, which you have set in place, what is man that you are mindful of him, the son of man that you care for him?"

Upon viewing God's creation, even King David realized the greatness of its Creator. As we consider God's creation in our own lives, our response should likewise be one of worship and awe.

What do we discover about creation in John 1:3 and Colossians 1:16?

_____

_____

_____

Here, we find that Jesus Christ was involved in creation just like the Father. All three persons of the Trinity (Father, Son, and Spirit) were involved in the creation of the universe (Genesis 1:2).

Scripture records several other times when God the Son, our Lord Jesus, showed His power over creation during His earthly life, including:

■ Jesus demonstrated His power over physics by turning water into wine (John 2:1–11)

■ Jesus showed power over nature when He walked on the Sea of Galilee and stopped the storm (Matthew 14:24–33)

■ Nature shook at His crucifixion by an earthquake and eclipse (Matthew 27:50–54).

■ In His resurrection He conquered death and promised those who believe in Him, even though they die, that they will live eternally (John 21:1–18).

The psalmist writes in Psalm 104:31–34 (NIV) that:

> *May the glory of the LORD endure forever; may the LORD rejoice in his workss—he who looks at the earth, and it trembles, who touches the mountains, and they smoke.*
>
> *I will sing to the LORD all my life; I will sing praise to my God as long as I live.*
>
> *May my meditation be pleasing to him, as I rejoice in the LORD.*

Here we find that the writer's reflection on God's creation resulted in singing praise to Him. What are some songs of worship that come to mind that focus on God's power and wisdom in creation?

_____

_____

_____

APPLY When was a time you were in creation and sensed God's majesty and power because of your surroundings?

_____

_____

_____

_____

Near the end of the Bible, the elders mentioned in Revelation 4:11 provide an appropriate response to God's creative power.

📖 Read Revelation 4:10–11. What do these elders say about God's work of creation?

_____

_____

When you see Christ someday, will you offer worship to Christ for the same reasons? Their reasons for worshiping Christ on the throne included: **1)** He created all things, **2)** they were created by His will, and **3)** because of Christ they have their being.

📖 God also sustains His creation. Read Jeremiah 10:12–13 and note how God continues to intervene in His creation today.

_____

_____

_____

Jeremiah teaches that God made the creation and controls it still today. Rather than a deistic God who set a plan in motion and remained distant, our God is involved with every aspect of our universe's operation. Otherwise we would never pray for rescue during a storm.

God also uses the record of nature (general revelation) to point people toward His Word (special revelation). Isaiah 55:8–13 shares how God's ways are far higher than our ways and thoughts:

"For my thoughts are not your thoughts, neither are your ways my ways," declares the LORD.

"As the heavens are higher than the earth, so are my ways higher than your ways and my thoughts than your thoughts.

As the rain and the snow come down from heaven, and do not return to it without watering the earth and making it bud and flourish, so that it yields seed for the sower and bread for the eater, so is my word that goes out from my mouth: It will not return to me empty, but will accomplish what I desire and achieve the purpose for which I sent it.

You will go out in joy and be led forth in peace; the mountains and hills will burst into song before you, and all the trees of the field will clap their hands.

Instead of the thornbush will grow the pine tree, and instead of briers the myrtle will grow. This will be for the LORD's renown, for an everlasting sign, which will not be destroyed."

What does God say His Word does according to these verses?

_____

_____

_____

_____

How should we live regarding what God has made? First, we should live as if God did create our environment. This would apply in practical ways through recycling, picking up trash, and to promote balanced use of human development of land.

Another area of application regarding God's creation is the role of Christians and the environment. How should we live regarding what God has made? First, we should live as if God did create our environment. This would apply in practical ways through recycling, picking up trash, and to promote balanced use of human development of land. However, in the Bible, we always see that people are valued over both the environment and animals or pets. In terms of priority, we are to store up treasures for heaven (Matthew 6:19–21). The one thing that will last forever from this earth is people.

Read Genesis 1:26. What are some practical ways you could show obedience to God's Word through how you treat the environment? What is something your church could do to help in this area?

_____

_____

_____

_____

_____

_____

Spend some time in prayer to God right now, reflecting on our Creator's greatness in Psalm 95:2–7:

"Let us come before him with thanksgiving and extol him with music and song.

For the LORD is the great God, the great King above all gods.

In his hand are the depths of the earth, and the mountain peaks belong to him.

The sea is his, for he made it, and his hands formed the dry land.

Come, let us bow down in worship, let us kneel before the LORD our Maker; for he is our God and we are the people of his pasture, the flock under his care."

Write your own words of praise to God for His creation of the universe and of your life:

_____

_____

_____

_____

_____

_____

_____

_____

Notes

WHAT EVIDENCE EXISTS FOR THE RESURRECTION?

The main event of Jesus' life is His resurrection from the dead. If he didn't rise from the dead, it doesn't matter what he taught. Why? Jesus claimed to be God, God doesn't lie, and Jesus said that He would rise from the dead on the third day. If there was no resurrection of his literal, physical body from the tomb, then he is not God and Christianity is false.

But what if Jesus did come back to life from the dead? Then this is proof that His claim to be God is true. Therefore, Christianity's message *is* true. It would also indicate we should listen to Jesus and not to someone else. In fact, the Christian faith has been willing to put itself on the line down through the centuries with the assertion that if the resurrection happened, then Christianity is true. If it didn't, then Christianity is false.

A rabbinic lawyer who persecuted Christians one day met the risen Jesus. We know him today as the apostle Paul. He wrote to the Christians in Corinth, *"If Christ has not been raised, our preaching is <u>useless</u>, and so is <u>your faith</u>. . . . If only for this life we have hope in Christ, <u>we are to be pitied more than all men</u>"* (1 Corinthians 15:14, 19).

> **The main event of Jesus' life is His resurrection from the dead. If He didn't rise from the dead, it doesn't matter what he taught.**

Over the last few years, television networks have aired the latest popular conceptions of Jesus. Guests and scholars have issued many new radical and controversial opinions about what happened at the end of Jesus' life. Some of these controversial opinions include:

- Jesus really didn't die on the cross. He survived and became a traveler to Egypt or to Spain.
- Jesus' body was secretly taken out of the tomb by his mother Mary and his brother James. The other disciples never discovered what they had done.
- The Family Tomb of Jesus has been "discovered" in a tomb near Jerusalem along with his so-called wife and son.
- The disciples had hallucinations of a resurrected Jesus, saw psychologically induced visions, or they just made up the story that Jesus came alive again to comfort others who loved Jesus and wanted to remember him in a unique way.

How can a person sift through these theories and get to the truth of what really happened at the end of Jesus life?

In this session, we'll look at five historical facts that nearly all scholars agree upon regarding the end of Jesus' life. From these five facts, one must make a decision: Do the facts best support a supernatural resurrection or some other conclusion? These five facts include:

- The death of Jesus on the cross
- The honorable burial of Jesus
- The empty tomb of Jesus
- The post-resurrection appearances of Jesus
- The growth of the early church

I (John) discussed many of these issues during a television program with Dr. Gary Habermas, one of today's foremost authorities on the resurrection of Jesus. He argued that there are more than twelve historical facts that the vast majority of critical scholars, regardless of personal bias, will typically admit today about the end of Jesus' life. Some will give twenty, thirty, or more. But Habermas says, just using twelve facts he can prove the resurrection of Christ happened. According to Habermas, these twelve facts include:

- Jesus died by crucifixion.
- Jesus was honorably buried.
- Jesus' death caused his followers to lose hope.
- Jesus' tomb was soon empty.
- The followers of Jesus believed they had seen Jesus alive.
- The followers of Jesus regained hope and communicated a risen Jesus.
- This message was the center of preaching in the early church.
- This message was communicated in and around Jerusalem shortly after the death of Jesus.
- The church was started and quickly grew.
- Sunday became the primary day of worship for Christians.
- James, a former skeptic, became an early leader of the Jerusalem church after he "believed" he had seen Jesus alive after his death.
- Paul later had an experience of the risen Jesus and became a leader in the early Christian movement.

In tracking over one thousand different scholarly sources on the resurrection, Habermas observed, "What I'm saying is that with the exception of the empty tomb, virtually all critical scholars accept this list as historical, and most of them will even grant the empty tomb. And by the way, these facts have two prerequisites. It's not only that they are admitted by virtually all critical scholars, but they are also individually attested by other data."

THE DEATH OF JESUS ON THE CROSS

I asked Dr. Habermas in the same interview mentioned on the previous page, "What do you think about those who claim Jesus really didn't die on the cross?" He sat up in his chair and quickly responded:

Jesus *died*. Why do scholars today rarely question the death of Jesus? Why do the founders of the Jesus Seminar, for example say that the fact that Jesus died is the surest fact we have in his career? It's because the data is so strong.

What is some of this data? First, death by crucifixion is essentially death by asphyxiation. When you hang on a cross and the weight of your body pulls down on the intercostal pectoral and deltoid muscles around your lungs, you reach a state where when the weight is dragging down on them, you can inhale, but you are increasingly unable to exhale until you reach a place of near paralysis and can't exhale at all.

In the 1950s an experiment was performed in West Germany in which male volunteers were tied to a 2 x 4. These males lost consciousness at a maximum of 12 minutes. Now, on the cross you can push up on the nails. When you push up, you relieve those muscles in your lungs. But when you pull down on them again, because you can't stay up there for long, you're in a low position on the cross and you asphyxiate. The Roman Centurion did not require a degree in medicine. If the person was hanging low on the cross for any amount of time, even thirty minutes, he's dead.

The Trials
Shortly after midnight, temple officials arrested Jesus in the garden at Gethsemane. Between that time and sunrise on Friday, Jesus stood trial before Caiaphas and the political Sanhedrin. Here Christ experienced his first major physical trauma. The guards blindfolded Jesus, spat on him, taunted him, and struck him in the face with their fists.[26] Soon after daybreak, the religious Sanhedrin with the Pharisees and the Sadducees tried Jesus again and found him guilty of blasphemy for His response to one of the High Priest's questions. The priest asked, *"Are you the Christ, the Son of the Blessed One?"* Jesus responded: *"I am"* (Mark 14:60–61). To the religious leaders, Christ's answer represented a crime punishable by death.

Unfortunately for the Jewish leaders, only the Romans had permission to execute a traitor or conspirator. Later that morning, Jesus was taken to the Praetorium, the residence of Pontius Pilate. Pilate made no charges against Jesus and sent him to Herod Antipas, the tetrarch of Judea. Herod in turn returned Jesus to Pilate. Due to the crowd's adamant demand for crucifixion (*"We have no king but Caesar"* in John 19:15), Pilate finally granted their wishes. He agreed to hand Jesus over for Roman whipping and eventual crucifixion on a cross.

The Seven Trials of Jesus

Trial	Scripture
Before Annas	John 18:12–14, 19–23
Before Caiaphas	Matthew 26:57, 59–68; Mark 14:53, 55–65; Luke 22:54, 63–65; John 18:24
Before the Sanhedrin	Matthew 27:1; Mark 15:1; Luke 22:66–71
Before Pilate	Matthew 27:2, 11–14; Mark 15:1b–5; Luke 23:1–5; John 18:28–38
Before Herod	Luke 23:6–12
Before Pilate	Matthew 27:15–23; Mark 15:6–14; Luke 23:13–22; John 18:39–19:6
Rejection by the People	Matthew 27:24–31; Mark 15:15–20; Luke 23:23–25; John 19:7–16

What physical torture die Jesus suffer during his trial in Luke 23:63–65?

_____

_____

Read John 19:2–3. What abuse did Jesus endure here? Why did they mock Him?

_____

_____

_____

_____

The Scourging

After Jesus had been turned over to Roman hands, he experienced the torture of whipping, also known as flogging or scourging. According to scholars, flogging was a legal preliminary to every Roman execution.[27] The usual flogging instrument was a short whip with several single or braided leather thongs of variable lengths. Each braid contained small iron balls or sharp pieces of sheep bones tied at intervals.[28]

In preparation for this whipping, soldiers stripped the individual of his clothing. Hands were tied to an upright post.[29] The back, buttocks, and legs were flogged either by two soldiers or by one soldier who alternated positions. The severity of the scourging depended on the attitude of the soldiers and was intended to weaken the victim to a state just short of collapse or death. After the scourging, the soldiers often taunted their victim.

Read Matthew 27:26–31. What additional suffering did Jesus endure before the cross?

_____

_____

According to one medical doctor's investigation of the Roman flogging, "When it was determined by the centurion in charge that the prisoner was near death, the beating was finally stopped."[30] Even before His suffering on the cross, Jesus would have endured enough pain to soon end His human life without it.

Why is this important? Sometimes people like to make the accusation that Jesus didn't really die. They claim that He simply passed out on the cross and was later able to exit the tomb, either on His own or with the help of His buddies. After reading a little bit about the torture Jesus experienced that day, it would be physically impossible to claim any human could have walked out alive.

Death on the Cross

Imagine this scenario: the heavy crossbeam was tied across his shoulders. Jesus, the two thieves, and supervising Roman soldiers led by a centurion began their slow journey along the path, which was known as the Via Dolorosa. Despite Jesus' efforts to walk, the weight of the heavy beam combined with the pain of earlier beatings and a brutal scourging left Him only to stumble in a heap. The beam likely smacked his head and shoulders, producing additional pain. The centurion, undeterred, selected a North African man, Simon of Cyrene, to carry the cross. Jesus followed, still bleeding and sweating the cold, clammy sweat of shock. Traveling the length of over six football fields, the journey from the Fortress Antonia to Golgotha was finally completed. Jesus was once again stripped of his clothing except for a loincloth.

Simon placed the cross on the soil along with the heavy beam. Then the soldiers made Jesus lie down upon it. One soldier reached for a hammer and felt for the depression at the front of the wrist. He drove a heavy, square wrought-iron nail through his flesh and deep into the wood. Quickly, he moved to the other side and repeated the action, being careful not to pull the arms too tightly, but to allow some flexion and movement. The left foot was pressed backward against the right foot. With both feet extended, toes down, a nail was driven through the arch of each, leaving the knees moderately flexed. The victim thus started his crucifixion, which could last hours or even days. A person would not be removed from a cross until confirmed dead.[31]

Soldiers could speed up a crucifixion by breaking the bones of one of the victim's legs. This prevented the victim from pushing himself upward. Rapid suffocation would occur, quickly ending hours of suffering. According to the Gospel writers, soldiers broke the legs of the two thieves, but when they prepared to do the same to Jesus, they saw that it wasn't necessary. Most likely, the soldiers realized Jesus had not pulled himself up on the cross in order to breathe. He had been hanging in the down position for long enough to assure the soldiers he had already died.

Read John 19:31–35. What did the soldier do to confirm Jesus was dead?

_____

_____

This passage of Scripture provides conclusive evidence that Jesus died if not by asphyxiation, then certainly due to heart failure. As one article on the issue states, "This is rather conclusive post-mortem evidence that Jesus died, not the usual crucifixion death by suffocation, but of heart failure due to shock and constriction of the heart by fluid in the pericardium."[34]

Did You Know?

PROOFS OF CHRIST'S CRUCIFIXION

A first-century skeleton of a young crucified man was discovered in ancient Palestine in 1968? He still had a large nail pierced through his feet![32]

Archaeological expert J. H. Charlesworth stated: "It is not a confession of faith to affirm that Jesus died on Golgotha that Friday afternoon; it is a probability obtained by the highest canons of scientific historical research."[33]

The result, according to Dr. Norm Geisler, founder of Southern Evangelical Seminary, was that:

> Clearly, the weight of historical and medical evidence indicates that Jesus was dead before the wound to his side was inflicted and supports the traditional view that the spear, thrust between his right rib, probably perforated not only the right lung but also the pericardium and heart and thereby ensured his death. Accordingly, interpretations based on the assumption that Jesus did not die on the cross appear to be at odds with modern biblical knowledge.[35]

APPLY Why is it important to understand that Jesus physically died while on the cross?

_____

_____

_____

_____

In what ways does the sacrifice of Jesus' life on the cross impact you today?

_____

_____

_____

_____

THE HONORABLE BURIAL OF JESUS

In an interview that I (John) conducted, Dr. William Lane Craig noted that, "With respect to the second historical fact, the honorable burial of Jesus, the majority of New Testament scholars who have written on this subject agree that Jesus of Nazareth was buried by Joseph of Arimathea in a tomb."

📖 Read Mark 15:42–46. How does Mark describe the account of Jesus' burial?

_____

_____

All four Gospels report that Joseph of Arimathea requested permission from Pilate to bury Jesus, and that His body was laid in a tomb cut out of solid rock. Three of the writers say the tomb was new—that no one had ever been laid in the tomb before. But does this information agree with what archaeologists in Israel have discovered in their investigations?

Jewish archaeologist Dr. Gabriel Barkay, considered one of the foremost authorities on first–century Jerusalem tombs, shared on this aspect of Jesus' burial. I asked him, "What current archaeological evidence supports the description given in the gospels about the tomb in which Jesus was buried?" According to his research, he confidently shared,

We have the fact that it was a rich man's tomb. We have, most probably, the allusion to the fact that it was outside the city of Jerusalem. We have the stone found unrolled three days later. Altogether we have about a thousand burial caves from the time of Jesus surrounding Jerusalem. The details that we have in the gospels about the burial of Jesus fit well with the evidence we have in the field.

The People Involved
According to the Gospels, two men buried Jesus.

📖 Read John 19:38–42. Who were the people involved in Jesus' burial?

_____

How did the burial process described in these verses confirm that Jesus was dead?

_____

_____

_____

Dr. Craig also stated,

> The gospels say that Jesus of Nazareth was laid in a tomb by this enigmatic figure, Joseph of Arimathea, who appears out of nowhere in the gospels. Contrary to expectation, he gives Jesus of Nazareth an honorable burial in a tomb with what would be about 75 pounds (34 kg) of spices by present standards. Moreover, Mark tells us that this man was a member of the Sanhedrin, the very council that had just condemned Jesus to be crucified. Then Joseph singles out Jesus among the trio of men who had been crucified for special care by giving him an honorable burial in a tomb rather than allowing the body to simply be dispatched into a common grave reserved for criminals. This is extraordinary and requires some sort of explanation.

> The historical credibility of the burial account of Jesus by Joseph of Arimathea leaves skeptical critics in an extremely awkward position. If Jesus was in fact buried by a Jewish leader in Jerusalem, as the gospels claim, that means that the location of Jesus' tomb was known to both Jews and Christian alike. But in that case, it's impossible to imagine how a movement founded on belief in the resurrection of a dead man who had been publicly executed in Jerusalem could arise and flourish in the face of a tomb containing his corpse. So those scholars who want to deny such things as the empty tomb and the resurrection appearances also find themselves forced to deny the fact of the honorable burial of Jesus, despite the fact that this is one of the earliest and best-attested facts about the historical Jesus that we have.

Where Was Jesus Buried?
One of the most impressive stops during my time in Israel was at the Church of the Holy Sepulcher in Jerusalem. According to archaeologists, it traditionally marks the actual site of the tomb in which Joseph of Arimathea (with the help of Nicodemus) buried Jesus.

📖 Read Luke 24:1–12. How would the followers of Jesus have known the location of the tomb?

> ## "Without the belief in the resurrection the Christian faith could not have come into being."
> ### —Dr. William Lane Craig

_____

_____

_____

In this account, the women and Peter actually knew where the tomb was so they could confirm whether Jesus was there. Joseph and Nicodemus buried Jesus and knew where the tomb was. The Roman soldiers would have known the location of the tomb, as would those who had assigned them to guard it. The historical tradition reveals too many witnesses to suggest his burial site would be unknown.

While standing in front of this Garden Tomb, I spoke with Dr. Magen Broshi, a respected Jewish archaeologist and scholar on the Second Temple period. He is the former curator of the Shrine of the Book Museum in Jerusalem in which the Dead Sea scrolls are housed. Based on his research, when asked about whether he thought the Garden Tomb was the location where Jesus had been buried, he answered, "There is high probability. A very high probability." When I asked him why, he revealed,

> Two reasons. One reason is that the tradition should be trusted. It was too important to be forgotten, and there was a Christian community in and around Jerusalem that would have carried it on and handed it down from one generation to the other. The second reason is that this area was a graveyard at the time of Jesus, and there are several graves around here now. There were more, but they have been obliterated by later building activity.

What about the Burial Stone?
📖 Read Matthew 27:59–60. What does it say about the stone in front of the tomb?

_____

_____

All four Gospel accounts mention a stone that was rolled against the entrance to the tomb. Mark added that it was a "very large stone."[36] So I asked Dr. Broshi about it, saying, "The Gospel accounts talk about a stone that was rolled in front of the tomb. Does that make sense to you?"

"Why not? We found it."

"You found it?" I clarified.

"Not here [at the Garden Tomb], but in many other places, the rolling stone. Sometimes they weigh more than a regular car. But being round, you know, you can roll it."

"Why did they place a stone in front of the tomb?" I asked.

"To keep the robbers out, to keep the places of the tombs away from animals."

According to Dr. Broshi, the New Testament description of Jesus' burial that included a large stone over its entrance accurately fits the burial pattern of first century Jerusalem.

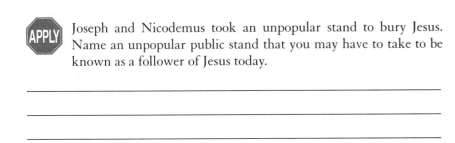 Joseph and Nicodemus took an unpopular stand to bury Jesus. Name an unpopular public stand that you may have to take to be known as a follower of Jesus today.

_____

_____

_____

_____

THE EMPTY TOMB OF JESUS

LESSON SEVEN — DAY THREE

How do we know the tomb of Jesus was empty when the stone guarding the entrance was rolled away? This is the third major fact historians must evaluate. All of the early sources report that Jesus' tomb was found empty, first by women, then by his disciples, and finally, by the Jewish leaders themselves. Dr. Craig shared that, "Today, the majority of scholars who have written on this subject agree that the tomb of Jesus was probably found empty by a group of his female followers early on Sunday morning. That represents the historical core of the empty tomb narrative as we find it in Mark."[37]

📖 Who were the first people to discover the empty tomb in Luke 24:1–10?

_____

According to Dr. Habermas,

> The empty tomb is preached very early. You have Paul in 1 Corinthians 15 saying Jesus died, he was buried, and what went down is what came out, and what came out is what appeared. First Corinthians is already early, about 25 years after the cross. But then the creedal passage that he [Paul] reports in 1 Corinthians 15 is earlier still. In Galatians, Paul has apostolic confirmation of his message about the resurrection events. These come from Peter and James in Galatians 1 and from Peter, James, and John in Galatians 2. This testimony was given to Paul *within five years of Jesus' resurrection* [30–35 or 33–38 AD] from those preaching since day one. So you have this intricate, interwoven, and accredited eyewitness messenger [via James and Peter] with an early book, with an even earlier creed. Ultimately, it's teaching our fact here in question—the empty tomb.

The Jewish Leaders
In addition, the Jewish leaders confirmed the early story of the empty tomb of Jesus. Dr. Craig notes that,

> The earliest Jewish response to the proclamation of the resurrection was not to point to the occupied tomb, but rather, to say that the disciples had stolen the body. It was itself an attempt to explain away why the body was missing.

> What we have here is evidence from the very enemies of the earliest Christian movement in favor of the empty tomb, evidence that is sim-

ply top drawer, because it comes not from the Christians, but from the very opponents of the early Christian movement.

📖 Read Matthew 28:11–15. How did the Jews react to the empty tomb?

_____

_____

_____

_____

The Jews did not deny the empty tomb. Instead, they offered a different reason to explain why it was empty. They claimed the disciples had stolen the body.

The Roman Guards
📖 Read Matthew 27:62–65. What security measures had been provided for the tomb of Jesus?

_____

_____

_____

It is interesting that the Romans, knowing of Jesus' claim of resurrection placed twelve Roman soldiers to guard the tomb of Jesus. These soldiers were always under penalty of death if they failed in their task in a matter such as this. The Bible does not say what happened to the soldiers assigned to Jesus' tomb, but if contemporaries agree his body was not there after three days, it stands to reason that the guards would have fought to the death to stop anyone who might attempt to steal Jesus' body. This is an inconvenient fact for those that would argue that Jesus' body was removed by the apostles so they could propogate a myth. Surely such a battle would not have gone unnoticed to historians. It also seems credible that the apostles would have no reason to propogate the myth in the first place if Jesus did not in fact raise from the dead.[38]

In addition, would the soldiers have accepted a bribe for the body of Jesus as the Jewish leaders accused? There are significant problems with this concept. First, where would Jesus' followers obtain a large sum of money within three days of His death?

Second, even if his followers somehow obtained a large sum of money to pay off the guards, would the guards have taken it?

📖 Read Acts 16:25–30. Why was the guard mentioned in this passage planning to kill himself?

_____

_____

_____

Here we see that for Roman soldiers assigned to guard duty, if one or more of their inmates escaped, somebody in charge was likely to pay for this security breach with his life. This guard at the jail in Philippi was aware of this fact and thought that taking his own life was the best possible scenario for him.

> *It is interesting that the Romans, knowing of Jesus' claim of resurrection placed twelve Roman soldiers to guard the tomb of Jesus.*

📖 Another example is found in the passage of Peter's imprisonment in Acts 12:18–19. What did Herod state would happen to the guards if Peter escaped?

_____

_____

In this episode we read that Herod specifically ordered the guards to be executed if Peter escaped. These examples help us to see the problems with the claim that the guards at Jesus' tomb would have accepted a bribe for his body. However, the attitude of the disciples prior to the resurrection, fleeing in fear of being captured, presents yet another problem to those who wish to discredit Christ's resurrection.

The Disciples
Instead of planning a "tomb rescue," what were the disciples doing while Jesus was in the tomb, according to John 20:19?

_____

_____

Rather than stealing the body of Jesus, how did the disciples react when the women told them about the empty tomb in Luke 24:11–12?

_____

_____

After the death of their friend and leader, the disciples were in mourning. In addition, they feared that they might be the next targets, so they gathered behind locked doors during the days after the crucifixion.

APPLY How would you explain the empty tomb of Jesus to a skeptic?

_____

_____

_____

_____

_____

How does the evidence of the empty tomb of Jesus strengthen your faith today?

_____

_____

_____

_____

_____

_____

THE POST-RESURRECTION APPEARANCES OF JESUS

A ccording to Dr. Craig,

The fourth fundamental fact that any responsible historical hypothesis has to account for in explaining the fate of Jesus of Nazareth is the fact that after his death different individuals and groups of people claimed to have seen Jesus of Nazareth alive from the dead on different occasions and under varying circumstances. Now, this general fact is one that is universally acknowledged today among New Testament critics.

The Post-Resurrection Appearances of Jesus

Appearance	Scripture
To Mary Magdalene	Mark 16:9; John 20:15–28
To Mary Magdalene, Mary mother of James, and Salome	Mark 16:1
To two men on the road to Emmaus	Luke 24:30–31, 33; Mark 16:12–13
To Simon Peter	Luke 24:33b–34, 1 Corinthians 15:5
To ten disciples (without Thomas)	Luke 24:36–43; John 20:19–23
To eleven disciples (Thomas present)	John 20:24–29
To seven disciples	John 21:1–14
To over five hundred people at one time	1 Corinthians 15:6
To James, the half-brother of Jesus	1 Corinthians 15:7
To eleven disciples at Galilee	Matthew 28:16–17a
To eleven disciples near Jerusalem	Luke 24:50–53
To Paul during his walk on the Damascus Road	1 Corinthians 15:8; Acts 9:1–9

According to historical sources, how many people claimed to have actually seen Jesus? The key list is in 1 Corinthians 15. In that list you have individuals, including leaders of the church. Paul starts with Peter, ends with himself, and in the middle has James, the brother of Jesus—three key individuals who saw the risen Jesus.

But you also have *groups* (and that's a very important fact in itself) to ascertain some evidence for these appearances. You have the Twelve—a group Paul calls 'all the apostles'—and you have more than five hundred people, most of whom remain alive at the point Paul wrote the document.

According to Dr. Habermas,

Now, when you go to the gospels, I think also with good grounds we have, for example, the women. You have several women at the tomb and probably Mary Magdalene alone as she returns. So you see them sighting Jesus as well as the empty tomb. But if the apostles were going to put their best foot forward [to prove that Jesus was alive again], they would not use women because women couldn't go to a law court. This would not have impressed people in first century Palestine. By far the best reason for starting with the women and secondarily with Mary is very simple—they saw the risen Jesus.

📖 Read 1 Corinthians 15:3–8. Identify our four historical facts about Jesus from this passage:

The death of Jesus (verse 3):

_____

_____

The burial of Jesus (verse 4a)

_____

_____

The resurrection (empty tomb) of Jesus (verse 4b)

_____

_____

The post-resurrection appearances of Jesus (verses 5–8)

_____

_____

_____

How many people saw Jesus alive?

- 3 women (Luke 24:10)
- 2 men on the Emmaus road (Luke 24:13–35)
- 11 disciples (multiple times)
- 500 people at one time (1 Corinthians 15:6)
- James, the brother of Jesus (1 Corinthians 15:7)
- Paul (outside of the 40 post-resurrection days in Acts 9)

TOTALS: 518, unless some of the 500 were the same as other sightings. In Acts 1:3, Luke alludes that there were *additional* eyewitness accounts of the resurrected Jesus.

Why is the fact of multiple witnesses important in the resurrection accounts?

_____

_____

_____

_____

Today, certain scholars look at these appearances very differently. Dr. Ben Witherington, professor of New Testament at Asbury Theological Seminary shared in an interview that,

Most scholars would certainly say that the disciples believed that they saw Jesus, and many of them would want to just leave it there and say,

"Okay, it was subjective phenomenon that happened here." But if you interpret the gospel documents about the resurrection appearances of the risen Lord, and you interpret the Pauline evidence, and the rest of the New Testament evidence, they were claiming far more than that. They were claiming to actually have a *physical encounter* with Jesus after his death—that he ate, was tangible, could be touched, and that he was still moving in space and time as a real person. They were claiming more than just having had a vision of Jesus.

📖 Read Luke 24:42–43 and John 21:13. How do these details prove that Jesus appeared in a physical body?

_____

_____

_____

_____

Other scholars use the word "vision" to describe what they think the disciples saw. A vision is defined as seeing an object in the mind without the use of the five senses. Further, there are two kinds of visions: a truthful vision and a false vision. An example of a true vision would be a prophet who receives accurate information from God.

📖 Read Acts 7:55–56. How is this vision of Jesus by Stephen different from what the disciples experienced?

_____

_____

_____

_____

Stephen saw a true vision of Jesus Christ, but not a physical appearance. Again, on this issue, Dr. Craig observes,

> It's interesting that the New Testament draws a clear distinction between *appearances* of Christ and *visions* of Christ. The appearances of the risen Christ were to a limited circle and soon ceased. But visions of the exalted Christ continued in the New Testament Church. Paul saw them when he was praying in the temple in Jerusalem. Stephen saw a vision of Christ at his stoning. In the Book of Revelation you have a vision of the throne room of God that John sees. So the visions in the church were something that did not cease, yet these were distinct from a resurrection appearance.

Some scholars even suggest that the resurrection appearances of Jesus were simply hallucinations. But Dr. Habermas points out four major problems with this opinion:

Problem #1: Groups Do Not See the Same Hallucination. A hallucination is something you believe so firmly that you invent the mental picture. Two cannot share a hallucination any more than two can share a dream.

Problem #2: The disciples were not expecting to see the risen Jesus. It's granted by everybody, both from Scripture and from psychology, that you can't have exuberant, expecting disciples after this calamity. They were not in the right frame of mind to have such positive hallucinations.

Problem #3: Too many people, times, and places. To believe that every one of these people manufactured a private, individual hallucination is unrealistic. We rarely even see hallucinations today, but they were just supposed to have them on demand. That's too problematic.

Problem #4: The empty tomb. It wouldn't be empty. The leaders could have easily proven these hallucinations wrong by digging up the body and placing it on public display. They didn't because it wasn't there.

In 1 Corinthians 15, Paul wrote that Jesus appeared to all of the disciples, to James, and to over 500 people at one time, most of whom were still alive at the time of Paul's writing.

How could Paul's opponents have proven him wrong about the resurrection of Jesus?

_____

_____

_____

Ultimately, opponents could have rounded up some of the witnesses Paul mentioned so they could say that he was lying. They could have also responded by finding the body of Jesus in the tomb. Yet there were numerous people who claimed to physically see Jesus and no corpse to prove otherwise.

 Read Paul's words regarding the importance of the resurrection in 1 Corinthians 15:14. Where do you see the resurrection under attack in our world today?

_____

_____

_____

_____

How do the historical facts regarding the resurrection strengthen your faith in Christ?

_____

_____

_____

_____

> *"To believe that every one of these people [eyewitnesses of the resurrection] manufactured a private, individual hallucination is unrealistic."*
>
> *Dr. Gary Habermas*

THE GROWTH OF THE EARLY CHURCH

LESSON SEVEN — DAY FIVE

I n continuing my (John's) interview with Dr. William Lane Craig, he explained that the fifth fundamental fact concerning the fate of Jesus of Nazareth is the very origin of the disciples' belief that God had raised Jesus from the dead. In his words, "You see, it's an indisputable fact that Christianity sprang into being in the middle of the first century. Now, why did this movement arise? Where did it come from?"[39]

N.T. Wright, bishop of Durham and former Canon theologian of Westminster Abbey, provided a colorful explanation of this growth during my interview with him at his home office in England. He shared that,

> The origin of Christianity is actually itself one of the most extraordinary phenomenon in the history of the world. In 20 AD there's no such thing as a Christian church. By 120 AD, the emperor in Rome is getting worried letters from one of his proconsuls off in northern Turkey about what to do about these Christians. So in that century, you have this extraordinary thing suddenly appearing out of nowhere. All the early Christians for whom we have actual evidence would say, "I'll tell you why it's happened. It's because of Jesus of Nazareth and the fact that He was raised from the dead."[40]

📖 Read Luke 24:9–12. What was Peter's initial response to hearing and then seeing the empty tomb?

_____

_____

Now read Peter's preaching in Acts 2:22–36. How did his attitude about the empty tomb change from the previous passage? What changed him? (see also Mark 16:7; 1 Corinthians 15:5–8)

_____

_____

_____

_____

Instead of wondering what happened to Jesus or hiding behind closed doors, as a result of Jesus appearing and talking to him, Peter now boldly preached the resurrection of Jesus on the streets of Jerusalem. As a result, over three thousand people became followers of Jesus in one day, including many from distant nations who had traveled to the city to celebrate Pentecost.

Another example can be found in the life of James, the half-brother of Jesus. Early in the ministry of Jesus, James and his other siblings didn't understand what He was doing. Yet after the resurrection, James the skeptic became a believer and led the early church in Jerusalem (along with Jesus' other half-brother, Jude, author of the Book of Jude). James ultimately gave his life as a martyr for his belief in the resurrection of Jesus.

📖 Read Mark 3:20–21. How did Jesus' family respond to His miracles and teachings?

_____

_____

📖 What happened to James to change his mind about Jesus as recorded in 1 Corinthians 15:7?

_____

_____

The same change that occurred in the life of James also took place among the other disciples. James saw Jesus alive again! As a result, he changed his

"If the resurrection had not happened, . . . There would have been no Christian movement."

–Dr. Edwin Yamauchi[41]

thinking, the direction of his life, and gave his life for this belief. The other disciples did the same. The only reasonable explanation for their change of mind is that the resurrection actually happened and that they were eyewitnesses of this fact.

Finally, let's look at the example of the apostle Paul.

📖 Read Acts 9:1–2. What did Saul/Paul do before his conversion?

_____

_____

Paul once acted as a persecutor of Christians and despised their beliefs. What changed this person who didn't believe what Christians were saying and was throwing them in prison for their beliefs?

📖 Read Acts 9:3–19. What happened to Saul/Paul on the road to Damascus?

_____

_____

Now read Acts 9:20. What did Paul do immediately after seeing Jesus?

_____

The examples of Peter, James, and John are only three of countless examples of how the resurrection of Jesus has changed the lives of people in dramatic ways. Worldwide, the message of the resurrection has provided evidence for Christians that no other religion in the world can claim. Nations and cultures have been altered. Bedrock changes have been made in people's view of themselves, God, society, and others. For two thousand years, millions of families have been reunited by belief in Christ. After conflict, hateful people have become loving, have seen addictions broken, and selfish individuals have turned selfless. Incredible sacrifices have been made by countless Christians, impossible to explain unless the resurrection really occurred.

Further, we need only compare the practical results of the Judeo-Christian faith worldwide to that of any other faith to note the radical differences—differences that can *only* be explained by the person and resurrection of Jesus Christ. Think of what Christ endured to provide this evidence so we could believe in His resurrection and have faith. He will also give us eternal life as we believe in Him.

Spend a few moments in prayer to God based on Ephesians 3:14–20 (NIV):

"For this reason I kneel before the Father, from whom his whole family in heaven and on earth derives its name. I pray that out of his glorious riches he may strengthen you with power through his Spirit in your inner being, so that Christ may dwell in your hearts through faith. And I pray that you, being rooted and established in love, may have power, together with all the saints, to grasp how wide and long and high and deep is the love of Christ, and to know this love that surpasses knowledge—that you may be filled to the measure of all the fullness of God.

"Now to him who is able to do immeasurably more than all we ask or imagine, according to his power that is at work within us, to him be glory in the church and in Christ Jesus throughout all generations, for ever and ever! Amen."

> The examples of Peter, James, and John are only three of countless examples of how the resurrection of Jesus has changed the lives of people in dramatic ways.

Write down any personal thoughts, prayers, or applications based on your study of Christ's resurrection this session:

_____

_____

_____

_____

_____

_____

_____

_____

_____

_____

_____

How Can God Allow Suffering and Evil?

The problem of evil is one of the greatest challenges to the Christian faith today due to questions posed by skeptics. Many Christians have difficulty tackling questions like:

- "If God really is all-powerful and loving, then why am I suffering this way?"

- "Why does a good God allow his creatures, and even his children to suffer?"

- "We see wars, hunger, violence, and natural disasters on television and question how God could really care about the predicament of those in need. Is God really there at all?"

In the Bible, "evil" is mentioned over 440 different times. God is familiar with the reality of evil and addresses it directly. God is also intimately familiar with suffering. He addresses it 145 times in Scripture. One of the larger books of the Bible, the book of Job, is given solely to this question. The books of Jeremiah and Habakkuk have much to say about it. About one third of the Psalms, the prayers of the Old Testament, are cries that arise out of doubt, disappointment, or pain. Even our Lord Jesus Christ experienced suffering and evil at the hands of others during His crucifixion.

The problem of evil is one of the greatest challenges to the Christian faith today due to questions posed by skeptics.

Yet often we still feel that God doesn't seem to be there when times are tough. Dr. Erwin Lutzer writes, "We must be careful about what we say about tragedies. If we say too much, we may err, thinking we can read the fine print of God's purposes. But if we say nothing, we give the impression that there is no message we can learn from calamities. I believe that God does speak through these events, but we must be cautious about thinking we know the details of his agenda."[42]

During this session together, we'll explore different ways people discuss evil and examine several examples of God at work through the sufferings experienced by His people.

PROBLEMS WITH THE PROBLEM OF EVIL

For starters, it's important to distinguish between two kinds of evil: moral evil and natural evil. Moral evil results from the actions of free creatures. Murder, rape, and theft are examples. Why doesn't God turn the knife or gun or the murderer into Jell-O? Why doesn't He stuff a person's mouth with cotton every time they want to say hurtful words? He could, but then people could say, "That's not fair. I'm not free to act or make my own decisions." God has given us freedom, and the majority of evil comes from the free decisions of human beings.

Natural evil results from natural processes such as earthquakes and floods. Of course, sometimes the two are intermingled, such as when flooding results in loss of human life due to poor planning or shoddy construction of buildings. About these, Dr. Lutzer writes:

If natural disasters are out of God's control, then my life and my future are out of God's control. The weak God of modern liberalism is hardly able to speak comfort to those who seek it.

The God of predestination, the God of worldwide providence, the God who created all and sustains all and thus ultimately is responsible for all—this God has revealed to us only glimpses of the divine cosmic plan. God has not let us see in any comprehensive way the sense in suffering, the method in the madness. God has chosen, instead, to remain hidden in mystery.[43]

Moral Evil	Murder, rape, theft, lying, cheating
Natural Evil	Earthquakes, floods, hurricanes, human disease, famine
Combined	Poverty due to war, human disease spread through illegal drug use

Name some other evils people commonly use to argue against a loving God:

_____

_____

_____

It's also important to identify two aspects of the problem of evil and suffering. First, there is the philosophical aspect. This is the problem of evil approached from the perspective of the skeptic who challenges the belief

> "The world is full of suffering, it is also full of overcoming it."
>
> —Helen Keller

that there is a God who exists who would allow such suffering. In meeting this philosophical challenge, we must follow the New Testament command to always be ready to give *"a reason for the hope within us"* (1 Peter 3:15).

Second, we will examine the religious or emotional aspect of the problem of evil. This is the problem of evil approached from the perspective of the Christian like Job whose faith in God is tested by life's difficult situations. How can we love and worship God when He allows us to suffer in these ways? Answers to experiencing God personally are found in the numerous teachings on this issue in the Bible.

Philosophical Problem of Evil   How can a loving God allow evil to exist?

Emotional Problem of Evil   How could God allow *me* (or have allowed me) to suffer?

APPLY Which of these two problems regarding evil and suffering do people in your circle of acquaintances bring up the most?

_____

_____

_____

_____

Which of these two problems do you personally struggle with the most?

_____

_____

_____

_____

Some argue that since God created everything, then He must be the maker of evil as well. But this is not the case.

📖 Read Genesis 1:31. What did God say about everything He had created?

_____

If everything God created was good, then where did evil come from? God was perfect; what He made was good; but now the world is full of pain. What happened?

These questions address the issue of free will. If God had created robots, pre-programmed with no ability to choose right and wrong, then evil would not have existed. It would not have been an option. However, God did give Adam and Eve one rule: to not eat from a certain tree. He gave them the ability to choose whether they would obey or not obey this rule. God did not create evil, but He created people with a capacity to make wrong choices. They chose to use a good thing (free will) in a bad way.

Dr. Norm Geisler explains this through the following lines of logic:

God made everything perfect.

One of the perfect things God made was free creatures.

If God had created robots, pre-programmed with no ability to choose right and wrong, then evil would not have existed. It would not have been an option.

Free will is the cause of evil.

So, imperfection (evil) can arise from perfection (not directly, but indirectly through freedom).[44]

The Origins of Human Evil

How did evil begin? To answer this question, we must travel with Adam and Eve back to the Garden of Eden as recorded in Genesis 3. In verses 1–7, we find the progression of circumstances that led this couple from obedience to disobedience and the beginnings of evil.

📖 Read Genesis 3:1–6 and answer the following questions:

Who questioned God's command?

_____

How did Eve respond?

_____

_____

What lie die the serpent offer?

_____

_____

How did Adam and Eve respond?

_____

_____

Notice the factors involved in this first human sin. First, the serpent (Satan, see Revelation 12:9) questioned God's words. Sin entered humanity because of false information regarding God, not because of something God did directly.

Second, notice Eve's response in verses 2–3:

> *The woman said to the serpent, "We may eat fruit from the trees in the garden, but God did say, 'You must not eat fruit from the tree that is in the middle of the garden, and you must not touch it, or you will die.'"*

Is this really what God said? If we rewind to His original statement in 2:16–17, we read:

> *"And the LORD God commanded the man, 'You are free to eat from any tree in the garden; but you must not eat from the tree of the knowledge of good and evil, for when you eat of it you will surely die.'"*

Interestingly, Eve added to God's words, saying that God commanded that they not even *touch* it. She knew that it was best to stay away from that particular tree altogether.

How did the serpent respond? He told her a lie. The serpent (Satan, who also freely chose to disobey God and fell) is known as the father of lies (John 8:44) and used one with Eve to deceive her in this situation.

Next, we are told that Eve did four things that marked her part in this entry of sin into the human race:

In Genesis 3:1–7, we find the progression of circumstances that led this couple from obedience to disobedience and the beginnings of evil.

- She *saw* that the fruit looked good (temptation).
- She *took* the fruit (initiation).
- She *ate* the fruit (execution).
- She *gave* the fruit to Adam to eat (extension).

📖 Read Genesis 3:7–24 and answer the following questions regarding the effects of sin in the world:

What was the first thing Adam and Eve did after eating the fruit (verse 7)?

_____

How did they respond toward God (verses 8–10)?

_____

_____

How did Adam and Eve answer regarding their sin (verses 11–13)?

_____

_____

What were the consequences of Adam and Eve's sin (verses 16–19, 23)?

_____

_____

_____

We find that when Adam and Eve disobeyed, they instantly became self-conscious rather than focused on God. They were now concerned about clothing, a need that was never an issue before. They hid from God and answered Him by blaming their sin on others. God dealt with the sin problem through several consequences, including expulsion from the Garden of Eden.

Ever since, humans have continued in this tradition of individually making wrong choices and dealing with the consequences. While not all evil or suffering is due to personal choices, sin entered the world through the wrong actions of humans whom Satan tempted, a pattern that continues today.

Evil had its origin in the Garden of Eden, but its impact has continued into our time. But what about natural disasters or natural evils such as earthquakes or hurricanes? Why would God allow such horrible events to occur?

The reasons for such tragedies are often never understood, but that does not mean they do not have purpose. As we will investigate over the next four days, such suffering offers God a myriad of ways to work in people's lives.

APPLY In what ways can you relate to the feelings Adam and Eve experienced when they disobeyed God? How do you respond when someone asks why bad things are happening?

_____

_____

_____

_____

_____

APPLY How does understanding the origin of sin help confront sinful issues in your life? What is an area of temptation you are facing where you need to turn to God for help rather than run from Him? What are the consequences if we don't?

_____

_____

_____

_____

_____

_____

LESSON EIGHT   DAY TWO

REASONS FOR SUFFERING

Human suffering is not without purpose. It is not enjoyable, but as C. S. Lewis wrote, "Pain is not good in itself. What is good in any painful experience is, for the sufferer, his submission to the will of God, and, for the spectators, the compassion aroused and the acts of mercy to which it leads."[45]

While we often do not understand why we must endure pain and suffering, the Bible offers several reasons why people suffer in this world. We will discuss these over the next two days as we learn how God addresses the issue of why we suffer.

Suffering as an Example to Others

One reason God allows Christians to suffer is to allow them to serve as an example to others. When we live with joy and perseverance in the face of difficult situations, it becomes a wonderful testimony to others of the power of Christ at work in us, because they too experience difficult and painful situations.

📖 Read 2 Timothy 2:8–10. Why does Paul say here that he suffered as a criminal for his faith?

_____

_____

_____

Paul endured hardship in order to help other people come to faith in Jesus. His suffering helped others enjoy the privilege of new life and freedom from their own sins.

📖 Read Peter's words in 1 Peter 3:13–17. Why did he claim it is better to suffer for doing good rather than for doing evil?

_____

_____

_____

Peter also mentions that our suffering can provide a blessing in the way of an example to others who may come to know Christ. Even when we are mistreated for doing what is right, there are other blessings God has in store for us.

📖 According to 2 Corinthians 12:9, how can we rejoice in our sufferings and weaknesses?

_____

📖 Read 2 Corinthians 4:8–11. What additional insights does Paul provide as to how suffering can serve as an example for others?

_____

_____

_____

Paul believed that his suffering ultimately resulted in others receiving eternal life in Christ. Because of this, he was willing to suffer greatly to further the work of Christ.

Suffering So We Can Sympathize

Another reason God allows us to suffer is so we can better sympathize with others. Who could better help a couple mourn the loss of a child than someone who has personally experienced such loss themselves? Who could better help a person struggling with debt than someone who has personally encountered this dilemma? Who could best help someone through a difficult marriage situation than a person who has dealt with this trauma in his or her own life?

📖 Read Paul's words in 2 Corinthians 1:3–5. What does he say comes to the believer along with suffering?

_____

_____

What are some areas in your life in which you can comfort others because of something you have suffered? For example, maybe you can comfort someone who is a single parent because you have been or are currently in that same situation.

_____

_____

_____

_____

_____

We Sometimes Suffer to Remain Humble

The apostle Paul experienced a "thorn in the flesh" that forced him to remain humble in his walk with God. As a person who had experienced amazing visions (2 Corinthians 12), healed others, and served as a missionary with unprecedented results, God allowed a dose of suffering to keep Paul dependent upon Him. Scripture does not tell us what Paul's predicament was, but the personal pain caused by it kept him in a humble yet desirable attitude toward God.

> "... suffering produces perseverance; perseverance, character; and character, hope."
>
> Romans 5:3–4

📖 Read 2 Corinthians 12:7. Why does this verse say Paul was given a thorn in the flesh?

_____

_____

_____

Paul knew that God had allowed personal pain for a reason. If personal discomfort was required to keep him humble and dependent upon the Lord, rather than himself, then Paul willingly accepted it.

God Uses Suffering as an Educational Tool
Another reason God allows suffering is for our learning. Sometimes, the best way to learn is through personal experience. There are at least three major ways God uses suffering as an opportunity for learning.

📖 First, God sometimes allows us to suffer in order **to help us mature.** Read James 1:2–4. Why does James say we should face life's problems with joy?

_____

_____

_____

_____

📖 Other times, God allows us to suffer in order **to show us some bad habits that need to be removed.** John 15:1–7 compares this to pruning a vine to help it grow stronger. Read Psalm 119:67, 71. Why does the psalmist write that it was good to be afflicted?

_____

_____

_____

_____

📖 Read John 15:1–7. What does Jesus say about our efforts apart from Him?

_____

_____

_____

Finally, sometimes God allows suffering **in order to discipline** us. Hebrews 12:5–11 uses the analogy of a father who disciplines his son when this child is wrong out of his love for the child.

📖 Read Hebrews 12:5–11. What do these verses say about the purpose of discipline and the motive behind it?

_____

_____

_____

Here, the author of Hebrews provides several comments regarding God's discipline in our lives:

- Do not make light of it (verse 5)
- Do not lose heart (verse 5)
- The Lord loves you (verse 6)
- Discipline is a sign you are a child of God (verse 8)
- It helps us mature (verse 11)

Suffering itself is not the thing that produces faith or maturity. It is only a tool that God uses to bring us to Himself so we will respond to Him and His Word. It forces us to turn from trusting in our own resources to living by faith in God's resources. It causes us to put first things first. Ultimately, it is the Word and the Spirit of God that produces faith and mature Christ-like character (Psalms 119:67, 71). We will see four additional ways God uses suffering in Day Three, but we have already discovered many ways God can and does use suffering for His purposes.

In James 1:2–4 and 1 Peter 1:6–7 the key word is "proof." The word "proof" in these passages comes from the word *dokimion,* which looks at both the concept of testing which purifies, and the results, the proof that is left after the test. The Lord uses trials to test our faith in the sense of purifying it, to bring it to the surface, so we are forced to put our faith to work.[46]

APPLY Identify an area or difficult situation in your life of which you have seen God at work. How has this situation helped to strengthen your relationship with God?

_____

_____

_____

_____

_____

REASONS FOR SUFFERING, PART 2

LESSON
EIGHT DAY THREE

In Day Two, we focused on four ways God uses suffering in our lives. But God has other ways, and we will look at some of these in this study section. Let's begin by reviewing the life of someone who suffered greatly—the apostle Paul. In 2 Corinthians 11:24–31, he lists many of the difficulties he had experienced to this point in his life:

> *"Five times I received from the Jews the forty lashes minus one. Three times I was beaten with rods, once I was stoned, three times I was shipwrecked, I spent a night and a day in the open sea, I have been constantly on the move. I have been in danger from rivers, in danger from bandits, in danger from my own countrymen, in danger from Gentiles; in danger in the city, in danger in the country, in danger at sea; and in danger from false brothers. I have labored and toiled and have often gone without sleep; I have known hunger and thirst and have often gone without food; I have been cold and naked. Besides everything else, I face daily the pressure of my concern for all the churches. Who is weak, and I do not feel weak? Who is led into sin, and I do not inwardly burn?*

If I must boast, I will boast of the things that show my weakness. The God and Father of the Lord Jesus, who is to be praised forever, knows that I am not lying.

Suffering enables us to walk in God's ability, power, and provision rather than our own. This passage shows us our fifth reason for suffering:

5. Suffering Enables Us to Depend on God's Power
Paul encountered the worst of persecutions. He was whipped, beaten, left for dead, shipwrecked, lived in dangerous environments, and even been betrayed by false brothers. If anyone had a reason to be upset about suffering for Jesus, it was Paul. Yet he continued to honor God, claiming that these situations helped reveal to him his weakness so that he would depend more on God's power.

Another illustration of this dependence can be found in the life of Moses. In Exodus 17:8–16, we find a remarkable story in which Moses was required to hold up his hands toward heaven during one of Israel's military battles. When Moses' hands were up, God's people had the upper hand. When his hands were down, they began to lose.

📖 Read Exodus 17:8–16. Why do you think God provided victory for his people in this unique way?

_____

_____

_____

📖 Psalm 20:7 offers another illustration of this dependence. What does this verse say about turning to God for help?

_____

_____

Suffering is never enjoyable, but dependence on God provides the proper attitude toward the Father that He desires.

6. We Sometimes Suffer to Grow in the Fruit of the Spirit
Though this is similar to some of the reasons already mentioned, this reason for suffering specifically emphasizes a development of a Christ-like lifestyle.

📖 Read about the fruit of the Spirit in Galatians 5:22–23. Which of these areas do you find to be the easiest to develop? Which are the most difficult?

_____

_____

_____

_____

Growing in the fruit of the Spirit involves both negative and positive aspects. On the negative side, suffering involves removing (or pruning) sinful areas of our lives, including apathy, selfish ambition, wrong priorities, greed, and personal pride. Suffering in itself does not remove the impurities, but is a tool God uses to cause us to exercise faith in the provisions of God's grace. It is God's grace in Christ (our new identity in Christ, the Word, and the Holy Spirit) that changes us.

"If I am to go on living in the body, this will mean fruitful labor for me."

Philippians 1:22

God uses two negative or harsh ways to grow us in the fruit of the Sprit. First, He disciplines us when we are out of fellowship with Him. In this case, suffering is discipline from God, as we read about in Hebrews 5:5–11. Another example is found in Paul's explanation of the Lord's Supper in 1 Corinthians 11:28–32. There, we are taught to examine ourselves before taking Communion in order not to come under God's judgment. Second, God makes us aware of sins that are causing a less effective relationship with Him. In these cases, we are told God prunes us (John 17:1–7) in order to help us grow.

Read 1 Corinthians 11:28–32. How is a person to take the Lord's Supper? What does Paul say can happen to those who take it without personal examination?

_____

_____

_____

_____

On the positive side, we are instructed to deal with suffering joyfully (see James 1:2–5). When we do, Christ's character becomes more evident in us as we grow stronger through suffering (2 Corinthians 4:9–10).

Read 1 Corinthians 11:28–32. How is a person to take the Lord's Supper? What does Paul say can happen to those who take it unworthily?

_____

_____

7. Suffering Sometimes Reveals the Need for God's Judgment

When we suffer for doing what is right, it reveals the need for God to judge the evil that exists in this world. It shows the evil character of those who persecute others and the justice of God's judgment when it falls.

Read 1 Thessalonians 2:14–16. How does the evil shown toward Paul and the Thessalonian believers reveal the need for God's judgment?

_____

_____

_____

In 1 Thessalonians, Paul comforts his readers by acknowledging that those who mistreat them would ultimately come under God's judgment for their actions. It is an encouragement even to us today that to stand firm in our faith even when others ridicule us for our beliefs or Christ-like lifestyles.

Read Romans 12:14–20. How do these verses teach us to respond to those who persecute us?

_____

_____

_____

8. We Sometimes Suffer to Expand Christian Ministry

In addition to personal growth and outreach opportunities to others, suffering can at times open new possibilities to reach out to new groups of people.

How did Paul's suffering as a prisoner help him in reaching a new group of people according to Philippians 1:12–14?

_____

_____

_____

As a result of Paul's imprisonment, he was able to speak about Christ to guards in the Roman palace and other who had business where he was detained. In addition, his example strengthened others to speak boldly about their faith (verse 14).

How would Paul's outreach have been different if he had complained or sulked as would be expected of a prisoner?

_____

_____

_____

_____

QUESTIONS AND ANSWERS ABOUT SUFFERING

During an interview I (John) conducted with Dr. Geisler on the question of evil and suffering, I asked him a series of questions that are commonly raised on this issue. In our times together for the next two days, we'll share some of these questions and answers together to help grow in our understanding of God's Word.

Q: Why Do We Have Evil in the World?

A: *The key word in that particular argument against the existence of the God of the Bible is the word "destroy": "If God is all good, He would destroy evil; if He is all powerful He could destroy it; but He hasn't destroyed it, therefore there is not such a God."*

Sure God could destroy all the evil of the world, but in destroying it, He would destroy good. Because one of the good things God made was freedom. God could destroy all evil, by destroying all freedom, but He would be working against the good He has made.

The atheist is assuming that, because God hasn't defeated evil yet, that He never will. But as Christians we believe that it was officially defeated on the cross and Jesus will return and will actually defeat it at his second coming. So we just say to him, "Hold on, pal. It's coming. God's going to defeat evil."

📖 Read Revelation 21:3–4. How do we know that God will end evil in the end?

> **The atheist is assuming that, because God hasn't defeated evil yet, that He never will. But as Christians we believe that it was officially defeated on the cross.**

_____

_____

Q: Is Evil Only an Illusion?

A: *Well, illusionism is probably one of the oldest non-Christian solutions to the problem of evil. It arises out of the pantheistic worldview where God is all and all is good, and therefore there is no evil. It is manifest in Christian Science, and Unity, and Hare Krishna, and the Hindu background, and Baha'i. A lot of American religious groups have picked up this pantheistic background. What they are saying in essence is, to quote Mary Baker Eddy, "evil is an error of mortal mind"; that it is like darkness; it doesn't exist; it goes out of existence when the light comes there; it is like a zero; it is like a dream. It isn't real, therefore death and sin and hell and suffering are all a figment of one's imagination.*

It's denying the obvious. No philosophy should start with denying the obvious; we should start with the obvious and work our way from there. Besides that, they have no explanation for the origin of the illusion. Where did the illusion come from? Secondly, why is this illusion so universal? Why is it *everybody* has this illusion? Why is this illusion so persistent? And why does the illusion seem so real? After all it doesn't make any real difference to somebody who believes. If you stick him with a pin, he hurts just as much as I hurt.

How are we to respond to evil according to Romans 12:9?

_____

_____

Q: What do you say to a person who says, "There is just too much suffering. There is just too much evil in this world and I've come to the conclusion that God just can't be there because there is just too much evil."

A: *Well, let me tell you what actually happened. I've had a number of debates with atheists around the country. I pointed out to an atheist in a process of a debate once this very dilemma. I said that C. S. Lewis was an atheist. He said that atheism is circular, it is arguing in a circle for this reason. I said there is no God because there is injustice. Then I started to think, injustice. That means "not just." I must know what justice is. And then the atheist has to say not only is this unjust, but it has to be ultimately unjust. If you get a ticket for speeding when you weren't speeding, then you go to the judge and he throws it out, it was immediate injustice, but ultimately it wasn't unjust.*

How does God teach us to respond to evil in Romans 12:21?

_____

_____

Q: Where did the evil come from that is in this world?

A: *According to the Bible, God is absolutely good, and He made an absolutely good world. Everything He made, He said it is good. Every creature of God is good, according to 1 Timothy 4. One of the good things that he gave some of those good creatures was free will. It is good to be free. Hardly anyone would say freedom was bad because, if they did it would be at least self-defeating because they* *are exercising their freedom, which they enjoy as a good, in order to say freedom is bad. So freedom is undeniably good. Freedom is the source of evil, because if you are really free to love God, you are also free not to love Him, because forced love is a contradiction in terms. If you are free to worship him, you are free to blaspheme him. So evil arose from free will. Freedom is a good. God created the good of freedom. Man performs the acts of evil by misusing his freedom.*

What caused man to sin? It was his own freedom. And if his freedom is the first cause, it is meaningless to ask, what caused his freedom, because that is like asking, "Who made God?"

According to Dr. Geisler, God did not create evil, but he did allow for it by giving people the ability to make free choices. These free choices mean that we will often be tempted to make a choice inconsistent with God's Word. The book of James discusses the source of temptation in our lives today.

📖 Read James 1:13–14. What does James say is the source of our evil temptations?

_____

We can respond to the evil in today's world in several ways. First, we can deny it. Second, we can ignore it. Third, we can embrace it. Or fourth, with God's help, we can fight it.

📖 Read Ephesians 6:10–20. How do the various parts of the armor of God assist in combating against evil?

Belt of truth

_____

_____

Breastplate of righteousness

_____

_____

Feet fitted with readiness

_____

_____

Shield of faith

_____

_____

Helmet of salvation

_____

_____

Sword of the Spirit

_____

_____

Prayer

_____

_____

APPLY What personal struggles are you struggling with now? How can you apply some of God's answers in your life?

_____

_____

_____

_____

_____

QUESTIONS AND ANSWERS ABOUT SUFFERING, PART 2

As we continue our questions and answers to common questions regarding evil and suffering, we investigate how God can work despite the suffering His Son endured on the cross, how God can work despite natural disasters, and what His ultimate plan is for dealing with evil in our world. Once again, Dr. Norm Geisler provides wisdom from God's Word to address some of the probing questions of our time.

Q: How could an all-knowing, all-loving God allow his Son to be murdered on a cross in order to redeem my sins?

A: That's like saying, "How could a soldier fall on a hand grenade to save his whole company from destruction?" *"Greater love has no one than this, that one lay down his life for his friends"* (John 15:13) and *"While we were yet sinners, Christ died for us"* (Romans 5:8). So I would think that this is the highest act of love rather than [by] implication of the question . . . a very unloving thing to do. In fact, that is the most loving thing that could be done.

📖 How can the crucifixion be seen as a loving act by God according to 1 John 3:16?

_____

_____

Q: Why doesn't God prevent natural disasters?

A: *God of course could miraculously intervene in everything. But if He did He would be violating our freedom. If God miraculously intervened all the time, it would no longer be a miracle, because a miracle [is] a rare, abnormal occurrence. So He permits us our freedom, and intervenes only when it is necessary to keep the whole plan going, such as He did at the cross. If somebody wanted to throw*

Jesus off a cliff and Jesus never got to the cross, God would miraculously inter-vene, as some believed He did [while Jesus ministered on earth], so that His sal-vation could be accomplished for all mankind.

📖 Read Job 1:18–22. How did Job respond to the disaster that he experi-enced? In what ways does his example apply to our lives?

_____

_____

_____

_____

Q: Does God have a purpose for evil?

A: *I think one of the best books on this topic on a practical level is Phillip Yancey's book,* Where Is God When It Hurts? *The book is built on the research done by a Christian who spent time with lepers. He found out three very interesting things. First of all, ninety-eight percent of the deformed fingers and toes in lepers are not caused by the disease; it is caused by the leper knocking off his own finger or putting it in the fire, because leprosy destroys the ability of the nerves to sense pain. So the leper will go to the fire and burn his finger off. So the first lesson is: <u>God permits suffering in the world to keep us from self-destruction.</u> If there were no pain and suffering in the world, we would destroy ourselves. Second, they fit-ted little alarm systems to lepers, something like a buzzer system, so when they got near fire, they would move, get a mild electric shock, and would get away from it. They found out that didn't work because it wasn't strong enough. So the sec-ond lesson they learned was that <u>in order for pain to be effective it has to be real-ly strong.</u> So then they hooked up a stronger system on the leper and when they got near a fire, they would get a painful shock. That didn't work because on the second time when they got near a fire, they would turn the system off before they got in danger. So they discovered that the third necessity is that <u>in order for pain to be effective, it has to be out of our control.</u>*

Now that is the kind of universe God has. One with pain to keep us from self-destruction, hard enough to really hurt and it has to be out of our control. So as C. S. Lewis said, "Pain is God's megaphone to arouse a morally deaf world."

Read Psalm 30. What lessons does it share about how God can draw us clos-er to Him through the pains of life?

_____

_____

Q: Is there anything encouraging about evil?

A: *Let's take the classic example in the Book of Job. [Job] himself said, "When He has tried me, I shall come forth as gold" (Job 23:10). The book of James says, "You have heard of the patience of Job and have seen the end [literally "design"] of the LORD" (James 5:10). God has a design in your suffering. The divine architect of the universe doesn't build staircases that lead to nowhere. There is a purpose and there is a greater day.* "For our light and momentary troubles are achieving for us an eternal glory that far outweighs them all" (2 Corinthians 4:17).

> ## "Shall we accept good from God, and not trouble?"
> ## Job 2:10

📖 Read 2 Corinthians 4:16–18. What do these verses share about our response to evil?

_____

_____

_____

The existence of evil and suffering in our world poses a very personal religious and emotional problem for the person who is enduring great pain. Although our painful experiences may not challenge our belief that God exists, what may be at risk is our confidence in a God we can freely worship and love.

First, Scripture reveals that when we suffer it is not unnatural to experience emotional pain or express it. An entire portion of the Psalms is called a lament, or words of sorrow and mourning. The psalmist encourages us to pour out our hearts to God (Psalms 62:8). When we do, we can rest assured that God understands our pain. Jesus Himself expressed sorrow when John the Baptist was beheaded (Matthew 14:13). When His friend Lazarus died, it is recorded that Jesus openly wept at his tomb (John 11:35). At the cross, Jesus confessed to being filled with anguish of soul in contemplating it (Matthew 26:38).

Second, when we suffer we should draw comfort from God's promises. We have already reflected on many of these promises during this session. As Psalm 1:2 shares, we are to meditate on them day and night. We are to remember this life is not the whole story. In eternity God will heal our bodies, judge the guilty, and reward the righteous. He will fix the inequities and injustices we have experienced in this life.

Finally, even in severe trial God is working all things together for the good of those who love Him (Romans 8:28). Joseph provides an amazing example of having learned this truth, when after years of unexplained suffering due to the betrayal of his brothers, he was able to say to them, *"You meant it for evil, but God meant it for good"* (Genesis 50:20). Though God did not cause his brothers to betray him, He was able to use their betrayal in furthering his good intentions.[47]

Spend some time in prayer to God now, meditating on the following Scripture:

To you, O LORD, I lift up my soul; in you I trust, O my God. Do not let me be put to shame, nor let my enemies triumph over me.

No one whose hope is in you will ever be put to shame, but they will be put to shame who are treacherous without excuse.

Show me your ways, O LORD, teach me your paths; guide me in your truth and teach me, for you are God my Savior, and my hope is in you all day long.

Remember, O LORD, your great mercy and love, for they are from of old.
(Psalms 25:1–6)

> "And we know that in all things God works for the good of those who love him, who have been called according to his purpose."
>
> **Romans 8:28 (NIV)**

Write down any specific prayers or applications God brings to mind from this session:

_____

_____

_____

_____

_____

_____

_____

_____

WHAT HAPPENS AFTER WE DIE?

Every one of us must address the ultimate issue of what happens after we die. Whether the answer is reincarnation, nirvana, annihilation, heaven, or hell, all religious movements must provide a response to what happens next?

In this session, we'll take some time to study what the Bible teaches on this important issue. First, we'll discuss what happens when we die? Do we simply rot in the ground? Do we reincarnate and begin again in another form? Do we all go to heaven? Is there a hell?

Second, we'll address the question of future judgment. The Bible discusses it frequently, mentioning judgment over 120 times. How will it be different for those who follow Christ and those who do not?

Third, we will discuss what the Bible shares heaven is really like. It is the future home of all believers, a place where we will live with Jesus forever. Yet cultural ideas of heaven have often polluted the true biblical concept of heaven.

Fourth, we'll look at the Bible's description of hell. Is it a real place? If so, what is it like? We know it will be bad, but in this portion we'll find out what the Bible specifically says about this dreadful destination.

Every one of us must address the ultimate issue of what happens after we die.

Finally, we'll respond to some of the key questions about the afterlife. The Bible doesn't answer every detail regarding the afterlife, but we'll share regarding some of the major insights.

For the believer, a study of the afterlife reminds us of the home Christ has for us in eternity. It also motivates us to share Jesus with those who do not know Him as we focus upon their future predicament. Let's begin together the adventure of understanding what God has in store for the afterlife.

Common Views Regarding the Afterlife

Annihilation	Reincarnation	Purgatory	Universalism	Works-based Afterlife	Biblical Christianity
Life ends at physical death	Life repeats in various forms	A "middle ground" between heaven and hell where many temporarily go before heaven	All people go to heaven upon death	Those who know Jesus by faith go to heaven; those who do not go to hell	Rejects the other four views

LESSON NINE

DAY ONE

WHAT HAPPENS WHEN WE DIE?

The Bible presents the concept of death as separation. At the moment of physical death, a person's spirit leaves the body. For example, just before Stephen died he prayed, *"Lord Jesus, receive my spirit"* (Acts 7:59). He understood that death would not be the end of his life, but rather a separation of spirit and body.

📖 Read 2 Corinthians 5:6–9. How does Paul contrast the issues of life and death?

_____

_____

_____

Paul spoke of life in his current body as being away from the Lord. Being with God in heaven is understood as separated from this life's body temporarily. Physical death involves no loss of our soul (Revelation 6:9–11). The soul passes immediately into the presence of Christ for the believer (Luke 23:43; Philippians 1:23) until a future time (1 Thessalonians 4:13–17), when the believer's soul and body will be reunited to be with the Lord forever (Philippians 3:21; 1 Corinthians 15:35–44).

📖 Read Ecclesiastes 12:6–7. What do these verses indicate about death?

_____

_____

_____

These poetic verses describe the soul as returning to God. Though this should not be understood as meaning the soul has always existed, it does indicate that the soul separates from the physical body upon death. In these verses, the writer anticipates his soul returning to God in heaven.

The Bible indicates that at death, a believer's spirit departs from the physical body and immediately enters the presence of the Lord in heaven. Death for the believer is an extremely joyful experience.

📖 Read Philippians 1:21–26. How does Paul describe leaving this life to enter heaven?

_____

_____

_____

In Paul's words, to live is Christ and to die is gain. Death is our exit from this life to experience and enjoy in heaven according to Scripture. While we deeply mourn the loss of a loved one, the believer who passes away experience something much better than anything available on earth. Our attitude should be as Paul wrote, *"I am torn between the two: I desire to depart and be with Christ, which is better by far; but it is more necessary for you that I remain in the body"* (verse 23).

For the unbeliever, however, death is quite the opposite. Rather than something to greatly anticipate, it is a reason for fear and of being judged by God Himself. At death, the unbeliever's spirit departs from the body and immediately enters a place of great suffering.

📖 Read Luke 16:19–31. How does Jesus describe the resting place of the unbeliever in these verses?

_____

_____

_____

In this account, we are even told angels accompanied Lazarus to heaven, but that the soul of the rich man entered torment upon dying. The unbeliever has nothing to look forward to in the afterlife and will understand his predicament in only a few moments after he dies.

The Bible is very clear that there are certain key facts about the afterlife that apply to all people. In fact, Scripture provides three specific guidelines about eternity that apply to our study here of death and dying.

1. Everyone Will Exist Eternally.
A person's body may decompose in the ground upon death, but not the soul. In Matthew 25, Jesus tells the story of two kinds of people: those who exhibit faith through helping others and those who show unbelief by doing the opposite. At the end of the account, judgment is given and each person awaits one of two destinations.

📖 Read Matthew 25:46. What are the two destinations provided by Jesus in the afterlife?

_____

_____

Again, Jesus offers only two options, eternal joy with Him or eternal punishment.

2. Everyone Has Only One Life to Determine His or Her Eternity.

Unlike the teachings of Eastern religions, the Bible teaches that we have only one life in which to determine our future. Joshua wrote to God's people in his day, *"But if serving the LORD seems undesirable to you, then choose for yourselves this day whom you will serve, whether the gods your forefathers served beyond the River, or the gods of the Amorites, in whose land you are living. But as for me and my household, we will serve the LORD"* (Joshua 24:15). He understood that there were only two real choices. He also knew that the time to make that choice was then and now. There is only one life in which to determine your eternal future.

Read Hebrews 9:27. What does it say about the time people have to determine their eternal destiny?

_____

_____

_____

_____

In contrast with reincarnation, the author of Hebrews wrote that *"we are appointed* **once** *to die."* What happens next? Immediately following death, we face judgment. The time to make up our minds is now. At death, will then spend eternity in the destination we chose while living on earth.

3. A Person's Destination in Eternity Is Based upon Faith in Jesus Christ.

The Bible also clearly states that a person's destination in eternity is based upon a choice. That "choice" is faith in Jesus Christ who alone can forgive all our sins and give us eternal life.

What does Romans 6:23 call eternal life?

_____

_____

_____

To live in heaven with Jesus is a gift. It is nothing anyone can earn. As Paul wrote in Ephesians 2:8–9: *"For it is by grace you have been saved, through faith—and this not from yourselves, it is the gift of God—not by works, so that no one can boast."*

Of the forty-two times the phrase "eternal life" is used in the New Testament, fourteen of them are in the Gospel of John. Why? Because, *"these are written that you may believe that Jesus is the Christ, the Son of God, and that by believing you may have life in his name"* (John 20:31).

Eternal Life According to John's Gospel

Quotation	Scripture Reference in John
*...that everyone who believes in him may have **eternal life.***	3:5
*...whoever believes in him shall not perish but have **eternal life.***	3:16
*Whoever believes in the Son has **eternal life.***	3:36
*...the water I give him will become in him a spring of water welling up to **eternal life.***	4:14
*...even now he harvests the crop for **eternal life.***	4:36
*You diligently study the Scriptures because you think that by them you possess **eternal life.** These are the Scriptures that testify about me, yet you refuse to come to me to have life.*	5:38–39
*Do not work for food that spoils, but for food that endures to **eternal life,** which the Son of Man will give you.*	6:27
*everyone who looks to the Son and believes in him shall have **eternal life.***	6:40
Whoever eats my flesh and drinks my blood has eternal life, and I will raise him up at the last day.	6:54
*Lord, to whom shall we go? You have the words of **eternal life.***	6:68
*I give them **eternal life,** and they shall never perish...*	10:28
*The man who loves his life will lose it, while the man who hates his life in this world will keep it for **eternal life.***	12:25
*For I did not speak of my own accord, but the Father who sent me commanded me what to say and how to say it. I know that his command leads to **eternal life.***	12:49–50
*For you granted him authority over all people that he might give **eternal life** to all those you have given him.*	17:2

Death awaits each of us. Our goal must be to be prepared in our own lives and in helping others (See Lesson 12).

Apply: How confident are you about your destination in the afterlife? How would you explain what you believe about the afterlife to a skeptic?

_____

_____

_____

_____

_____

DOES JUDGMENT AWAIT US?

LESSON NINE DAY TWO

Does judgment really await us in the afterlife? Many people, even Christians, are unclear on what will happen upon death. Few people in our culture live as if they will be held accountable for their actions at a future judgment. Though many prefer to ignore any advice that sounds judgmental, the fact remains that the Bible teaches that every person will face a judgment.

Judgments in Scripture

Appearance	Scripture
Judgment of Jesus Christ	John 12:31
Judgment of the believer's works	2 Corinthians 5:10
Judgment of the individual believer	1 Corinthians 11:31–32; 2 Samuel 7:14–15
Judgment of the nations	Matthew 25:31–46; Joel 3:11–16
Judgment of Israel	Ezekiel 20:33–44
Judgment of the fallen angels	Jude 6; 2 Peter 2:4, 1 Corinthians 6:3
Judgment of unbelievers	Revelation 20:11–15

The Bible teaches that the purpose of judgment for a believer, however, is much different from the judgment that awaits the unbeliever. Believers are not judged regarding whether they enter heaven or hell, but are judged regarding rewards received or not received. Judgment for the unbeliever, in contrast, results in one being sent into what we call hell, or the lake of fire. We will spend time today studying each of these judgments.

Judgment for Believers
Did you know that all believers will one day stand before the judgment seat of Jesus Christ? What does Romans 14:8–10 say about this judgment?

_____

_____

_____

Paul makes it very clear that those who have placed their faith in Christ will stand at the judgment. Our concern will not be whether we were good enough to make it or not. Our basis of judgment for entering heaven will be based our relationship with the Son of God.

The concept of a judgment seat comes from the athletic competitions of Paul's day. When the races were over, a dignitary would sit on an elevated throne in the arena. Then, one by one, the winning athletes would come up to the throne to receive a reward. This reward was usually a wreath of leaves, a victor's crown. For believers, each of us will stand before Christ the Judge and receive or lose rewards. According to verse 10, "*We will all stand before God's judgment seat.*" The Bible indicates some believers may have a reason for some degree of shame.

📖 Read 2 John 8. What does this verse indicate about our eternal rewards as believers?

_____

_____

📖 Why does 1 John 2:28 say we should continue to grow in our relationship with Christ?

_____

_____

_____

It is possible for some disobedient believers to actually find themselves ashamed at the return of Christ or at the judgment. The way to avoid this is to continue to grow in the grace of Christ. Regardless of our level of rewards in heaven, however, all believers will experience everlasting joy with Christ in heaven.

But what are these rewards Scripture mentions? Explained as crowns, the following crowns can be found in the Bible:

Crown	Purpose	Scripture
The crown of life	Given to those who persevere under trial	James 1:12; Revelation 2:10
The crown of glory	Given to those who faithfully teach God's Word	1 Peter 5:4
The crown that will last forever	Given to those who are self-controlled and persevere	1 Corinthians 9:25
The crown of righteousness	Given to those who long for Christ's return	2 Timothy 4:8

Jesus endured a crown of thorns, yet offers us crowns as rewards for following Him. What do those in Revelation 4:10 do with their crowns in the presence of Jesus?

_____

_____

At the same time, when Greek or Roman athletes received their garland wreaths, they quickly disintegrated. But there were personal rewards that continued into the future. Some were given homes, education for their children, and no tax payments for the rest of their lives. Even so, we may throw our crowns at Jesus' feet, but His rewards will continue on into eternity. As with all of Christ's gifts, they are ultimately for His glory. Everyone's cup in heaven will be full, but some will have bigger cups.

The Judgment of Unbelievers
Believers face a judgment of rewards. Unbelievers face the judgment of being cast into what the Bible calls the lake of fire. The judgment that unbelievers face is called the Great White Throne Judgment.

Read Revelation 20:11–15. What do these verses say about the judgment of the unbeliever?

_____

_____

_____

_____

Notice the details of this passage. First, the unbeliever is in a place away from God. Second, the unbeliever is sent into a place of eternal suffering. Both aspects are utterly painful and terrifying in contrast with the joys of heaven.

A fuller biblical picture of the destiny of unbelievers in the afterlife includes:

- Weeping and gnashing of teeth (Matthew 13:41–42)
- Condemnation (Matthew 12:36–37)
- Destroyed, yet not annihilated (Matthew 10:28; Philippians 1:28)
- Eternal punishment (Matthew 25:46)
- Separation from God's presence (2 Thessalonians 1:8–9)
- Trouble and distress (Romans 2:9)

Comparing these negative aspects with what the Bible teaches regarding heaven, we find that the two realities are complete opposites.

📖 Read Revelation 20:3–4. How do these verses describe heaven in contrast with hell?

_____

_____

_____

In contrast with hell, which will be a place of weeping and pain (Matthew 13:41–42), heaven will be a place without tears and without pain. Also, just as believers will experience varying degrees of rewards in heaven, Scripture appears to indicate that unbelievers will also experience varying degrees of punishment in hell.

📖 Read Matthew 10:15 and Luke 12:47–48. How do these verses describe future judgment?

_____

_____

_____

Here, Jesus seems to indicate that even among unbelievers there will be some variation in levels of judgment. However, regardless of the degree of judgment, eternity without God is a dreadful future to consider.

APPLY How do the rewards of heaven motivate us to life a life that is pleasing to God? In what ways do you desire to be changed today to a life fully devoted to Him?

_____

_____

_____

_____

LESSON
NINE   DAY THREE

WHAT IS HEAVEN LIKE?

Heaven will be a great and glorious experience for the believer. While we are limited in our knowledge of what heaven will look like and be like, Scripture gives us several indications of what to expect. In addition, Scripture also describes many of heaven's blessings that motivate our earthly lives.

There are several names used to describe heaven in the Bible. How does Jesus describe this city of glory in John 14:2–3?

_____

_____

_____

Here, we are told heaven is described as the Father's house with many rooms. Jesus is personally preparing a place for His believers to live with Him.

📖 Read 1 Corinthians 2:9. How does Paul describe what heaven will be like?

_____

_____

Revelation 21 provides a window into this place called heaven. We are told in verse 23 that, *"The city does not need the sun or the moon to shine on it, for the glory of God gives it light, and the Lamb is its lamp."* This description is in line with what we read from Isaiah 60:19, where the prophet wrote, *"The sun will no more be your light by day, nor will the brightness of the moon shine on you, for the LORD will be your everlasting light, and your God will be your glory."*

Where Is Heaven?
Some people become confused about heaven because of Paul's discussion in 2 Corinthians 12:2 of a third heaven. However, this idea of three heavens simply refers to the following:

> "There is no more comparison to be made between heaven and earth than there is between a piece of rusty iron and refined gold."
>
> —Rev. William Secker, a 17th century British minister

The Three Heavens

Heaven	Location	Scripture
First Heaven	Sky Above	Jeremiah 4:25
Second Heaven of glory	Space (stars, sun, and moon)	Isaiah 13:10
Third Heaven will last forever	Sphere of God (heaven)	2 Corinthians 12:2

In fact, the Greek word for heaven was the same word translated "sky." We speak of the heavens above, but there is a place called heaven where Jesus Himself lives and rules where all believers will one day live and worship Him.

Heaven is also called a heavenly country. How does Hebrews 11:13–16 describe the future home of believers?

_____

_____

The faithful believers in Hebrews 11 were not content with what this world had to offer. They longed for a greater reality where they would dwell in the direct presence of God.

How does Revelation 21:1–2 describe heaven?

_____

_____

_____

Here, we find heaven called a "holy city." This description helps us to understand that no sin or evil will exist there. Those of us who believe in Christ will be like Him, *"because we shall see him as he is"* (1 John 3:2).

Read 2 Peter 3:13. How does Peter describe heaven?

_____

_____

_____

Heaven will be a perfect environment. There will be no need to worry about someone breaking into our home. There will be no washing dishes or taking out the trash. Heaven will be a perfect place with no need for "home improvement." While our current world is filled with much evil, our new home in heaven will be one of perfection.

What does Colossians 1:12 call heaven? Why is this significant?

_____

_____

_____

Jesus is called the light of the world (John 8:12). It is only appropriate that His kingdom is also called a kingdom of light. In fact, we read in Revelation 21:23 that Christ is even the source of light that illumines the entire holy city in the new heaven.

What does Revelation 2:7 call heaven?

_____

_____

_____

> **"Earth is a pilgrim's stay, a pilgrim's journey, a pilgrim's tent. Heaven is a city, permanent, God-planned, God-built, whose foundations are as stable as God's throne."**
>
> **—E. M. Bounds**

This is the same paradise Paul saw in 2 Corinthians 12:4. It was considered so amazing that Paul was commanded not to write about it. Interestingly, Jesus also mentioned this paradise of God as He hung on the cross. When the thief asked Jesus to remember him when he came into God's kingdom, Jesus answered: *"I tell you the truth, today you will be with me in paradise"* (Luke 23:43). Also mentioned here in Revelation 2:7 is the "tree of life," which alludes back to the Garden of Eden where we are told that if a person eats from the tree of life that they would live forever (Genesis 3:22).

Revelation 21 provides perhaps the most detailed description of the heavenly city, the New Jerusalem. It is approximately 1,400 miles on each side and 1,400 miles high. These dimensions would require that its shape be a cube or possibly a pyramid shaped city. A river called the "water of life" flows through it (Revelation 22:1–2). It will be the most magnificent location ever created.

📖 Read Revelation 21:15–27. What are some of the special features of the New Jerusalem?

_____

_____

_____

Heaven will also offer several unique benefits for the believer. We mentioned some of these earlier, but there are further details in some of these blessings that God has shared as an encouragement for us today.

📖 Read Isaiah 25:8. According to this verse, what will happen in heaven?

_____

_____

Here we read that death will end in heaven. Paul speaks of this also in 1 Corinthians 15:54: _"When the perishable has been clothed with the imperishable, and the mortal with immortality, then the saying that is written will come true: 'Death has been swallowed up in victory.'"_ Revelation 21:4 also tells us there will be no more death in heaven. This incredible blessing serves as a great encouragement even in this life as we sometimes struggle with the loss of loved ones and friends. Yet this will end as we celebrate eternity with our Lord.

📖 Where does 1 Thessalonians 4:17 teach believers will be alive forever? How should this encourage us today?

_____

_____

_____

Paul also writes that when we are in heaven we will be with our Lord Jesus Christ (2 Corinthians 5:6–8). Believers know Him now; then they will see Him face to face. In heaven, we will be reunited with believers who have died in the past (1 Thessalonians 4:13–17), have all of our needs satisfied (Revelation 7:16–17), and enjoy perfect rest (Revelation 14:3).

📖 What will we share with Christ in heaven according to Romans 8:17?

_____

_____

_____

As believers, we will share in His glory. This does not mean we will become divine, but rather that we will be in a state of glory as citizens of the kingdom of heaven.

APPLY How does discovering what the Bible says about heaven motivate your life today?

_____

_____

_____

_____

"Then we who are alive and remain will be caught up together with them in the clouds to meet the Lord in the air, and so we shall always be with the Lord."

I Thessalonians 4:17

IS THERE REALLY A HELL?

The Bible clearly teaches that hell is a real place. It was designed for Satan and his fallen angels who rebelled against God (Matthew 25:41). Yet many are confused as to whether hell really exists, what it is like, and who will go there. One author notes:

Many things we don't know about hell. But Jesus and the New Testament writers used every image in their power to tell us that hell is real, it's terrible, it's something to be feared, and something to avoid. In his description of the last judgment, Jesus taught that some would go to eternal punishment, some to eternal life (Matt. 25:46). In other words, hell will be as real and as lasting as heaven.[48]

There are a variety of terms used in the Bible to describe hell. We will look at each of these below to help develop a biblical perspective on this issue. The common Old Testament word used to describe a place of punishment is *Sheol* (used in older English translations). Sometimes it simply referred to the grave (Psalm 49:15). Other times it was described as a place of dread (Psalm 30:9), sorrow (Isaiah 38:3), or punishment (Job 24:19).

Biblical Terms Referring to Hell °

Name	Definition	Scripture
Hades	The dwelling place of the wicked dead	Used 11 times in New Testament
Tartaros	Home of wicked angels	Jude 6–7
Lake of Fire	The second death	Revelation 20:15 (5 times in Revelation)
Bottomless Pit	The lower regions as the home of demons	Revelation 9:1 (used 6 times in Revelation)
Gehenna	Place where children were sacrificed to Molech in fire	Jeremiah 7:31; Matthew 23:33
Outer Darkness	Place where there is weeping and gnashing of teeth	Matthew 8:12; 22:13:25:30
Place of Torment	Used in same context as Hades	Luke 16:28
Fiery Furnace	Place angels will throw evildoers	Matthew 13:42
Everlasting Destruction	Where those who do not know God will be sent	2 Thessalonians 1:8–9
Eternal Punishment	Place Jesus says the wicked will go	Matthew 25:46
Exclusion from God's Presence	The result of each of the above	John 16:11

📖 In the New Testament, the corresponding word to *Sheol* is *Hades* (Greek). Read Luke 16:19–24. How did Jesus describe hell?

_____

_____

_____

Hades is used eleven times in the New Testament and refers to dwelling place of the wicked dead. Though it is sometimes used a general reference to the grave like *Sheol*, it is often used with very negative associations, as in Luke 16.

Another term the Bible uses to describe the concept of hell is *Gehenna*. In ancient Israel, horrible acts occurred at the valley of Ben Hinnom. These included human sacrifice and even children burned as sacrifices to the Moabite god Molech (2 Chronicles 28:3; 33:6; Jeremiah 32:35). Later, garbage, dead animals, and even human corpses of criminals were discarded there. It was a place in a perpetual state of burning where the smoke continually rises. It is used in Matthew 23:33 (translated "hell" in the NIV) as the place where evildoers will reside.

Non-Biblical Viewpoints Regarding Hell

- Hell does not exist: "There is no such place. Christians just made it up."
- Hell is the suffering we experience on earth: "Hell is what you go through on earth."
- Hell is simply to cease to exist upon death (annihilation): "It refers to the final destruction of all evil persons."
- Hell is temporary: "All persons will ultimately be saved."

Jesus Speaks about Hell

Jesus Himself spoke plainly about the reality and suffering in hell. In fact, He talked about hell more anyone else. Read Matthew 10:27–30. How does Jesus describe hell in these verses?

_____

_____

_____

Clearly, Jesus believed hell would be a place of perpetual decay and destruction and that it clearly existed.

How did Jesus describe hell in Matthew 25:41–46?

_____

_____

_____

Here we see hell described in terms of an eternal fire, a place for the devil and his angels (demons), and a place of eternal punishment. Some believe this fire will be literal, while others interpret fire as a metaphor for God's wrath (Deuteronomy 4:24; Hebrews 12:29). While these verses seem to indicate a place of literal fire, either way, the meaning is that hell will be a place of great agony.

Read Matthew 8:10–12. How did Jesus describe the fate of those who rejected Him?

_____

_____

_____

> "If people can ignore what the Bible calls sin, then they can quite logically discount what it says about the reality of hell."
>
> —Billy Graham

Here Jesus notes four aspects of the afterlife for unbelievers. First, those who reject Him will be outside of the kingdom. Second, they will be in darkness. Because of these verses, some people think hell will be painful, yet not fiery. However, Jesus mentions the darkness in connection with being outside, which could simply refer further to unbelievers being outside of heaven. Third, the fate of unbelievers would involve weeping and gnashing of teeth. Hell will clearly be a place of sadness and pain for those who reject Christ.

📖 Read 1 Thessalonians 1:8–9. How does Paul describe what hell will be like for unbelievers?

_____

_____

_____

Here, Paul clearly notes three significant details of hell. First, he writes that those who go to hell will be punished. Next, he mentions that this punishment will be everlasting. It will not be a temporary place of pain. Just as heaven will be a place of everlasting joy for those who are believers, hell will be a place of everlasting sorrow for unbelievers. Third, hell will be a place of separation from God's presence and majesty. This will serve as the greatest suffering of all. There will be no hope for reversal through all eternity.

Along with these verses, there are several other places that describe the duration of hell. Hell according to the Bible is:

- Everlasting punishment: Matthew 25:46.
- Eternal condemnation: Mark 3:29 (sin).
- Eternal judgment: Hebrews 6:2.
- Everlasting destruction: 2 Thessalonians 1:9.
- Eternal fire: Matthew 18:8–9 (*Gehenna*); Matthew 25:41; Jude 7.
- Unquenchable fire: Mark 9:43–38 (see also Isaiah 66:24).
- Eternal torment: Revelation 19:20; 20:10.[49]

📖 Read Revelation 20:10. What does this verse say regarding how long punishment in hell will last?

_____

_____

_____

God is clear in His Word that just as believers will spend all eternity in heaven, unbelievers will spend all eternity in hell.

APPLY What does the Bible tell us about the need for Jesus giving His life for us, so we could stand perfect before God and be given the gift of eternal life? In what ways does it encourage you to share Jesus with those who do not know Him?

_____

_____

_____

_____

_____

OTHER QUESTIONS ABOUT THE AFTERLIFE

The afterlife is a fascinating topic in our culture today. Many of today's bestselling books and several of today's top films build upon the afterlife in ways that have attracted the attention of many. However, most people have unanswered questions regarding the afterlife that need to be addressed from a biblical perspective. Today, we've selected some of the common questions not addressed in our previous sections in this lesson regarding the afterlife, including reincarnation, purgatory, and near-death experiences.

What Does the Bible Say about Praying for the Dead?
Praying for the dead is not a practice taught in the Bible. Our prayers have no bearing on someone once they have died. At that point their eternal future has already been confirmed. The story of the rich man and Lazarus the beggar in Luke 16 is a good illustration of this.

  📖 Read Luke 16:19–31 once again. What do these verses say about altering the destiny of a person in hell?

_____

_____

_____

Here Jesus indicates that once a person is in heaven or hell, the decision regarding that person's eternity is final. Paul was confident that to be absent from the body was to be at home and present with the Lord (2 Corinthians 5:1–8). He also said, *"For to me, to live is Christ and to die is gain. Now if I am to go on living in the body, this will mean productive work for me; yet I don't know what I prefer: I feel torn between the two, because I have a desire to depart and be with Christ, which is better by far"* (Philippians 1:21–23). There is no reason to pray for a believer or unbeliever who has already died. It is far better to pray for the person's loved ones who must handle the loss of someone dear to them.

What about Those Who Claim to Have Near-Death Experiences?
Researchers have suggested a variety of explanations for those who claim to experience near-death experiences. First, some explain these experiences as a lack of oxygen to the brain, a condition known as hypoxia. This causes the sensation of going through a tunnel and seeing a bright light. However, this is a highly debatable and inconclusive view. Others, such as the astronomer Carl Sagan, have suggested the concept of seeing light at the end of a tunnel is a deeply embedded birth memory. A third medical explanation is that certain accompanying injuries release chemicals into the brain that create such experiences.

Christian researchers also note that these experiences could be caused by evil spiritual forces. Satan, the father of lies, has the ability to counterfeit miracles, cause people to see a great white light, see loved ones in a beautiful place, and feel great love, deceiving with a counterfeit (2 Thessalonians 2:9). Those who claim out of body experiences in which they speak with spirit guides, sometimes impersonating angels, would fall into this same category.

> *In Luke 16:19–31, Jesus indicates that once a person is in heaven or hell, the decision regarding that person's eternity is final.*

However, some near-death experiences seem to have unexplained causes that could indicate a true vision from God. While Scripture does not share the thoughts of Christians who returned from the dead in the Bible (such as Lazarus, the man Jesus raised from the dead), it is not impossible for God to use such an experience to help someone grow in his or her relationship with Christ. Yet it is important to point out that much of what is described as near-death experiences today arise from psychic or new age backgrounds, practices condemned by Scripture (Deuteronomy 18:10–13).

📖 Read Deuteronomy 18:10–13. What do these verses say about psychic practices?

_____

_____

_____

What about Reincarnation?

The word reincarnation literally means to "come again in the flesh." The process of a soul experiencing birth and death multiple times in different human bodies allegedly continues until the soul has reached a state of perfection and reaches nirvana. But upon what authority does reincarnation rest? Since Jesus is the only one who ever claimed to be God, and resurrected from the dead, he has the only authority to speak on this topic.

📖 What does Bible state in Hebrews 9:27 about the concept of reincarnation?

_____

_____

_____

Hebrews clearly notes that a person dies once, then faces judgment in the afterlife. People do not have a second chance by reincarnating into another body. 2 Corinthians 5:8 also indicates that at death the Christian immediately enters the presence of the Lord, not into another body. Luke 16:19–31 indicates that unbelievers at death go to a place of suffering, not into another body. This is why the apostle Paul emphasized that "now is the day of salvation" (2 Corinthians 6:2).

What about Purgatory?

Roman Catholic theology teaches that those who are perfect at death are admitted to heaven. Those who are not perfectly cleansed and are still tainted with the guilt of "venial sins" (to Catholics: insignificant or inconsequential sins as opposed to "mortal sins" that may lead to damnation), however, do not go to heaven but rather go to purgatory where they allegedly go through a process of cleansing or purging. Such souls are oppressed with a sense of deprivation and suffer certain pain. How long they stay in purgatory and how much suffering they undergo while there depends upon their particular state of sin.

Roman Catholics also teach that the faithful prayers and good works of those still alive may shorten a person's time in purgatory. The sacrifice of the Mass is viewed as especially important in this regard. Catholics find support for this doctrine in the apocryphal book 2 Maccabees 12:42–45. Yet purgatory is never mentioned in the 66 books of the Bible accepted by Protestants.[50]

Did You Know?

？ FAMOUS REINCARNATION ADHERENTS

- Edgar Cayce (American mystic)

- Henry Ford (automobile magnate)

- L. Ron Hubbard (founder of Church of Scientology)

- General George S. Patton (World War II hero, believed he fought in many famous battles throughout history in past lives)

- William Butler Yeats (Irish Poet and Nobel Laureate)

Also, when Jesus died on the cross, He paid for all our sins, "venial" and "mortal." The Bible does not teach we do our part and Jesus does His. The Bible says we are dead in our sins. You can ask a dead man to just reach out his hand so you can pull him out of the casket, but it won't happen. He's dead. We, as sinners, need the gift of salvation and new life that only Jesus can give us.

As we have seen in our study of heaven and hell, only two options are presented in Scripture when describing the afterlife. There is no "penalty box" as in hockey where a person stays temporarily before entering heaven.

APPLY How has this study of the afterlife affected your thinking about who Jesus is and what He promises to those dead in their sins? What applications do you desire to take from this session?

_____

_____

_____

_____

_____

_____

Spend some time in prayer with the Lord now. Use the following Scriptures from John 3:16–18 to reflect on God's desires for our future:

"For God so loved the world that he gave his one and only Son, that whoever believes in him shall not perish but have eternal life. For God did not send his Son into the world to condemn the world, but to save the world through him. Whoever believes in him is not condemned, but whoever does not believe stands condemned already because he has not believed in the name of God's one and only Son. This is the verdict: Light has come into the world, but men loved darkness instead of light because their deeds were evil. Everyone who does evil hates the light, and will not come into the light for fear that his deeds will be exposed. But whoever lives by the truth comes into the light, so that it may be seen plainly that what he has done has been done through God."

Write down any prayer concerns you have as you seek to apply the material from this session:

_____

_____

_____

_____

_____

_____

_____

Notes

Does the Bible Accurately Predict Future Events?

One of the strongest evidences that Christianity is true is the testimony of fulfilled prophecy. No other religion can claim the accuracy predicted by the Bible. At best, the scriptures of other religions contain a small number of vague predictions, along with many inaccurate prophecies. Nothing compares to the large number of detailed prophecies in Scripture that have come true.

Those who seriously study Bible prophecy will quickly discover that it is a subject of great importance in Christianity. There are more than six hundred direct references in the Bible to "prophecy" and "prophets." An incredible twenty-seven percent of the Bible's verses mention Bible prophecy. Out of sixty-six Bible books, only four contain no prophetic statements. The apostle Peter writes that we *"will do well to pay attention to"* God's prophetic Word (2 Peter 1:19–21). Jesus rebuked his own disciples for ignoring it (Luke 24:25) and taught that the Old Testament predictions about Him were of special importance (Luke 24:44).

> *At best, the scriptures of other religions contain a small number of vague predictions, along with many inaccurate prophecies. Nothing compares to the large number of detailed prophecies in Scripture that have come true.*

Surprising Facts Concerning Bible Prophecy

- Approximately 27% of the entire Bible contains prophetic material. Half of that has already come true. Half remains to be fulfilled.

- Of the Old Testament's 23,210 verses, 6,641 contain prophetic material, or 28.5%.

- Of the New Testament's 7,914 verses, 1,711 contain prophetic material or 21.5%.

- Of the Bible's 31,124 verses, 8,352 contain prophetic material, or 27% of the whole Bible.

- 1,800 verses deal with the Second Coming of Christ.

- In the New Testament, 318 verses deal with the Second Coming of Christ.

- Every 25th Bible verse in the New Testament refers to the Second Coming.[51]

LESSON TEN DAY ONE

Over one-fourth of the entire Bible is prophetic in nature.

WHY STUDY BIBLE PROPHECY?

Over the past thirty years, I (John) have spoken on the issue of prophecy at numerous conferences and events. From these experiences, there have been seven core principles that I have consistently used to help individuals understand the importance of Bible prophecy for today.

1. Prophecy Is the Study of God Speaking Directly to Humanity

Prophecy makes up a major portion of the Bible. As noted in the statistics above, over one-fourth of the entire Bible is prophetic in nature. Certainly God desires such a significant portion of Scripture to be studied and understood by its readers.

📖 Read 2 Peter 1:19–21. What does it state about the origin of prophecy?

_____

_____

_____

Peter wrote that *"men spoke from God as they were carried along by the Holy Spirit"* (verse 21). The ultimate origin of prophecy is from God Himself.

📖 Read 1 Peter 1:10–13. How important did the prophets consider their writings?

_____

_____

The prophets wrote with the utmost care and diligence. Their writings were considered so sacred that even angels longed to look into these things.

2. God Himself Commands Us to Study Prophecy

God has not only provided prophecy. He has *commanded* us to study it. In Isaiah 45:21, the prophet writes:

"Who foretold this long ago? Who declared it from the distant past? Was it not I, the Lord? And there is no God apart from Me, a righteous God and a Savior, there is none but Me. Turn to Me and be saved, all you ends of the earth, for I am God and there is no other."

📖 The apostle Paul spoke to Timothy regarding this issue as well. Read 2 Timothy 3:16–17. How do these verses apply to the study of prophecy?

_____

_____

_____

If all Scripture is inspired by God and useful, then all prophecy is inspired as well. The natural application of this verse regarding prophecy is that we would study prophecy diligently because they are the very words of God Himself.

3. Jesus Personally Encouraged the Study of Prophecy

Jesus clearly stated that the study of prophecy was of great importance. Matthew 13 reveals this emphasis Jesus gave to His followers to understand the predictions of the Bible:

Matthew 13:5: *"Jesus said to them: Watch out that no one deceives you."*

Matthew 13:9: *"You must be on your guard."*

Matthew 13:23: *"So be on your guard; I have told you everything ahead of time."*

Matthew 13:29: *"When you see these things happening, you know that it is near, right at the door."*

Matthew 13:33: *"Be on guard! Be alert! You do not know when that time will come."*

Matthew 13:37: *"What I say to you, I say to everyone: Watch!"*

In addition to Christ's positive warnings, He also called those "foolish" who did not study and believe what God said, especially regarding His future teachings. After His resurrection, He rebuked two men during a walk to Emmaus, saying, *"How foolish you are, and how slow of heart to believe all that the prophets have spoken! Did not the Christ have to suffer these things and then enter His glory? And beginning with Moses and all the prophets, He explained to them what was said in all the Scriptures concerning Himself."*[52]

📖 Read Luke 24:44–45. What did Jesus teach here about the value of the Old Testament's predictions concerning Him?

_____

_____

_____

_____

Jesus taught that His life fulfilled the Law, the Prophets, and the Psalms.

Finally, Jesus also taught that the entire Old Testament was about Him—all thirty-nine books written by thirty different authors over a period of a thousand years predicted the events of His life in specific detail.

Jesus taught that His life fulfilled the Law, the Prophets, and the Psalms.

📖 Read Luke 24:27. How did Jesus use prophecy to speak of Himself?

_____

_____

4. Prophecy Is Evidence That God Exists.

All it takes is one false prophecy to discredit the claim that the Bible is God's Word to us. Yet Scripture has proven repeatedly that prophecy reveals God's existence. "In all the writings of the world, the accuracy of biblical prophecy is unique and stands as one of the great evidences of the God-breathed nature of the Bible."[53]

The prophet Isaiah stated this from God's point of view when he wrote in Isaiah 44:6–8:

> _This is what the LORD says—Israel's King and Redeemer, the LORD Almighty: I am the first and I am the last; apart from me there is no God. Who then is like me? Let him proclaim it. Let him declare and lay out before me what has happened since I established my ancient people, and what is yet to come—yes, let him foretell what will come. Do not tremble, do not be afraid. Did I not proclaim this and foretell it long ago? You are my witnesses. Is there any God besides me? No, there is no other Rock; I know not one._

Even the archaeological accuracy of the Scripture is difficult to explain if the Bible is only written by erring men. For example, over twenty-five thousand archaeological sites from the biblical era have been confirmed by modern discoveries. Knowing that prophecy helps prove God's very existence, it stands as vital for those seeking God to passionately study these words for their personal growth and for sharing with others.

5. Prophecy Gives Us Hope for the Future

Dr. Wilbur M. Smith suggests that there are three different attitudes one can take toward the future. The first is **indifference**, the second is **fear,** and the third is **hope.** No intelligent person would take the first; no one needs to be trapped in the second; but all can possess the third. There is comfort and hope for all believers who love and study the prophecies of the Bible.[54]

📖 What does 1 Corinthians 14:3 teach about the hope prophecy provides?

_____

_____

_____

Prophecy's intent is to encourage people regarding God's future for the world.

Prophecy's intent is to encourage people regarding God's future for the world. As the apostle Peter records, "But in keeping with his promise we are looking forward to a new heaven and a new earth, the home of righteousness. So then, dear friends, since you are looking forward to this, make every effort to be found spotless, blameless and at peace with him" (2 Peter 3:13–14). For follows of Christ, the future is not a source of horror; it is a source of hope.

6. Prophecy Encourages a Lifestyle of Integrity

According to Renald Showers, "Believers in the early church held vigorously to belief in the imminent coming of Jesus Christ, and that belief powerfully motivated them to holy living."[55]

📖 What does the apostle John teach that prophecy does for our spiritual lives in 1 John 3:2–3?

_____

_____

_____

Regarding the study of the Book of Revelation, Dr. Tim LaHaye observes, "I have found that the proper understanding of Revelation motivates Christians to consistent dedication and service."[56] Prophecy is a motivator of holy living.

C. H. Spurgeon once said, "A good character is the best tombstone. Those who loved you, and were helped by you, will remember you. So carve your name on hearts, and not on marble." To fully embrace the belief that Jesus will return at any moment fuels a lifestyle of integrity.

7. Prophecy Shapes Our Personal Thinking and Worldview

Showers, comments further, "It [the Rapture] should make a major difference in every Christian's values, actions, priorities, and goals."[57] No one can be unconcerned about future events, especially if God is the One who has purposely revealed this information. It is important that we know and understand God's message to us.

📖 Read 2 Peter 3:10–12. What does it teach concerning our response to God's prophecies?

_____

_____

_____

_____

Dr. LaHaye makes an important point in his book _Are We Living in the End Times?_ He says that when people have taken prophecy seriously in the past, three things have occurred: **1)** believers were challenged to holy living in an unholy age; **2)** Christians were greatly challenged to evangelize; and **3)** the church was more missionary-minded as it realized it must continue to fulfill the Great Commission until Christ returns.[58]

APPLY In what ways does studying prophecy help motivate you to live out your faith?

_____

_____

_____

_____

_____

_____

_____

_____

SURPRISING STATISTICS FROM THE BIBLE REGARDING PROPHECY

Consider the following statistics regarding Bible prophecy:

Prophetic Material in the Bible

	NUMBER OF PREDICTIVE VERSES	TOTAL VERSES	PERCENTAGE OF PREDICTIVE VERSES
Old Testament	6,641	23,210	28.5%
New Testament	1,711	7,914	21.5%
Entire Bible	8,352	31,124	27%

Source: Adapted from statistics in J. Barton Payne, *Encyclopedia of Biblical Prophecy* (New York: Harper & Row, 1973).

According to Payne's *Encyclopedia of Biblical Prophecy*, approximately half of the Bible's prophecies have been fulfilled. Half remains to be fulfilled. Only four of the sixty-six books of the Bible are without prophecy: Ruth, Song of Solomon, Philemon and 3 John. Even the shortest book in the Bible contains Bible prophecy (Jude 14). Out of sixty-six Bible books, seventeen are devoted primarily to prophecy (16 in the Old Testament and Revelation in the New Testament).

What are the chances that so many prophecies could be predicted accurately? Dr. Hugh Ross has conservatively calculated the accuracy of all of the Bible's already fulfilled prophecies at 10 to the 2000th power (10 followed by 2,000 zeros!).

What are some of the common views today regarding Bible prophecy?

_____

_____

_____

_____

If over one-fourth of the Bible consists of prophecy, how should we view its importance?

_____

_____

_____

_____

The Bible also contains numerous geopolitical prophecies. For example, Isaiah, Jeremiah, Ezekiel, Daniel, and others all predicted future events in stunning detail, including the rise and fall of every major world empire that left its mark on the Middle East. For example, the prophet Daniel predicted the rise of the Medo-Persian, Greek, and Roman empires hundreds of years before events unfolded that led to their establishment.

Read Revelation 1:3. What does it say about the person who studies its prophecy?

_____

_____

Jesus teaches that we are blessed if we read and take to heart His prophecies.

Read Genesis 20:7. What does this verse indicate about the importance of God's prophets in the Bible?

_____

_____

God's prophets were highly valued in His sight as communicators of His words. Our goal should be to value His words with the greatest importance.

The prophet Samuel provides many insightful thoughts regarding our understanding of prophecy. In his life, he was raised as a young man who heard the voice of God, anointed the two kings of Israel, and taught God's people spiritual truth.

Read 1 Samuel 3:1. What does this verse imply about some of the things a prophet does?

_____

_____

In this one verse from Saul's early life, we find implied that a prophet was a person who heard God's word and saw visions from God.

Read 1 Samuel 9:8–9. What was another name for a prophet? What does this name indicate about the role of a prophet?

_____

_____

_____

A "seer" sees things revealed to him by God and communicates what he sees to others. Though there are some who claim to see into the future today, the Bible's prophets were one hundred percent accurate in all issues they addressed.

Prophets were also used by God to serve in other ways in addition to foretelling events. Read 2 Chronicles 24:19. What was the purpose for God sending prophets to His people?

_____

_____

God gave a great number of prophecies about the Messiah for at least two reasons: to make identifying the Messiah obvious and to make an impostor's task impossible.

God is not the only one, however, who uses forecasts of future events to get people's attention. Satan does, too. Through clairvoyants (such as Jeanne Dixon and Edgar Cayce), mediums, spiritists, and others, come remarkable predictions, though rarely with more than about 60 percent accuracy, never with total accuracy. Messages from Satan, furthermore, neither match the detail of Bible prophecies, nor do they include a call to repentance.[59]

📖 According to 2 Peter 2:1–3, what are some of the characteristics of false prophets?

_____

_____

Several aspects are shared in these verses. We find that false prophets or teachers will teach unbiblical concepts, deny the traditional beliefs about Jesus, lead people to believe lies, are marked by greed, and make up stories for their own gain.

📖 Read 1 John 4:1–3. How are we supposed to evaluate those who claim to be a prophet?

_____

_____

False prophets are identified by what they believe about Jesus. According to John, anyone who claims that Jesus did not come in the flesh (in the incarnation) is a false prophet. Mark 13:21 also notes that Jesus said that a mark of a false prophet is someone who predicts a date for Christ's return.

Finally, we find that the power of false prophets is limited in comparison with God's power. Read Acts 13:4–12. What happened to the false prophet who troubled Paul?

_____

_____

Christians have a power through God's Spirit that is far greater than any false prophet.

The Bible's sheer number of prophecies provides more than enough evidence to reveal their importance for our lives today. For critics to maintain that the Bible does not accurately predict the future is nonsense. The words are there for everyone to see. Only God can successfully predict that future, and He has done so in the Bible.

LESSON
TEN

DAY THREE

Is There Evidence from the Old Testament Prophecies about Jesus?

Is there evidence in history that God gave specific information hundreds of years in advance about a person He knew would live? The Bible provides a clear answer to this question. 456 different prophecies have been identified from the Old Testament that directly predict aspects of the life of Jesus Christ. In fact, twenty-four prophecies were fulfilled just within the final twenty-four hours of Jesus' earthly life:

24 Prophecies Fulfilled within 24 Hours of Jesus' Death

Prophecy	Prediction	Fulfillment
Betrayed by a friend	Psalm 55:12–14	Matthew 26:49–50
Money thrown to the potter	Zechariah 11:13	Matthew 27:5–7
Abandoned by his followers	Zechariah 13:7	Matthew 26:56
Accused by false witnesses	Psalm 35:11	Matthew 26:59–60
Beaten and spat upon	Isaiah 50:6	Matthew 27:30
Silent before his accusers	Isaiah 53:7	Matthew 27:12–14
Wounded and bruised	Isaiah 53:5	Matthew 27:26, 29
Fell under the cross	Psalm 109:24	John 19:17
Hands and feet pierced	Psalm 22:16	Luke 23:33
Crucified with thieves	Isaiah 53:12	Mark 15:17–18
Prayed for those who killed Him	Isaiah 53:12	Luke 23:34
People shook their heads	Psalm 109:25	Matthew 27:39
People ridiculed Him	Psalm 22:8	Matthew 27:41–43
People astonished	Psalm 22:17	Luke 23:35
Clothes taken and cast lots	Psalm 22:18	John 19:23–24
Cries for the forsaken	Psalm 22:1	Matthew 27:46
Given gall and vinegar	Psalm 69:21	John 19:28–29
Committed Himself to God	Psalm 31:5	Luke 23:46
Friends stood at a distance	Psalm 38:11	Luke 23:49
Bones not broken	Psalm 34:20	John 19:33, 36
Heart broken	Psalm 22:14	John 19:34
Side pierced	Zechariah 12:10	John 19:34–37
Darkness over the land	Amos 8:9	Matthew 27:45
Buried in a rich man's tomb	Isaiah 53:9	Matthew 27:57–60

Prophecy experts have evaluated these predictions in a multitude of ways. We'll focus on twelve specific areas of Jesus' life, briefly comparing the Jewish prophecies with their fulfillment during the life of Jesus to better determine if the prophecies really line up with the life of Jesus Christ.

1. The Messiah Would Be Born in a Specific City

Micah claimed concerning the town of Bethlehem, *"But you, Bethlehem Ephrathah, though you are small among the clans of Judah, out of you will come for me one who will be ruler over Israel, whose origins are from of old, from ancient times"* (Micah 5:2). When was this written? 700 BC.

Nearly seven hundred years later, Matthew records that Jesus was born in Bethlehem in Judea, during the time of King Herod.

📖 Read Matthew 2:1–8. What did the Jewish religious leaders claim about the coming Messiah?

_____

_____

Even the Jewish religious leaders alive during the time of Jesus understood Micah's prediction. When the wise men came from the East in search of this Jewish king, the experts in the Law turned right to Micah.

2. The Messiah Would Come from One of the Twelve Jewish Tribes

At the end of Jacob's life, he offered words of blessing to each of his twelve sons. Read Genesis 49:10. What did Jacob promise to his son Judah?

_____

Jews would have understood the references to the "scepter" and "ruler's staff" as symbols of leadership. Whoever the reference concerned, it would be a person from the family line of Judah who would serve as the greatest of leaders.

Both Matthew and Luke record the family genealogy of Jesus, one through Joseph's family and the other through Mary's family (Matthew 1; Luke 3). In each account, the family line traces Jesus' origins to Judah, the very tribe mentioned in the prophecy by Jacob.

3. The Messiah Would Be Preceded by a Messenger

Isaiah wrote over six hundred years before the life of Jesus. In fact, one of the best finds among the Dead Sea Scrolls includes the Isaiah Scroll dated to approximately two hundred years before the birth of Christ.

📖 Read Isaiah 40:3 and Matthew 3:1–2. Who does this prophecy identify?

_____

Notice that Isaiah claims this person will come *from the desert*, his message will prepare the way for the Messiah, and even that this messenger would refer to the coming Messiah as "God." Matthew shares that Jesus is the one John spoke of, and we learn that John baptized Jesus as Messiah before Jesus began public service. Just as Isaiah predicted, John the Baptist preached in the desert, spoke about the soon-coming Messiah, and considered Jesus as God.

Did You Know?

PROPHECY AND JESUS

456 different prophecies in the Old Testament were fulfilled in the life of Jesus Christ.[60]

4. The Messiah Would Enter Jerusalem on a Colt

Yes, even Jesus' mode of transportation on what is now known as Palm Sunday (see Luke 19:28–38) was prophesied centuries earlier.

📖 What did prophet Zechariah predict in Zechariah 9:9?

_____

_____

_____

While utilizing donkeys for travel was common in the first century, to have a specific reference to a *"colt, the foal of a donkey"* provides an eerie accuracy that seems to have no other explanation than a prophecy revealed by God. Remember, Zechariah penned these words around 550 years before the earthly life of Jesus!

5. The Messiah Would Be Betrayed by a Friend

One of Christ's own followers, Judas, betrayed Jesus on the eve of his crucifixion. While the gospels communicate that Jesus himself had foreknowledge of who would hand him over for death, a much earlier account also speaks on this event.

📖 What did King David prophesy in Psalm 41:9?

_____

_____

In the gospels, we see Judas as one of Jesus' twelve closest friends, who shared bread with him (including the Last Supper), yet conspired against him. As Matthew reports:

> *"While he was still speaking, Judas, one of the Twelve, arrived. With him was a large crowd armed with swords and clubs, sent from the chief priests and the elders of the people. Now the betrayer had arranged a signal with them: 'The one I kiss is the man; arrest him.' Going at once to Jesus, Judas said, 'Greetings, Rabbi!' and kissed him. Jesus replied, "Friend, do what you came for." Then the men stepped forward, seized Jesus and arrested him."* (Matthew 26:47–50)

Are similarities between David's lyrics and accounts of Judas' betrayal only a coincidence? Perhaps one could get away with such thinking if this was the only spot to connect the Jewish scriptures with the life of Jesus. However, this is the fifth *very specific* connection we have mentioned to Jesus' life.

6. The Messiah Would Be Sold for Thirty Pieces of Silver

Matthew also shares the financial motivation behind Judas' betrayal:

"Then one of the Twelve—the one called Judas Iscariot—went to the chief priests and asked, 'What are you willing to give me if I hand him over to you?' So they counted out for him thirty silver coins." (Matthew 26:14–16)

Interestingly, even this specific monetary amount was prophesied in Old Testament Scriptures. Read Zechariah 11:4–13. What similarities do you see between these verses and the verses from Matthew above?

_____

_____

After a dispute about his work, Zechariah ended his shepherding. In his wrap-up with his employer, he remarked, *"I told them, 'If you think it best, give me my pay; but if not, keep it.' So they paid me thirty pieces of silver"* (verse 12). Interestingly, this was also the price for the redemption of a servant according to the Law of Moses (Exodus 21:32). This visual form of teaching served as an additional prophecy of the set price for Jesus' betrayal.

APPLY How do these prophecies regarding Jesus strengthen your faith in the truth of God's Word?

_____

_____

_____

_____

LESSON TEN   DAY FOUR

IS THERE EVIDENCE FROM THE OLD TESTAMENT PROPHECIES ABOUT JESUS? (PART 2)

Yesterday we began our investigation regarding just six of the prophecies regarding the life of Jesus and found they included amazing details and accuracy. Yet these are only a small sampling of what the Bible predicts about the life, death, and resurrection of Jesus. Today we continue with six more prophecies fulfilled in the life of Christ.

7. The Messiah Would Be Spit upon and Beaten
The "Servant," understood as the Messiah in Isaiah's prophecies, undertakes a graphic beating in prophecy: *"I offered my back to those who beat me, my cheeks to those who pulled out my beard; I did not hide my face from mocking and spitting"* (Isaiah 50:6). Sound familiar? Maybe because this is *exactly* the type of violent treatment Jesus received prior to his crucifixion.

Matthew details the brutality of Jewish leaders as they accused Christ of blasphemy: *"Then they spit in his face and struck him with their fists. Others slapped him and said, 'Prophesy to us, Christ. Who hit you?' "* (Matthew 26:67–68). Later, Roman soldiers would torture him similarly.

Read Matthew 27:28–30. What details of prophecy did Jesus fulfill here?

_____

_____

Notice what they called Jesus. The Jewish leaders mocked him as *the Christ*. The Roman soldiers mocked him as *King of the Jews*. This was not the treatment of an ordinary criminal but a religious mocking of a man who claimed to be the Messiah. This mocking included spitting and beating and was predicted centuries earlier.

"The secret things belong to the LORD our God, but the things revealed belong to us and to our sons forever, that we may observe all the words of this law."

Deuteronomy 29:29

8. The Messiah Would Be Wounded by His Enemies

In a later prophecy, Isaiah 53:5 also notes that the Messiah was, *". . . pierced for our transgressions, he was crushed for our iniquities; the punishment that brought us peace was upon him, and by his wounds we are healed."*

Notice the specifics of this prediction. First, it included a piercing. This is a prophecy regarding the nails used in Jesus' feet and hands at the cross. Second, Jesus was *"crushed for our iniquities."* What would it mean to be crushed? In the Gospels, we find that after the Roman governor Pilate was persuaded to execute Jesus, *"he had Jesus flogged, and handed him over to be crucified"* (Matthew 27:27). A flogging would have been carried out with a lead-tipped whip, sometimes even laced with chips of bone or other sharp materials. According to Jewish tradition, forty lashes minus one were the maximum number of lashes allowed. History also notes that criminals sometimes died during these whippings. This could definitely be classified as being "crushed."

9. The Messiah Would Be Silent before His Accusers

One striking observation made by the Gospel writers was that Jesus refused to argue for his own release before his sentencing. Pilate didn't quite know how to handle him: *"Don't you hear the testimony they are bringing against you?' But Jesus made no reply, not even to a single charge—to the great amazement of the governor"* (Matthew 17:12–14).

📖 Read Isaiah 53:7. How does this prophecy relate to Matthew's words about Jesus?

_____

_____

_____

Using the imagery of a lamb led to slaughter, Isaiah uniquely identifies another aspect of Jesus' life in stunning detail. In fact, during one specific period of research, revisionist scholars began disputing the traditional dating of Isaiah, claiming its predictions could not have been made before the lifetime of Jesus. However, in the mid-twentieth century, the discovery of the Dead Sea Scrolls revealed an intact Hebrew Isaiah scroll from approximately two hundred years before the life of Jesus. This, combined with the fact that Isaiah was translated into Greek prior to Jesus' earthly life, disproves any attempt to re-date the predictions made in Isaiah's work.

10. The Betrayal Money thrown in the Temple and Given for a Potter's Field

Continuing our earlier story from Zechariah, after receiving thirty coins from his employer, *"The Lord said to me [Zechariah], 'Throw it to the potter'—the handsome price at which they priced me! So I took the thirty pieces of silver and threw them into the house of the Lord to the potter"* (Zechariah 11:13). At first this prophecy appears confusing. What does a potter's house have to do with Jesus?

If we fast-forward to Matthew, we read that Judas became overwhelmed by guilt after betraying his leader.

📖 Read Matthew 27:3–5. What does it say about the potter's house?

_____

_____

> "He was oppressed and He was afflicted, Yet He did not open His mouth; Like a lamb that is led to slaughter, And like a sheep that is silent before its shearers, So He did not open His mouth."
>
> **Isaiah 53:7**

The chief priests found themselves in a touchy situation. If they invested the funds back into their treasury, they would be breaking their own law, the very law they had used to condemn Jesus. If they left the money there, someone would surely discover their involvement with Judas. Their decision? *"It is against the law to put this into the treasury, since it is blood money.' So they decided to use the money to buy the potter's field as a burial place for foreigners. That is why it has been called the Field of Blood to this day"* (Matthew 27:6–8).

Judas received thirty silver coins for his treacherous act yet remorsefully threw them into the temple. The coins eventually were used to purchase real estate from a potter, an eerie parallel to Zechariah's earlier notation of thirty coins on the floor of the Lord's house that were given to the potter.

11. The Messiah would have his hands and feet pierced

Psalm 22 finds David once again making predictions in the form of musical lyrics. Here he laments, *"Dogs have surrounded me; a band of evil men has encircled me, they have pierced my hands and my feet"* (Psalm 22:16). Those in David's day would have naturally attributed these woes to themselves, suffering Jews against outnumbered foes in the day of battle. Yet a more specific account, written at a later date, complements this Psalm 22 prediction quite nicely.

📖 Read Luke 23:33. How does this verse relate to Psalm 22:16?

_____

_____

_____

Notice the connections—piercing of hands and feet, just as in crucifixion; "a band of evil encircled me," perhaps a reference to those hanging to the right and left of Jesus; "Dogs have surrounded me," possibly a reference to Jesus' enemies, since David elsewhere refers to enemies as dogs (Psalm 59:6). Some have noted that the Roman method of crucifixion had not even been invented yet. For David to specifically mention the Messiah dying in this way would have been of utmost significance since it predicted a form of execution not in existence at the time of its writing.

12. The Messiah would be crucified with thieves

📖 Read Isaiah 53:12. What does it say would happen to the future Messiah?

_____

_____

Here, Isaiah mentions two aspects of the coming Messiah. First, he would pour out his life unto death. The death of Jesus at the cross fulfilled this part of Isaiah's prophecy. Second, in Matthew 27:38 we read that, *"Two robbers were crucified with him, one on his right and one on his left."* Transgressors were considered lawbreakers, just as the two robbers hanging to the sides of Jesus. Interestingly, Jesus also prayed from the cross, and "made intercession" as Isaiah recorded in this prophesy.

 How do these fulfilled prophecies strengthen your belief in Jesus as the Messiah? How would you explain the concept of fulfilled prophecy to an unbeliever?

_____

_____

"Therefore, I will allot Him a portion with the great, And He will divide the booty with the strong; Because He poured out Himself to death, And was numbered with the transgressors; Yet He Himself bore the sin of many, And interceded for the transgressors."
Isaiah 53:12

_____

_____

_____

_____

WHAT EVIDENCE EXISTS IN OTHER AREAS OF THE BIBLE?

The Bible is indeed the Word of God, and the evidence cannot be explained on the basis of any other supposition. There are many additional examples to prove skeptics wrong and demonstrate genuine fulfilled predictions in the Bible.

Josiah in the Book of Kings

First Kings 13:2 mentions King Josiah by name and describes his lineage three hundred years before he was even born. Josiah was a contemporary of Pharaoh Neco, King of Egypt (610–595 BC). Read 1 Kings 13:2. In addition to predicting King Josiah by name, what other significant detail is predicted in this verse?

_____

_____

In this verse God also predicts that this king would destroy the altar at Bethel after sacrificing the evil prophets and burning their bones upon it. All this happened exactly as prophesied—three hundred years later. In 2 Kings 23:15–16 we find:

> _"Even the altar at Bethel, the high place made by Jeroboam son of Nebat, who had caused Israel to sin—even that altar and high place he demolished. He burned the high place and ground it to powder, and burned the Asherah pole also. Then Josiah looked around, and when he saw the tombs that were there on the hillside, he had the bones removed from them and burned on the altar to defile it, in accordance with the word of the LORD proclaimed by the man of God who foretold these things."_

The Decree of Cyrus

Around 700 BC, Isaiah names Cyrus as a king who will allow exiled Israelites to return to Jerusalem and rebuild its Temple. Isaiah 45:13 records:

> _"I will raise up Cyrus in my righteousness: I will make all his ways straight. He will rebuild my city and set my exiles free, but not for a price or reward, says the LORD Almighty."_

At the time of this prophecy, there was no king named Cyrus, and there was no need to build a new temple. However, in 586 BC, more than one hundred years later, the Babylonian King Nebuchadnezzar defeated the nation of Judah while ransacking Jerusalem and destroying the Temple. Jews living in Jerusalem were either killed or taken in captivity to Babylon. In about 539 BC, a Persian king named Cyrus would conquer the Babylonian Empire and soon issue a decree allowing Jews to return to Jerusalem and rebuild the Temple.

📖 Read Ezra 1:1–4. What did Cyrus do for the people of Israel?

_____

_____

_____

Cyrus' decree is confirmed by secular archaeology in the form of a stone cylinder that details many events of Cyrus' reign, including the decree to rebuild the Temple in Jerusalem. Remarkably, Isaiah predicted that a man named Cyrus, who would not be born for close to another hundred years, would give a decree to rebuild a city and a temple, which were still standing and fully active at the time.

The Babylonian Captivity in the Book of Isaiah
Isaiah's prophecies were written approximately around 700–680 B.C. The Jewish captivity in Babylon began in 605 B.C. Yet Isaiah spoke profound words concerning these events.

📖 Read Isaiah 39:5–7. What does it say about what Babylon would do to Israel?

_____

_____

_____

In other passages throughout his book, Isaiah also makes predictions regarding Babylon. He claimed it would be defeated by the Medes (13:17–22). One hundred fifty years after his prediction, the Medes and Persians besieged the walls of Babylon, an unthinkable military feat during that time.

In the book *Evidence That Demands a Verdict*, author Josh McDowell discusses the Bible's prophecies regarding Babylon that were fulfilled in exact detail. The probability that these items could be fulfilled by chance alone is ridiculously miniscule.

How Hard Would It Be to Make These Predictions by Chance?
All of these fulfilled prophecies bring us to another question: How hard would it be to make these predictions by chance? Peter Stoner wrote in his book *Science Speaks* that by using the modern science of probability in reference to eight prophecies, we find that the chance that any man might have lived down to the present time and fulfilled only eight prophecies from the life of Jesus is 1 in 10^{17}. That would be 1 in 100,000,000,000,000,000.

In order to help us comprehend this staggering probability, Stoner illustrates it by supposing that we take 10^{17} silver dollars and lay them on the face of Texas. They will cover all of the state two feet deep. Then mark one of these silver dollars and stir the whole mass thoroughly, all over the state. Blindfold a man and tell him that he can travel as far as he wishes, but he must pick up one silver dollar and say that this is the right one. What chance would he have of getting the right one? Just the same chance that the prophets would have had of writing these eight prophecies and having them all come true in any one man.

Stoner later considers 48 prophecies and concludes that the chance that any one man fulfilled all 48 prophecies to be 1 in 10^{157}, or 1 in:

100,000,000,000,000,000,000,000,000,000,000,000,000,000,000,000,
000,000,000,000,000,000,000,000,000,000,000,000,000,000,000,000,
000,000,000,000, 000, 000,000,000,000,000,000,000,000,000,000,000,000,000.

The estimated number of electrons in the universe is around 10^{79}. It should be quite evident that no one could predict the future this accurately by chance. It had to be God!

APPLY How has studying the fulfilled prophecies of the Bible helped you in believing biblical prophecies yet to be fulfilled?

_____

_____

_____

_____

How does knowledge of fulfilled prophecy help in explaining the importance of the existence of God and the Christian faith to others?

_____

_____

_____

_____

Spend some time in prayer with God right now, using the following words from Psalm 57:7–11 as a guide:

My heart is steadfast, O God, my heart is steadfast; I will sing and make music.

Awake, my soul! Awake, harp and lyre! I will awaken the dawn.

I will praise you, O Lord, among the nations; I will sing of you among the peoples.

For great is your love, reaching to the heavens; your faithfulness reaches to the skies.

Be exalted, O God, above the heavens; let your glory be over all the earth.

Write down one or two applications regarding this session you will seek to apply:

_____

_____

_____

_____

_____

_____

_____

_____

WHAT ARE THE CHANCES?

According to French mathematician Emile Borel, once we go past one chance in 10 to the 50th power, the probabilities of the event happening are so small, it's impossible to think it will ever occur by chance.[61]

Notes

Do Miracles Really Happen Today?

The Bible is full of miracles. From the Creation to the Second Coming, from Moses at the burning bush to Daniel in the lions' den, from the Virgin Birth to the Resurrection, miraculous happenings seem to fill the pages of Scripture. To the believer, these are a wonderful confirmation of the power and message of God, but to the unbeliever, miracles are a stumbling block—a proof that religion is just a bunch of fairy tales. In the world of the skeptic, there is no divine intervention, no interruptions to the normal order; there is only what is seen. Fire consumes when it burns; lions eat whatever is available; and the dead stay dead. As far as they are concerned, the miracles of the Bible could no more be true than Mother Goose.

The purpose of this session is not to explain how every miracle of the Bible occurred. Neither will we attempt to convince anyone that miracles should be considered part of the normal operations of the universe. Our objective is to convince people that the naturalistic attitude toward miracles, which has been fostered for over two hundred years, goes against simple common sense. Rather, this naturalistic attitude is based on faulty logic and unsound thinking that has decided what it is going to find long before it finds anything. The chapter may be thought of as addressing three pairs of questions.

From the Creation to the Second Coming, from Moses at the burning bush to Daniel in the lions' den, from the Virgin Birth to the Resurrection, miraculous happenings seem to fill the pages of Scripture.

One naturalistic thinker said, "The first step in this, as in all other discussions, is to come to a clear understanding as to the meaning of the term" (miracle).[62] A miracle is divine intervention into, or interruption of, the regular course of the world that produces a purposeful but unusual event that would not have occurred otherwise. By this definition, then, natural laws are understood to be the normal, regular way the world operates. But a miracle occurs as an unusual, irregular, and specific act of a God who is beyond the universe. This does not mean that miracles are violations of natural law or even opposed to them. Miracles don't violate the regular laws of cause and effect, they simply have a cause that transcends nature.

Some Well-Known Miracles of Jesus[63]

Miracles	Scripture
Turns water into wine	John 2:1–11
Orders the wind and waves to be quiet	Mark 4:35–41
Raises Lazarus to life	John 11:17–44
Raises a dead girl to life	Matthew 9:18–26
Gives sight to a man born blind	John 9:1–41
Cures the woman who had been bleeding for twelve years	Matthew 9:20–22
Cures a man of evil spirits	Mark 5:1–20
Heals ten men with leprosy	Luke 17:11–19
Heals a crippled man	Mark 2:1–12
Heals a man who was deaf and could hardly talk	Mark 7:31–37
Heals the high priest's servant after the man's ear is cut off	Luke 22:49–52

LESSON ELEVEN — DAY ONE

ARE MIRACLES POSSIBLE?

The most basic question to ask about miracles is, "Are miracles possible?" If they are not possible, we have nothing further to discuss. If they are possible, then we need to address the argument that suggests that belief in miracles is absurd. We find the root of this argument in the writings of Benedict de Spinoza. He developed the following argument against miracles.

Miracles violate the laws of nature.

Natural laws are immutable.

It is impossible for immutable laws to be violated.

Therefore, miracles are not possible.

He was bold in his assertion that "nothing then, comes to pass in nature in contravention to her universal laws, nay, nothing does not agree with them and follow from them, for . . . she keeps a fixed and immutable order."[64]

Certainly we can't argue with the third step in that argument, for what is immutable can't be set aside. But are natural laws immutable? Is this the only definition of a miracle? Mr. de Spinoza built into his premises his own view that nothing exists beyond the universe. In advance, he defined natural law as "fixed and immutable," making it impossible for miracles to occur. But today, scientists understand that natural laws don't tell us what *must* happen, but only describe what usually *does* happen. They are statistical probabilities, not unchangeable facts. So we can't rule out the possibility of miracles by definition.

The definition de Spinoza uses also reflects his anti-supernatural bias. It assumes that there is nothing *beyond* nature that could act *in* nature. But if God exists, then miracles are possible. If there is anything beyond the universe that might cause something to happen in the universe, then there is a chance that it will do so. But once we have established that a theistic God exists, miracles cannot be ruled out.

📖 The basis for believing in the miraculous goes back to the biblical concept of God. Genesis 1:1 notes the first recorded miracle in the Bible. What was it?

_____

_____

_____

If this verse can be accepted at face value, then the rest should be possible as well. If God has the ability to do this, then a virgin birth, walking on water, feeding five thousand people with a few loaves and fish, and other miracles should not only be possible but expected.

📖 For those who believe in the existence of God, the miraculous is at least possible. What did Paul ask in Acts 26:8? How did Paul assume the king's belief in God's existence in asking his question?

_____

_____

_____

_____

_____

> "Miracles are not contrary to nature, but only contrary to what we know about nature."
>
> —St. Augustine

Are Miracles Credible?

Some people don't deny the possibility of miracles. They just can't see any reason for believing in them. To these, the miraculous is not impossible. It just doesn't make sense. The great English skeptic David Hume advanced this very famous argument against believing in miracles:

A miracle is a violation of the laws of nature.

Firm and unalterable experience has established these laws.

A wise man proportions his belief to the evidence.

Therefore, a uniform experience amounts to a proof; there is here a direct and full proof, from the nature of the fact, against the existence of any miracle.

Some think that this argument proves that miracles can't occur. However, Hume disproves the existence of miracles by creating his own definition of a miracle. It seems that his real point is that no one should believe in miracles because all of our experience suggests that they don't happen. For example, we have never gone to a funeral expecting the person to come back to life while we were there. Why? Because we have never experienced such a phenomenon. Dead people stay dead. The proper way of determining whether something happened is not whether we can explain it. The first question to be asked is not can it happen, but rather did it happen?

If an event can be determined as having happened but defies explanation, we still have to admit it happened, whether we can explain it or not. This fits the explanations of the disciples. They experienced the miracles of Jesus, including His resurrection. They did not have an explanation for these events, yet they witnessed them and knew that they had indeed happened. So the disciples proclaimed them, and no one denied them. Neither did the enemies of Jesus. They just argued that Jesus performed His miracles by the power of Satan. But the disciples didn't argue about how Jesus did them. To them, the miracles just happened, so they told what they had seen and heard.

As C. S. Lewis has mentioned, if firm and unalterable experience shows that miracles really don't happen, then they don't happen. But the only way to know that is to check the evidence that they *may* have occurred. That is exactly why the evidence for Jesus' resurrection is so important.

📖 Read 1 John 1:1–3. Upon what did John base his reports?

_____

_____

_____

📖 Read Luke 1:1–4. What did Luke use to verify his reports of miracles?

_____

_____

The New Testament writers note that many witnesses verified the miracles of Jesus. As a result, the biblical accounts of Christ's miraculous works are based on historical reality, despite the fact that the events seem contrary to the laws of nature.

In an interview for *The John Ankerberg Show* with Oxford scholar Dr. N. T. Wright, Dr. Wright revealed,

> It's one of the remarkable games of contemporary history on Jesus, that a majority of current Jesus scholars, including many who are not Christian believers, agree that Jesus *did* do remarkable healings. That is the main explanation for why he attracted crowds and drew so many followers. It wasn't just that his teaching was exciting, though it was. They came because things were happening. A great aunt who had been sick for 50 years: "Bring her and Jesus will heal her." That draws the crowds and would do so today if it happened.[65]

Yet there are those who continue to dispute that Jesus performed miracles. Why? Research Professor of Philosophy at Talbot School of Theology in La Mirada, California, Dr. William Lane Craig suggested in our discussion that, "Members of the Jesus Seminar who are skeptical in their approach to the New Testament have made many of their presuppositions abundantly clear. . . . Their number one pillar of scholarly investigation of the historical Jesus is the presupposition [or starting assumption] of naturalism—that miracles do not happen."

📖 Read Acts 3:1–16. What did Peter state about the following?

What miracle occurred?

_____

Who provided the power for the miracle?

_____

How did the man respond when healed?

_____

_____

How did the other people respond to the miracle?

_____

_____

Of the words used in the New Testament for miracles, one of the most common is the word "sign." John notes at the end of his Gospel that, *"Jesus did many other miraculous signs in the presence of his disciples, which are not recorded in this book. But these are written that you may believe that Jesus is the Christ, the Son of God, and that by believing you may have life in his name"* (John 20:30). The "signs" or miracles recorded in the Gospels were always for a specific purpose and were not intended to be showy or pretentious.

📖 Look at Luke 9:12–17. What immediate need did Jesus meet through this particular miracle?

_____

_____

_____

Jesus performed His miracles out of love and compassion for others. They were also intended to show evidence that He was the Messiah John the Baptist predicted would soon arrive (Matthew 11:4–5).

🛑 APPLY How would you explain the possibility of miracles to a skeptic?

_____

_____

_____

Knowing Jesus performed miracles when He walked on this Earth, what does this mean for your life today?

_____

_____

_____

_____

_____

QUESTIONS ABOUT MIRACLES

Many people refuse to believe in miracles because they feel that if God were allowed to intervene in nature, then there could be no scientific method. As Dr. Allan Bloom has written, "Scientists are to a man against creationism, recognizing rightly that, if there is anything to it, their science is wrong and useless. . . . Either nature has a lawful order or it does not; either there can be miracles or there cannot. Scientists do not prove there are no miracles, they assume it; without this assumption there is no [naturalistic] science."[66]

Yet miracles do not necessarily contradict science. In other words, the fact that miracles occur does not mean science is wrong. A miracle is a break from the normal laws of nature. That's exactly what defines it as a miracle.

According to an interview I (John) conducted with Dr. Gary Habermas of Liberty University, the miracles of Jesus are attested in all the Gospel strata. In his words, "If there is a Creator, a Designer of the universe, who has brought it into being, if such a being exists, then clearly he could intervene in the course of history and perform miraculous acts. It seems to me that we have to be open to *the possibility of miracles*."

Habermas also notes that,

> Most scholars, the vast majority today, would say that Jesus did at least the healing miracles and the exorcisms. Then they add, he did something *like* these but they weren't truly supernatural. So now the question is, what data do we have for the supernaturalness of Jesus' miracles? I'd say again, you're looking at a lot of reasons here that are very respectful.

Why would the fact that the miracles of Jesus are mentioned in multiple sources be important?

_____

_____

_____

How Do We Know?

Even many who do not follow Jesus agree with the idea that He performed miracles. Vanderbilt religion professor Dr. Amy-Jill Levine suggested in an interview that,

> I do think Jesus was a miracle worker, along with several other miracle workers we have both in Jewish sources and in pagan sources. Would his miracle working have been attributed to God? Certainly by some, but as we have even seen in the gospels, others would have said, "Oh, yes, we agree he did miracles, but he does them by the power of Satan." *The miracle working itself is unquestioned.*

I (John) asked Dr. Craig Evans what reasons have compelled so many non-Christian scholars to admit Jesus must have performed miracles? Looking at the past thirty years, he noted,

> I can remember, as a university student, the idea of any kind of a miracle story was laughed at. That has changed in the past thirty years. You

"The most astonishing thing about miracles is that they happen."

—G. K. Chesterton

can see it in popular culture. You can see it in the popular television program, *Star Trek*. Mr. Spock wants to be a machine, right? He wants to be *scientific*. Science can solve everything. In the new version of it, you have a machine who wants to be a human! You have characters who want to be in touch with the inner spirit and channel and do all kinds of strange things. That show reflects the change that has taken place.

In science, there's a recognition: "Hey, we don't have a closed universe any more. We have to be open. We're not real sure about our origins any more. Maybe there is something beyond the physical universe. Maybe there *is* a God. Maybe miracles *do* occur." That's a big change.

Read Mark 12:1–12. Answer the following questions regarding this miracle of Jesus:

What was the situation before the miracle?

_____

_____

What did Jesus say?

_____

_____

How did the Pharisees respond?

_____

_____

How did the rest of the people respond?

_____

_____

What role did faith play in the healing of the paralytic man?

_____

_____

In our interview with Dr. N. T. Wright that we mentioned earlier, Dr. Wright, commented:

> My history makes me say, "Hey, put that stuff on hold for a moment," just supposing Jesus of Nazareth really did rise from the dead. Don't start by saying, "Did He walk on water?" Don't start by saying, "Was He born of a virgin?" If you start with those questions, you go round and round in circles and you never get anywhere. Start by saying, "How do you explain the rise of early Christianity?" If [the answer] comes back and says, "It was Jesus' resurrection," then you're going to have to hold your mind open to the fact that in the world, as Shakespeare said, "There are more things in heaven and earth than are dreamed of in your philosophy."

How did the growth of the early church depend on the occurrences of miracles? What other explanation could account for the beginning of Christianity?

_____

_____

_____

According to Dr. Darrell Bock,

> If you come to the text and you believe miracles can't happen, you kind of have a dilemma on your hands. You read these texts about Jesus multiplying the loaves or you read these texts about Jesus healing the blind, and you have to come up with some kind of explanation of what goes on. In fact, the healing of the blind is an interesting one because in the Old Testament, blind people didn't get healed. No one did that miracle. And that's not one you can very easily fake.

Every scholar I (John) have interviewed on the issue of miracles agrees in this area. For instance, Dr. Craig remarked, "It would be bad methodology to simply dismiss these in advance before even looking at the evidence that they might have actually occurred. Otherwise, we could be ruling out the true hypothesis simply on the basis of a philosophical presupposition [a personal bias] for which we have no justification."

 If someone asked why you believe in miracles, what would you say?

_____

_____

_____

How could you question someone who refuses to accept that Jesus performed miracles?

_____

_____

_____

_____

 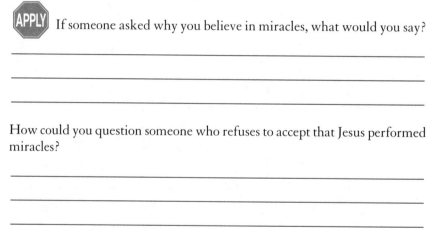 DAY THREE

OUTSIDE EVIDENCE FOR MIRACLES

In addition to New Testament accounts, a growing amount of information has been gathered to show the validity of miracles. Facts from psychiatry, medicine, and science are supplying evidence that may indicate miracles are happening in our world today. As I (John) asked the three researchers I interviewed about these new findings, I was surprised at the abundance of information that is beginning to show further support for miracles today.

Indicators from Psychiatry & Medicine
For example, Dr. Habermas revealed,

> I think another factor in favor of the miracles in the New Testament is that there is some very hard data I think that is difficult to explain away. I think of Marcus Borg who reports in one of his books on Jesus that there was a team of psychiatrists recently who could not explain a cou-

ple of possession cases by normal scientific means. I also refer to a dou-
ble blind experiment with almost 400 heart patients in San Francisco
where they were monitored in 26 categories and those who were prayed
for were statistically better in 21 out of 26 categories. Because the experiment was performed well, this was published in a secular journal, *The
Southern Journal of Medicine*.

So, if you can see some of these things today, maybe you can't say, "Oh,
there's a miracle right there," but it makes you wonder a little bit. I have
to say, can we be so quick to condemn the things Jesus did in the first
century?

How can information from psychiatry and medicine provide evidence for
miracles? What other stories or studies have you heard about that point
toward the reality of miracles?

_____

_____

_____

_____

_____

Read Matthew 9:27–34. How did the religious leaders of this time explain
the miracles of Jesus?

_____

_____

_____

Notice that these religious leaders did not deny that Jesus performed miracles. They instead chose to claim the source of His miracle working was evil.
They could not deny the miracles themselves. There were too many witnesses who had seen them.

Indicators from Science
Scientists claim that all events must have some natural explanation or have a
necessary cause. The supernaturalist makes a similar claim: *a miracle occurs
whenever God deems it necessary.* If we had all the evidence (if we knew all that
God knows), we could predict when God was going to intervene with as
much accuracy as the scientist can predict natural events.

But even contemporary science is changing. Dr. William Lane Craig noted,

It's interesting to note that in modern science, for example, in physics,
scientists are quite willing to talk about realities which are quite literally metaphysical in nature—realities which are beyond our space and
time dimensions; realities which we cannot directly perceive or know
but which we may infer by certain signposts of transcendence in the
universe to something beyond it.

A growing number of scientists now believe that the evidence for the
Big Bang theory points to a simultaneous beginning for all matter, energy, and even the space-time dimensions of the universe. This evidence
has led them to place the cause of the universe independent of matter,
energy, space and time. This evidence calls for the strong possibility of
the existence of God.

📖 How does the complexity of the universe show that miracles can occur? How does Psalm 104:24 confirm the wisdom of God in creating the universe?

_____

_____

_____

According to Dr. Craig,

> If there is a Creator and Designer of the universe, who has brought it into being, then clearly he could intervene in the course of history and perform miraculous acts. So in the absence of some sort of a proof of atheism, _it seems to me that we have to be open to the possibility of miracles._
>
> To give an analogy, in the field of cosmology, the evidence indicates that the universe came into existence in a great explosion called the Big Bang at some point in the finite past. Many physicists are quite willing to say that this event required the existence of a transcendent Creator and Designer of the universe who brought it into being. Now, when we come to the life and ministry of Jesus of Nazareth, could it be that this same Being has intervened in history in a dramatic and miraculous way as Jesus claimed? Shouldn't we be at least open to investigating those claims?

📖 Read 2 Peter 1:16. On what did Peter rely regarding the miracles of Jesus?

_____

_____

_____

Peter based his faith on what he had experienced; what he had seen and heard and touched. He based his teaching concerning Christ on his own testimony and the testimony of many others who had watched Jesus work miracles.

Dr. Gary Habermas argues that, "To me, a naturalistic theory has to, by definition, fill in the blank. A naturalistic theory is not, 'You Christians are crazy! Things like this don't happen. I don't see miracles in my life and Jesus wasn't raised from the dead.' That's not a naturalistic theory. That's a denial." Many of those who argue against miracles simply deny them based on their own predetermined bias.

Miracles also have purpose. God has a purpose and communicates something with each miracle. Moses' miracles confirmed that God had sent him and mocked the Egyptian gods whose domain the miracles overcame (Exodus 7:14—12:36). Elijah didn't call down fire for nothing (1 Kings 18:16–40). The whole day had been spent waiting for Baal to do something, but Elijah's God acted immediately, proving His reality and power.

📖 Read Acts 24:26–29. In Paul's defense to King Agrippa, what was the goal of his statements?

_____

_____

_____

Paul desired to help King Agrippa become a Christian. How? He spoke of God's miracles in his own life and the miracles of Jesus' life and resurrection.

APPLY Who could you speak to about the great things Jesus has done in your own life? What can you do to begin this process today?

_____

_____

_____

_____

_____

Miracles do not destroy science. But trying to explain miracles by means of natural causes is definitely unscientific! Science actually points to a miraculous cause for these events.

WHAT'S THE DIFFERENCE BETWEEN MIRACLES AND COUNTERFEIT MIRACLES OF THE OCCULT?

From a biblical perspective, Satan is not the same as God or even equal to God. In the beginning, God created everything good: the earth (Genesis 1:1), people (1:27–28), and angels (Colossians 1:15–16). One of the angels was named Lucifer (Isaiah 14:12), and he was very beautiful. But he was *"lifted up with pride"* (1 Timothy 3:6, KJV) and rebelled against God, saying, *"I will make myself like the Most High"* (Isaiah 14:14). In doing so, he also led many other angels to follow him, so that one third of all the angels left their home with God (Revelation 12:4). These beings are now known as Satan and his angels (verse 7; Matthew 25:41). They do have unusual powers and are said to be currently *"working in the sons of disobedience"* (Ephesians 2:2). Satan is able to disguise *"himself as an angel of light"* (2 Corinthians 11:14) and appear to be on God's side, but Satan is a deceiver and is always working against God.

How can we tell whether it is Satan or God at work? The Bible gives us some tests so that we can know who is a true prophet and who is false. The key is to distinguish miracles from the occult and counterfeit miracles. Miracles are God-ordained supernatural interventions; the occult involves supernormal forces. The chart below summarizes these differences.

One of the key distinctions between miracles and the occult is the use of spiritistic means to perform its acts. These are practices that claim to conjure powers from the spirit realm. In many cases they do just that; but it is demonic power, not divine. Some of the practices directly linked to demonic power in the Bible are:

- Witchcraft (Deuteronomy 18:10)
- Fortune-telling (Deuteronomy 18:10)

- Communicating with spirits (Deuteronomy 18:11)
- Mediums (Deuteronomy 18:11)
- Divination (Deuteronomy 18:10)
- Astrology (Deuteronomy 4:19; Isaiah 47:13–1 5)
- False Teaching (1 Timothy 4:1; 1 John 4:1–2)
- Immorality (Ephesians 2:2–3)
- Belief in self as God (Genesis 3:5; Isaiah 14:13)
- Lying (John 8:44)
- Idolatry (1 Corinthians 10:19–20)
- Legalism and self-denial (Colossians 2:16–23; 1 Timothy 4:1–3)

Divine Miracles	Counterfeit Miracles and the Occult
Under God's control	Under Satan's control
Supernatural power	A natural [mystical] power
Associated with good	Associated with evil
Associated with biblical teaching	Associated with unbiblical teaching
Can overpower evil	Cannot overpower good
Affirm Jesus is God in the flesh	Denies Jesus is God in the flesh
Prophecies always true	Prophecies sometimes false
Never associated with occult practices	Often associated with occult practices

Many of those who practice and teach pantheistic "miracles" not only admit that they use occult practices, but recommend them for others also. These characteristics show that the sources of these so-called miraculous powers are demonic.

Read Deuteronomy 18:9–13 and answer the following questions:

What were the Israelites to do to people who practiced witchcraft and magic?

_____

_____

What did God call such practices (verse 12)?

_____

Why did God tell them to stand against these practices (verse 13)?

_____

_____

What about those who claim to be prophets today? According to the Bible, a prophet had to be one hundred percent accurate. Yet today many claim to have a "word from God" or a prophecy, yet it does not come true.

Read Deuteronomy 18:21–22. What does it say regarding false prophets?

_____

_____

The Israelites were not to listen to prophets whose word did not come true. In fact, those who prophesied by any other god were to be put to death (18:20).

There are a lot of religions that claim to be "proven" by miraculous deeds. Moses' rod becoming a serpent has served as a proof text for Judaism; Jesus' walking on water and His many other miracles do the same for Christianity; Islam's Mohammed supposedly moved a mountain; and Hindu gurus claim to levitate themselves and others. Today, some pantheistic groups claim that they are performing miracles daily.

To make matters more complicated, there are many Christians making very similar claims today and, while some are valid, some have been exposed as frauds. Even the loose way we use the word "miracle" shows our confusion. Some say it's a miracle when a baby is born and some say it's a miracle when they pass an examination.

How can you tell what is truly miraculous and what is not? Is it possible to define a miracle in such a way that false claims and other kinds of unusual events are eliminated from the definition? Christians believe that miracles imply that there is a God beyond the universe who intervenes in it. Morally, because God is good, His miracles always lift up His truth. Miracles tell us which are true prophets and cannot lie, and which are false. They are never performed for entertainment, but have the distinct purpose of glorifying God and directing attention to Him.

The book of Acts reveals many examples of miracle working and the contrast between good and evil.

📖 Read Acts 3:11–16. Where did Peter and John direct the attention for their miracle?

_____

📖 Read Acts 13:6–12. What happened to Bar-Jesus? What was the result of this miracle?

_____

_____

📖 Read Acts 19:23–20. How did the demons respond to the non-Christian exorcists? How did the surrounding community respond as a result?

_____

_____

_____

🛑 APPLY Read Deuteronomy 18:9–13 again and answer the following questions: Are there any areas of spiritual darkness that need to be removed from your personal life (such as certain TV programs, movies, video games, music, or books)? How can you better fight forces of evil in your spiritual life today (Ephesians 6:10–20)?

_____

_____

_____

_____

FOR ME TO FOLLOW GOD

In contrast to dark spiritual powers, we see the superiority of biblical miracles. The magicians of Egypt tried to reproduce Moses' works by means of illusions and had some success at first (Exodus 7:19ff; 8:6ff), but when God brought forth gnats from the dust, the sorcerers failed and exclaimed, *"This is the finger of God"* (7:19). In the same way, Elijah silenced all claims of the prophets of Baal when he called down fire from heaven when they could not (1 Kings 18). Moses' authority was vindicated when Korah and his followers were swallowed up by the earth (Numbers 16). And Aaron was shown to be God's man for the priesthood when his rod budded (Numbers 17).

When Pharaoh's magicians could not duplicate the miracles of Moses, how did they respond in Exodus 8:16–19? How did miracles reveal to these men that the power was of God?

_____

_____

_____

_____

_____

📖 Read 1 Kings 18:36–39. What was the purpose for God's miracle through Elijah?

_____

_____

_____

What was Elijah's attitude when asking God to work in such a miraculous way?

_____

_____

📖 Read James 5:17–19. How can the life of a godly person influence others through the power available through prayer? How are you doing this in your life? How could you do it better?

_____

_____

_____

_____

_____

Jesus healed the sick (Matthew 8:14–15), made the blind to see (Mark 8:22–26), reached down and embraced lepers to heal them (1:40–45), and raised people from death (Luke 8:49–56). Jesus gave His apostles power, authenticating their testimony after He ascended. Following Jesus' example, Peter healed the beggar at the temple gate (Acts 3:1–11) and raising Dorcas from the dead (9:36–41). Hebrews 2:4 tells us the purpose of these miracles: "*God* [was] *also bearing witness with them, both by signs and wonders and by various miracles and by gifts of the Holy Spirit according to His own will.*" As far as purpose, goodness, and confirmation of God's message, these miracles are in an entirely different class to bending spoons and reading palms. There is no comparison.

📖 Read Acts 9:36–42 and answer the following questions:

What did Peter do?

_____

_____

_____

How did the people respond?

_____

_____

_____

Repeatedly, we find that miracles in the New Testament were used to help people come to faith in Jesus.

📖 What does Hebrews 2:3–4 about the role of miracles in confirming the truth for believers?

_____

_____

_____

Here we see that miracles are a witness and confirmation that the message of Jesus and his apostle are true. Through miraculous prophecies given hundreds of years in advance, predictions that were remarkably precise and accurate, God foretold not only the coming of the destruction of Jerusalem (Isaiah 22:1–25), but the name of the Persian ruler who would return them (Isaiah 44:28; 45:1) 150 years before it all happened. The very place of Jesus' birth is cited in about 700 BC (Micah 5:2). In 538 BC Daniel predicted Christ's triumphal entry into Jerusalem to the day (Daniel 9:24–26). No fortune–teller can boast of anything like this accuracy or consistency.

(APPLY) How does Bible prophecy strengthen your own trust in God's supernatural power?

_____

_____

_____

_____

_____

"I find it quite improbable that such order came out of chaos. There has to be some organizing principle. God to me is a mystery, but [He] is the explanation of the miracle of existence, and why there is something instead of nothing."

—Allan Sandage, winner of the Crafoord prize in astronomy[67]

A Sampling of the Prophecies Regarding Jesus as the Messiah

Prediction	Topic	Fulfillment
Genesis 3:15	seed of a woman	Galatians 4:4
Genesis 12:3	descendant of Abraham	Matthew 1:1
Genesis 17:19	descendant of Isaac	Luke 3:34
Numbers 24:17	descendant of Jacob	Matthew 1:2
Genesis 49:10	from the tribe of Judah	Luke 3:33
Isaiah 11:10	descendent of Jesse	Romans 15:12
Jeremiah 23:5–6	descendant of David	Matthew 1:1
Ezekiel 37:24	will shepherd His people	Matthew 2:6
Isaiah 9:7	heir to the throne of David	Luke 1:32–33
Psalms 45:6–7, Psalms 102:25–27	anointed and eternal	Hebrews 1:8–12
Micah 5:2	born in Bethlehem	Luke 2:4–5, 7
Daniel 9:25	time for His birth	Luke 2:1–2
Isaiah 7:14	to be born of a virgin	Luke 1:26–27, 30–31
Psalms 72:9	worshipped by shepherds	Luke 2:8–15
Psalms 72:10, 15, Isaiah 60:3	honored by great kings	Matthew 2:1–11
Jeremiah 31:15	slaughter of children	Matthew 2:16–18
Hosea 11:1	flight to Egypt	Matthew 2:14–15
Isaiah 40:3–5	the way prepared	Luke 3:3–6
Malachi 3:1	preceded by a forerunner	Luke 7:24, 27
Malachi 4:5–6	preceded by Elijah	Matthew 11:13–14

"No other religion has any miracle that can be compared to the resurrection of Jesus Christ in its grandeur or its testimony."[68]

—Dr. Norman Geisler[75]

Finally, Christ also predicted His own death (Mark 8:31), the means of death (Matthew 16:24), that He would be betrayed (26:21), and that He would rise from the dead on the third day (12:39–40). There is nothing like this anywhere in other religions. The resurrection of Jesus stands alone as the unique and unrepeatable event of history.

APPLY How is the resurrection the ultimate miracle? How does this miracle impact your life today and your view of the future?

_____

_____

_____

_____

_____

HOW CAN WE SHARE THE TRUTH WITH OTHERS?

We've shared together regarding eleven of the most important issues for Christians to understand in defending the faith with skeptics and seekers. In this session together, we'll transition from information for equipping you to application for evangelizing others. Now that we've learned more about addressing key Christian issues, it's vital to learn how to communicate these concepts with our friends, family, neighbors, classmates, and others in our lives.

Over the years, we have shared the truth of Christ with countless individuals in numerous contexts. Yet regardless of the situation, there are keys lines of reasoning that we have found helpful in discussing the issue of knowing Jesus. These concepts are shared in this session through eighteen principles that will guide our time together as illustrated in the chart below:

> *Now that we've learned more about addressing key Christian issues, it's vital to learn how to communicate these concepts with our friends, family, neighbors, classmates, and others in our lives.*

Truth-Sharing Principles for Communicating Christ

Principle	Biblical Basis
You must believe Jesus is God's Son.	John 8:24; 14:9
We must understand and be willing to admit that sin has separated us from God and keeps us from knowing and experiencing Him.	Romans 3:10, 23; 6:23
How good do I have to be to get into Heaven? Answer: Perfect!	Matthew 5:20, 48
When you die, the Bible says you will be judged by God, using His laws of right and wrong.	Hebrews 9:27; Romans 2:13

Principle	Biblical Basis
If we're going to be judged according to how we have obeyed God's Law, how are you doing?	Exodus 20:1–17; Romans 3:20
Wrong way of thinking: "Okay, I have committed a lot of sins, but here is how I will make it up to God."	Titus 3:5; Romans 3:20
If we have not lived a perfect life, if we have broken many of the Ten Commandments, then how will we ever be accepted perfect before God? Through Christ taking our place.	Romans 3:21,22; 1 Peter 3:18
On what basis will God credit Christ's righteousness to sinners? Faith in Christ.	Romans 3:22; 4:5
This sounds too good to be true. Do you mean to say that I don't have to do anything? I just have to admit I am a sinner, put my trust in Christ, and believe that He will save me, forgive me, and give me eternal life? Yes.	Ephesians 2:8–9
Why would God provide such a gift for me? Because of His love.	Romans 5:8; 6:23
God has provided only *one way of salvation*, not many ways.	John 14:6; Acts 4:12
How can I receive Christ into my life? By personally inviting Him to come in.	Romans 10:13; Revelation 3:12
We must believe in Christ.	John 6:40; Acts 16:31
Do I need a lot of faith to receive Christ? Answer: It's not the amount of faith; it's the object of faith.	Romans 10:9–10; Luke 17:6
What is saving faith? Answer: belief in Jesus as God's risen Son.	John 5:24
What is not saving faith? It's more than facts. It's entrusting yourself to Christ.	John 3:3
You can receive Christ now by faith through prayer (prayer is talking with God).	James 5:16
How do you know that Christ is in your life? Answer: You can know based on God's promises.	John 1:12; 1 John 5:13

LESSON TWELVE — DAY ONE

IT ALL BEGINS WITH JESUS

When you come across someone who is interested in discussing how to enter into a relationship with Jesus, you certainly want to respond positively and enthusiastically. This is the greatest life change anyone could ever consider.

At the same time, it is also important to be *prepared* to share. Ultimately, it all begins with Jesus. A relationship with Jesus is based on who He is, what He has done, and what He can do in the life of someone who accepts Him. The apostle John stated Christ's desire for us clearly when he wrote the famous words in John 3:16, *"For God so loved the world that he gave his one and only Son, that whoever believes in him shall not perish but have eternal life."*

If you want to know God personally, if you want God's forgiveness of your sins, if you want God to give you His gift of eternal life, He's willing to save you no matter how many sins you have committed, no matter what you have done, no matter how long you have done it. God's way of salvation is called the Gospel—or the good news. There are some things in the Gospel you must know about and believe.

1. You must believe Jesus is God's son.
Several verses in the New Testament emphasize that Jesus is truly the Son of God. Jesus Himself said:

"For unless you believe that **I am He** [God]*, you shall die in your sins"* (John 8:24).
"He who has seen **me** *has seen* **the Father***"* (John 14:9).

📖 What did the Apostle Paul say about Jesus in Philippians 2:6?

_____

_____

_____

"Who, being in very nature God" in this verse is an interesting phrase. The Greek word, *huparchon*, indicates that before Jesus came to earth and after His birth, He always and continuously existed in the form of God.

📖 What did Jesus say about Himself in John 8:58?

_____

_____

_____

MARK 14:61–62

"Again, the high priest was questioning Him, and saying to Him, 'Are you the Christ, the Son of the Blessed One?' And Jesus said, 'I Am; and you shall see the Son of Man sitting at the right hand of power, and coming with the clouds of heaven.'"

Here, Jesus was referring back to Exodus 3:10–15 where Moses was standing before God at the burning bush. Moses asked God for His name, *"And God said to Moses, 'I* Am *who I* Am'; *and He said, 'Thus you shall say to the sons of Israel, I* Am *has sent me to you. . . . This is my name forever and this is my memorial name to all generations'"* (emphasis added). In John 8:58 Jesus claims to all to be the "I Am," the very God who brought Moses and Israel out of Egypt.

In Matthew 25, Jesus claimed that He alone will come back at the end of the world and be the Judge of all people: *"When the Son of Man comes in His glory, and all the angels with Him, He will sit on His throne in heavenly glory. All the nations will be gathered before Him; He will separate* **the people** *one from another as a shepherd separates the sheep from the goats"* (emphasis added).

For a man to be excluded from heaven on the last day, all that will be needed is for Jesus to say, **"I never knew you"** (Matthew 7:23).

📖 Read John 10:30–33. What did Jesus say about His relationship with God the Father?

_____

_____

_____

The Greek word translated "one" in Christ's statement means one in essence or nature rather than one in purpose or agreement. The Jews tried to kill Him for this comment.

📖 What does John 1:1–3; 14 say about the identity of Jesus?

_____

_____

_____

That's why the apostle Paul could say, *"Believe in the Lord Jesus Chris, and you will be saved"* (Acts 16:31). Jesus is God's Son. A relationship with God means truly believing Jesus Christ is God the Son.

2. We must understand and be willing to admit that sin has separated us from God and keeps us from knowing and experiencing Him.
The Bible says no matter who we are, none of us have measured up to God's standard, none of us will make it—that is, be accepted by God and allowed into heaven on the basis of our good lives.

📖 Read Romans 3:10 and 3:21. What do these two verses tell us about our sinfulness?

_____

_____

_____

Here is how far we have failed to measure up to what God requires. Picture three people coming to the Grand Canyon being chased by an enraged mountain lion. One person says, "We'll have to jump. We have no choice." The problem is, the other side is a mile away. The first person runs as fast as he can, jumps ten feet, falls to the bottom, and dies. The second person tries even harder and jumps fifteen feet, but still is a long way from reaching the other side of the canyon. He, too, falls and dies. The third person is an Olympic long jumper. He runs and jumps much farther than the other two, but still doesn't come close to reaching the other side. Of the three people, even though two were better than the first, none came close to actually making it. The Bible says all of us *"have sinned and fallen short of the glory of God."* Isaiah 53:6 states, *"We all, like sheep, have gone astray, each of us has turned to his own way."*

📖 Read Romans 6:23. What does Paul say is the result of sin in our lives?

_____

_____

_____

Do you realize you are a sinner who will never be able to gain salvation by anything you do? Death is spiritual separation from God now and eternally. This leads us directly into our third principle:

3. How good do I have to be to get into heaven? Perfect!
The Jewish people knew that the Pharisees and the teachers of the Law tried to keep over five hundred laws in trying to please God. The common people believed they would never be able to keep all of these laws. In actuality, the Pharisees and the teachers of the Law didn't either.

📖 Read Matthew 5:20. According to Jesus, how good does a person have to be to reach heaven by his or her own efforts?

_____

_____

📖 Read Matthew 5:48. What is God's standard for entering heaven according to this verse?

_____

_____

Here, Jesus says we have to be perfect, just like God! In other words, if you're not as perfect as God, don't even think that you'll be admitted into heaven. Do you think you have lived a perfect life? Of course not! None of us have. Again, we are sinners who need a Savior to rescue us.

4. When you die, the Bible says you will be judged by God.
The Bible is very clear about what happens after human death. Rather than reincarnation or mere extinction, there is instead a time for judgment: _"It is appointed for men to die once and after this comes judgment"_ (Hebrews 9:27).

📖 Read Romans 2:13. When you stand before God, what will He be looking for?

_____

_____

We are not told in this verse that those who have _heard_ the Law will be just before God; but rather, those who have _obeyed_ it. Have you always obeyed God's laws? No one has, no matter how well he or she has lived in this life.

APPLY As we discuss these principles for sharing Jesus with others, evaluate your own spiritual life. How do you feel concerning your personal relationship with God? Second, who are the people God is bringing to your mind to pray for regarding a personal relationship with Him?

_____

_____

_____

_____

_____

_____

HOW GOOD DO I HAVE TO BE?

LESSON TWELVE · DAY TWO

Our first day began with who Jesus is, our sinfulness, and God's standard for entering heaven. Today, we'll launch into some of the questions that address the issue many ask, "How good do I have to be?" Many people believe if they just do enough good things, they'll be okay in the afterlife. But what does the Bible say? We'll begin our answer to this question with an answer of our own.

5. If we're going to be judged according to how we have obeyed God's Law, how are you doing?
When God gave the Ten Commandments, He said, _"You shall have no other gods before Me"_ (Exodus 20:3). You may say, "I'm not an idolater!" An idol-

ater, of course is one who worships idols. But what exactly is an idol? An idol is anything we put before God. In essence, it becomes our God. Any time we place fame, sports, money, prestige, relationships, or career before God, we have broken this law and are idolaters.

📖 Read Matthew 5:21–22. What does Jesus say about the law of murder?

_____

_____

_____

Jesus states that if you hate someone, you've broken this law of God. We may not be worried about murder, but when is the last time you've heard yourself say, "I hate that person."

The same can be true of other areas. The Ten Commandments instruct us not to lie (or bear false witness), but how often do we tell small lies or partial truths? In our culture, the issue of coveting is common as well. We often call it greed or materialism instead, but the desire for something we don't have, such as a new car, nicer house, or higher promotion are all examples of breaking God's law of coveting.

📖 Read Matthew 22:34–40. What does Jesus call the greatest commandment? How have you broken it?

_____

_____

_____

_____

_____

None of us have loved God with all of our hearts, souls, and mind every moment that we have lived. If so, then according to Jesus, we've broken the greatest commandment of them all. This is why the apostle Paul concluded, _"Therefore, no one will be declared righteous in God's sight by observing the Law"_ (Romans 3:20).

6. Wrong way of thinking: "Okay, I have committed a lot of sins, but here is how I will make it up to God."
Ray Pritchard, in his book, _An Anchor for the Soul_, tells a humorous story that depicts our situation before God. Picture a rich, well-dressed man coming up to Saint Peter at the entrance gate to Heaven. He rings the bell, and Peter says, "Yes. Can I help you?"

The man says, "I would like entrance into Heaven."

Peter responds, "Excellent, we always want more people in Heaven. All you need to enter is to earn 1,000 points."

The man says, "That shouldn't be any problem. I've been a good person all my life. I've been involved in civic things; always given money to charitable causes, and for 25 years I was chairman of the YMCA."

Peter writes it all down and says, "That's a marvelous record. Let me see, that will be one point."

> ## "Therefore, no one will be declared righteous in God's sight by observing the Law."
>
> ## Romans 3:20

With a look of fear on his face, the man says, "Wait a minute! There's more. I was married to my wife for forty-five years, and I was always faithful. We had five children—three boys and two girls. I always loved them, and I made sure they got a good education. I took care of them, and they all turned out all right. I was a very good family man."

Saint Peter then responds, "I am very impressed with your life. We don't get many people like you up here. That will be another point."

The man is really sweating now and starts to shake with fear. He says, "Peter, you don't seem to understand. I was a member in my church. I went every Sunday. Further, I gave money every time they passed the plate. I was a deacon, sang in the choir, and I even taught Sunday School class."

Saint Peter replies, "Your record is certainly admirable. That'll be another point. Now let me add this up: That's one, two, three points. I believe we only need 997 more."

Astonished and trembling, the man falls to his knees and in desperation says, "But for the grace of God, nobody could get in there!!"

Peter looks at him, smiles and says, "Congratulations! The grace of God is worth 1,000 points."

A lot of people think that the way they are going to have their sins forgiven and get into heaven is to believe in Jesus *and* do something! They think by believing in Jesus *plus* their good works, they will get into heaven.

📖 Read Titus 3:5 and Romans 3:20. What does the Bible say to those who believe that they can earn God's acceptance and forgiveness if they do enough good works?

_____

_____

_____

No level of human effort is good enough to blot out our sins. We need another basis for acceptance.

7. If we have not lived a perfect life, if we have broken many of the Ten Commandments, then how will we ever be accepted before God? Answer: Through Christ taking our place.

What if we could stand before God and use the record of Jesus' life as the record of how we lived? Jesus lived a perfect life. He never sinned. Certainly, if we could stand before God and use Jesus' track record, God would accept us. As unbelievable as it sounds, God has provided Jesus' righteous life as a gift for us. Christ has paid the total penalty for our sins, and offers this righteousness as a gift to those who trust Him to give it to them.

📖 Read Romans 3:21–22. What do these verses say about our acceptance before God?

_____

_____

_____

"He saved us, not on the basis of deeds which we have done in righteousness, but according to His mercy, by the washing of regeneration and renewing by the Holy Spirit."

Titus 3:5

> *"He made Him who knew no sin to be sin on our behalf, so that we might become the righteousness of God in Him."*
>
> *2 Corinthians 5:21*

How can you or I become as perfect as God in order to get into heaven? The good news is that God Himself made the way.

He did so by doing two things. He provided a substitute to pay the penalty for all of our sins. Second, He provides the righteousness we need as a gift, the moment we believe in Christ. The substitute God provided to pay for our sins is Jesus. *"For Christ died for sins once for all, the righteous for the unrighteous, to bring you to God"* (1 Peter 3:18).

Read 2 Corinthians 5:21. What did Jesus do on our behalf?

_____

_____

Notice, there is a transfer, a crediting of our sins to Christ legally. Jesus knew no sin. He never committed *any* sin of His own. Also, He died so that we might be credited the righteousness of God "in Him." As Isaiah predicted generations before Christ's crucifixion, *"For he was pierced for our transgressions, he was crushed for our iniquities, the punishment that brought us peace was upon him and by his wounds we are healed. We all, like sheep, have gone astray, and each of us has turned to his own way, and the Lord has laid on him the iniquity of us all"* (Isaiah 53:5–6).

8. On what basis will God credit Christ's righteousness to sinners? The answer: He will do so on the basis of a repentant faith in Christ.
God can change the life of anyone who believes in Him. Why? Because the change is based on a repentant faith in Christ.

On what basis will God credit Christ's righteousness to sinners? The answer: He will do so on the basis of a repentant faith in Christ. What is repentance? And what is the relationship of faith and repentance?

What do you think of when you think of the word "repentance"?

_____

_____

_____

Repentance means to change one's mind, to change one's resolve or purpose, to come to a different opinion, to change one's view. Repentance is a genuine change of mind that affects the life (see Acts 26:20). Repentance and faith are two sides of the same coin: repentance the tales, or the negative side; and faith is the heads, or the positive side. Before a person can believe, he must change his mind about God, Christ, and himself, and only then can he put his trust in Christ for salvation. Whatever a person thought of Christ before, he now changes his mind and trusts him to be the Savior of his life.

A purely intellectual faith will not save. Faith is not merely acknowledging that Christ can bring us to heaven; faith is also the willingness to place our very lives in his hands, to fully commit ourselves to him as the means of delivering us to our destiny. There are no conditions for God giving salvation and only one for receiving it—that is faith.

Faith and repentance are inseparable in the same way that the command to come "here" cannot be fulfilled without leaving "there." True faith and repentance regarding one's salvation involve embracing right and rejecting wrong—one cannot be exercised without the other. Repentance entails not only a genuine change of mind about whether we are sinners and need Jesus as our Savior, but also a willingness to have our lives changed by Christ so as to bear fruit for him (Matthew 3:8). Accordingly, there's only one condition for receiving God's gift of salvation—saving faith—the kind of faith that entails repentance.

So, while no outward acts of obedience and willingness are necessary in repentance to get saved, nonetheless, the very nature of saving faith and true inner repentance is such that it naturally tends to lead people to become willing and obedient to Christ, and to turn from their sins. Once we trust Christ as our Savior, our spiritual maturity in Christ usually grows as we grow in the Lord. Obedience leading to good works is a natural *result* of saving faith, but is not a *qualification* for being saved.

To help us understand the meaning of repentance, here is an illustration from marriage. While you are dating, there might be a number of people you go out with. But when you decide to get married, you change your mind about continuing to date others (you repent) and choose just one special person. You show your willingness and the inner desire of your heart when you say "I do." Your commitment doesn't necessarily mean you will always be a perfect husband or wife, but that you are willing to live with that person in a loving way. You realize your decision will entail changes after you are married. And even though you may not know all the changes that your loved one may want, with your whole heart you decide to give yourself to the other person and enter marriage.

The same is true with Christ. You realize your decision may entail changes once you are saved. Even so, with your whole heart you decide to give yourself to Him and receive His gift of full salvation. You enter into a personal relationship with Christ.

As Dr. Erwin Lutzer has written,

> Let me be clear. When you come to Christ, you do not come to give, you come to receive. You do not come to try your best [to be saved]; you come to trust. You do not come just to be helped, but to be rescued. You do not come to be made better (although that does happen), you come to be made alive. . . . We must believe that Christ did all that is necessary and ever will be necessary for us to stand in the sight of God. If we have such faith, we will have assurance; we'll know that we have eternal life.[69]

📖 What does Romans 4:5 say faith provides?

_____

_____

_____

Paul shares here that faith is counted as "righteousness." In other words, faith is how we receive Christ's gift that provides us forgiveness and entrance into heaven. As Paul writes elsewhere, any person, regardless of background, has the opportunity to have this faith in Christ: *"This righteousness from God comes through faith in Jesus Christ to all who believe, there is no difference, . . ."* (Romans 3:22).

9. This sounds too good to be true. Do you mean to say that I don't have to do anything? I just have to put my trust in Christ and believe that He will save me, forgive me, and give me eternal life? The answer: Yes.

According to God, this is the only way to eternal life. It is completely by God's grace rather than our human efforts.

📖 Read Ephesians 2:8–9. Why is salvation and eternal life the result of God's grace?

_____

_____

_____

If God allowed us to reach heaven by our own efforts, we could then brag and boast if we achieved it. But God has created salvation as a free gift, so no one can boast about it.

10. Why would God provide such a gift for me? Answer: Because of His Love.

The Bible says that even before you were born, God loved you and desired to have a personal relationship with you. Therefore, He went ahead and made it possible for you to know Him.

📖 Read Romans 5:8. What does this verse say about God's love for us?

_____

_____

_____

Here we find that God loved us love before we ever thought of Him. What does Ephesians 1:4 say about when God started preparing us for salvation?

_____

_____

_____

Amazingly, God chose us before the creation of the world. God _wants_ to give us His gift of salvation. We can't earn that gift. We can only accept it or reject it.

APPLY Have you accepted this free gift from God? If you are not sure, settle this issue today before seeking to communicate these life-changing principles to others. You can write your thoughts or commitment to God below:

_____

_____

_____

_____

_____

_____

What verse in today's material connected with you the most? Write it down on a note card or piece of paper to carry with you throughout the day to remind you of God's free gift of salvation.

Jesus Is the Only Way

Last time, we addressed many of the key questions regarding sin and salvation. Today we transition to issues regarding faith specifically in Jesus Christ as the only way to salvation. Maybe you have heard others say or maybe even wondered yourself whether there are other ways to heaven. Maybe you've wondered if there are other religions that may lead to heaven in addition to Christianity. Yet when we turn to the Bible, God makes it very clear that there is one way to God, not many. The Bible presents these truths not with a desire for intolerance but rather to provide a clear presentation of how a person can experience eternal life with Christ.

11. God has provided only one way of salvation, not many ways.
There is only one way to receive the forgiveness of your sins and the gift of eternal life.

📖 Read John 14:6. How does Jesus explain that a person comes to God? What does Jesus say about Himself?

_____

_____

_____

_____

Jesus made it clear that He is the Way, the Truth, and the Life. He is the only way to come to the Father.

📖 What does Acts 4:12 state about who provides salvation?

_____

_____

_____

Here, we are instructed even further that salvation can be found in no other person than Jesus.

In 1 Corinthians 15:1–3, Paul provides further details explaining that Jesus is the only way:

> *"Now brothers, I want to remind you of the gospel I preached to you which you received and on which you have taken your stand. <u>By this gospel you are saved</u> if you hold firmly to the word I preached to you, otherwise you have <u>believed</u> in vain. What I received I passed on to you as of first importance, that <u>Christ died for our sins</u> according to the scriptures, that <u>he was buried,</u> that <u>he was raised</u> on the third day according to the scriptures, . . . whether, then, it was I or they, <u>this is what we preach,</u> and this is what <u>you believe</u>."*
> (1 Corinthians 15:1–3 [emphasis added]; see also Galatians 1:9).

Clearly, the New Testament does not teach multiple ways to God or that many roads lead to heaven. Jesus is taught as the only way to God.

12. How can I receive Christ into my life? Answer: by personal invitation.
Jesus teaches that He is the only way, but He also provides a very accepting and loving way to begin a relationship with Him.

📖 Read Revelation 3:10. How does Jesus describe His invitation in this verse?

_____

_____

_____

Here, Jesus makes His offer to anyone: "*If <u>anyone</u> hears my voice.*" To the person who does open the door to allow Christ into his or her life, Jesus promises to come in. Notice, the Bible says Jesus is knocking on your heart's door. He is powerful enough to beat it down–but He doesn't. He won't force His way into your life. But, if you want Him, you must open your life to Him, and trust Him to give you His gift of salvation.

📖 Read Romans 10:13. According to this verse, who can call on the name of the Lord? What will Jesus do to the person who does?

_____

_____

_____

You can open your life by praying (calling) to Jesus, telling Him you are receiving Him and what He did for you by faith.

13. We must believe in Christ.
Again, there is faith, but there is also a clear object of our faith—Jesus Christ. We must believe, and we must believe *in* Him.

📖 Read John 6:40. What happens to the person who believes in Jesus?

_____

_____

Here, Jesus teaches that the person who believes in Him will have eternal life. According to Acts 16:31, those who believe in Jesus will be saved. To be "saved," means to be rescued—rescued from sin and eternal separation from God.

📖 Read Romans 5:1. What other benefit are we given when we believe in Jesus?

_____

_____

_____

In addition to eternal life and forgiveness, this verse promises that we have peace with God when we believe in Christ. Again, this is apart from any works on our own behalf. According to Jesus, the work of God is to believe in the One He has sent (John 6:29).

14. Do I need a lot of faith to receive Christ? Answer: It's not the amount of faith; it's the object of faith.

Some people ask, "What if I don't feel that I have enough faith?" In one sense, it is not the *amount* of faith that saves you–it is *in whom* you put your faith. The question you should ask: "Is Jesus strong enough and dependable enough to save me when I ask?"

Picture a two-story building that's on fire. You happen to be on the top floor. The fire is coming up from the bottom, and there is no escape. You run to the roof and see a fire truck pull up to the front. Five big firemen get out and unfold a great, big net. They look up at you and say, "Jump!"

Your first thought is, "You have to be kidding! I'm two stories up. I can't jump."

But the firemen say, "Trust us. We'll catch you."

Now, you don't have a lot of faith, but with fear and trembling, you jump off the roof. As a result, the firemen catch you. It's not your faith that saved you; the firemen did. But they couldn't save you until you jumped.

Now, let's change the story a little bit. Picture another person on the roof with the fire coming toward him. This man sees the firemen. And unlike you, he has a lot of faith. He confidently jumps off the roof, only to discover halfway down that the firemen have no net; they are just standing around holding hands. How much will the man's faith save him then? You better have real firemen holding a real net, or your faith won't save you.

In salvation, it's not how much faith you have or how sincere you are. Rather, everything depends on the object of your faith. Have you placed your faith in a real Savior? It's not your faith that saves you. It's Jesus who saves you. You just need to place yourself in His hands.

The more deeply we believe that Christ did all that is necessary in providing our salvation, the greater our assurance will be when we place our trust in Him. We might begin with a small faith, but Christ said that faith the size of a mustard seed is all that is required (Luke 17:6). Over time our faith will grow. But whether our faith is little or much, it must be directed to Christ alone, for God accepts only those who accept His Son.

📖 Read Romans 10:9–10. What faith is required to begin a relationship with Christ?

_____

_____

APPLY Have you begun a relationship with Christ based on faith? How did it happen? How is this relationship impacting your life today?

_____

_____

_____

_____

_____

> *"For Christ died for your sins once for all, the righteous for the unrighteous, to bring you to God"*
>
> *I Peter 3:18*

YOU JUST HAVE TO ASK

The emphasis in our last day was that a relationship with Jesus Christ is based on faith. But we have yet to answer what is and what is not saving faith? Finally, we also need to make a decision individually to begin a relationship with Christ and share that decision with others.

15. What is saving faith?

R. T. Kendall described what saving faith is: "We are saved because we are persuaded that Jesus Christ is the Son of God, the God-Man, and that He paid our debt by His shed blood on the cross. . . . If we are not persuaded that Christ has paid our debt, there can be no assurance of saving faith, hence no assurance of salvation."

📖 Read what Jesus said about saving faith in John 5:24. What two elements are involved according to this verse?

_____

_____

While these are not works to earn our salvation, we are told that saving faith includes hearing the good news of Jesus Christ and believing in Jesus.

📖 What does John 6:40 say about the Father's will regarding saving faith?

_____

_____

_____

According to Jesus, it is the Father's will that everyone who believes in Jesus will have eternal life (John 6:40).

Imagine a ship filled with people crossing the Atlantic. In the middle of the ocean there is an explosion. The ship is severely damaged and slowly sinking. Most are dead, and the rest are rushing for the lifeboats. Now suppose one man doesn't know about the lifeboats, so he does not get aboard any. He doesn't have knowledge, so he is not saved. Suppose another man knows about the lifeboats and believes one will save his life, but he is grief-stricken over seeing his wife killed, so he chooses not to get aboard and dies with his wife. He has knowledge and mental assent, but he is not saved. Others believe the lifeboats will save them, and they get into the boats. They are saved by faith, that is they have knowledge, mental assent, and trust. However, it is not their faith that saves them—no matter how much they have. It is the boat that each one climbs in. Saving faith trusts Christ, and Christ saves.[70]

16. What is not saving faith?

Believing on Jesus is not just accepting facts about Him: that He is God, that He loves you, that He died on the cross and paid for your sins, and is willing to forgive you. True belief is when you transfer all of your trust to Jesus to save you personally. Knowledge about the facts of Jesus' life, death, and resurrection for us is not enough. I can believe two plus two equals four and have no personal commitment or dependence on anyone in believing those facts.

> *"For this is the will of My Father, that everyone who beholds the Son and believes in Him will have eternal life, and I Myself will raise him up on the last day."*
>
> *John 6:40*

Nicodemus, a ruler of the Jews, came to Jesus by night (John 3). He believed Jesus was a teacher who had come from God, but this was not enough for Nicodemus to have saving faith. He still had to put his trust in Christ for salvation. Nicodemus had to believe in Christ.

📖 Read Acts 26:27–28. Why didn't King Agrippa have saving faith?

_____

_____

_____

In Acts 26, the apostle Paul was on trial before King Agrippa. This king also apparently believed many facts about Jesus' life, but he was still not saved. Paul said, *"King Agrippa, do you believe the prophets? I know that you believe"* (Acts 26:27). Yet Agrippa did not have saving faith, for later he said to Paul, "In a short time you think to make me a Christian" (Acts 26:28).

Belief in the biblical sense encompasses trust. Trust in Christ is not just belief in facts about Christ, but personally entrusting oneself to Christ. For example, I (John) have spoken at conferences at Niagara Falls many times. I've learned that in the past, a famous tightrope walker strung a wire across Niagara Falls from the Canadian to the American side. In front of a stunned audience, he walked on the wire across the falls. He then put a wheelbarrow on the wire, filled it with about 225 pounds of sandbags and took the wheelbarrow across the Falls. When he came back, he said to the many bystanders, "How many of you think that I could take a *person*, put that person in the wheelbarrow, and safely take that person across the Falls and back?"

Everybody in the crowd said, "Yes! We believe you can do that."

But then he said, "All right, who will be the first to get in?"

You see, it's one thing to say you *believe*. It's another thing to entrust yourself personally to Christ. Saving faith takes place when you are willing to put yourself in Christ's hands and totally trust Him with your sins and your eternal destiny.

17. You can receive Christ now by faith through prayer (prayer is talking with God).
God knows our hearts and is not as concerned with our words as He is with the attitude of our hearts. The following is a suggested prayer that a person could use to place faith in Jesus Christ.

"Dear Lord Jesus, I admit to you that I have sinned. I know that I cannot save myself. Thank you for dying on the cross and being my sin-bearer. I believe that your death was for me, and I receive your sacrifice on my behalf. As best I can, I now transfer all of my trust from myself and anything that I would do, to you. I open the door of my life to you and by faith receive you as my Savior and Lord. Thank you for forgiving my sins and giving me eternal life. Amen."

You can pray your own prayer. It's not the wording of a prayer, putting up your hand, or walking an aisle in a church that saves you. It is the attitude of your heart and of trusting in the sufficiency of Christ that saves you.

James 5:16 tells us that, *"The prayer of a righteous man is powerful and effective."* Through prayer, we call out to Jesus and come to know Him personally.

Have you prayed to trust Christ personally? If not, use the above prayer to begin a relationship with God right now, writing your own prayer to God below. If you already have trusted in Christ in the past, briefly describe the circumstances regarding how it happened:

_____

_____

_____

_____

_____

_____

18. How do you know that Christ is in your life?
The Bible provides several promises to help you know that Jesus has come into your life:

"But as many as received Him, to them gave He power to become the sons of God, even to them that believe on His name" (John 1:12).

"These things I have written to you who believe in the name of the Son of God in order that you may know that you have eternal life" (1 John 5:13).

If you have entrusted yourself to Christ and have believed in Him, the Scripture says God wants you to *know*—not guess—that you have eternal life. *"Everyone who calls on the name of the Lord will be saved"* (Romans 10:13). He promises to save when you call and trust in Christ.

📖 What does Hebrews 13:5 say about God's faithfulness to us?

_____

_____

If Christ is in your life, know that He will never leave you.

APPLY If someone asked you how you knew that Christ was in your life, what would you say?

_____

_____

_____

_____

LESSON TWELVE — DAY FIVE

BRINGING IT ALL TOGETHER

U p to this point in this session together, our focus has been to clarify what it means to know Christ for yourself. Today, we bring it all together to help you in sharing your faith with others. In doing so, we have adapted an approach used in several outreach contexts built around three words: "prayer," "care," and "share."

Begin by Praying

We have already learned several principles about prayer, including the fact that apart from God we can do nothing (John 15:5) and that the prayer of a person who follows God is powerful and effective (James 5:16). Therefore, the foundation in sharing our faith with others is to pray for them. In the appendix of this book, we have provided a clear list of biblical principles for praying for those who do not believe. Here we will discuss a few of these verses and how they can be applied to those you desire to reach with the truth of Christ.

📖 Read John 6:44. What does Jesus say about people believing in Him?

_____

_____

_____

Our first step is to pray for God to create a desire to know Him in the people we want to reach.

📖 Read Matthew 9:38. What is another area we are to pray for regarding those who do not know Christ?

_____

_____

_____

_____

In addition to praying for God to draw others to Him, we are to also pray for people to share Jesus with them. In some cases, these will be prayers for other people. In other cases, these prayers will be for you to personally share your faith with others.

It Deepens Through Caring

In addition to praying for individuals to come to faith in Christ, another way we can help reach others is by caring for their needs. This could be anything from car repair to child care and anything in between. Jesus often cared for people regarding daily needs (providing food, healing sickness) in addition to His preaching and teaching. In doing so, it drew the attention of those who had been helped. They were then much more willing to listen to the message He had to share.

📖 Read Matthew 14:13–21. Why did Jesus heal these people and provide food for them?

_____

_____

_____

_____

Verse 14 tells us Jesus had compassion on them. This was a common theme in the life of Jesus:

"Therefore beseech the Lord of the harvest to send out workers into His harvest."

Matthew 9:38

The Compassion of Jesus

Situation	Scripture
When he saw the crowds, he had **compassion** *on them…*	Matthew 9:36
When Jesus landed and saw a large crowd, he had **compassion** *on them and healed their sick.*	Matthew 14:14
"I have **compassion** *for these people…"*	Matthew 15:32
Jesus had **compassion** *on them and touched their eyes.*	Matthew 20:34
Filled with **compassion,** *Jesus reached out his hand and touched the man.*	Mark 1:41
…he had **compassion** *on them, because they were like sheep without a shepherd.*	Mark 6:34
"I have **compassion** *for these people…"*	Mark 8:2

Think of a person you would like to tell about Jesus. What are some practical needs in that person's life where he or she could use help?

_____

_____

_____

_____

 Choose one of the areas of care you listed above to practice this week. Specifically note what you will do to show the love of Christ in a practical, everyday way.

_____

_____

_____

"The Great Commission is not an option to be considered; it is a command to be obeyed."

—J. Hudson Taylor

It Continues Through Sharing

We have spent the majority of this session sharing particular aspects of the good news of Jesus Christ to help you better understand your faith in Christ. However, it is vital to not only know Christ yourself or even to just pray for and help others. Ultimately, you must be able to respond as Peter wrote in 1 Peter 3:15–16:

"But in your hearts set apart Christ as Lord. Always be prepared to give an answer to everyone who asks you to give the reason for the hope that you have. But do this with gentleness and respect, keeping a clear conscience, so that those who speak maliciously against your good behavior in Christ may be ashamed of their slander."

Notice the order here. First, you must know Christ as Lord. Second, be prepared to give an answer. Hopefully this study has helped in these two areas. Third, we must do so with gentleness and respect. We are not attempting to win a court hearing. We are seeking to help people know Christ's love. Our example must communicate this at all times.

The result of these applications will be that even those who speak against our faith would be ashamed of doing so because our lives and actions are so powerful. Only God can change a heart, but He uses people who love Him as factors in the change process.

APPLY If someone asked you why you follow Christ, how would you answer? We are told to be prepared, so spend some time writing a one or two sentence response you could use in everyday conversation:

_____

_____

_____

_____

Spend some time in prayer with God right now for your outreach to others. Use the following prayer of Paul as a starting point for your own thoughts:

"For this reason I kneel before the Father, from whom his whole family in heaven and on earth derives its name. I pray that out of his glorious riches he may strengthen you with power through his Spirit in your inner being, so that Christ may dwell in your hearts through faith. And I pray that you, being rooted and established in love, may have power, together with all the saints, to grasp how wide and long and high and deep is the love of Christ, and to know this love that surpasses knowledge—that you may be filled to the measure of all the fullness of God.

Now to him who is able to do immeasurably more than all we ask or imagine, according to his power that is at work within us, to him be glory in the church and in Christ Jesus throughout all generations, for ever and ever! Amen. (Ephesians 3:14–21)

_____

_____

_____

_____

_____

_____

"Evangelism is not a professional job for a few trained men, but is instead the unrelenting responsibility of every person who belongs to the company of Jesus."

—Elton Trueblood

Notes

Appendix

Praying for Those Who
Do Not Believe

The Scriptures provide several ways for us to pray for those who do not know Jesus. However, it's often a daunting task to choose where to begin in praying for others. The following outline of verses is designed to assist in offering biblical prayers for those who do not believe.

Pray for God to draw the person to Himself.
"No one can come to me unless the Father who sent me draws him" (John 6:44).

Pray that the person would desire God.

"But in their distress they turned to the LORD, the God of Israel, and sought him, and he was found by them" (2 Chronicles 15:4).

"God did this so that men would seek him and perhaps reach out for him and find him, though he is not far from each one of us" (Acts 17:27).

Pray for an understanding and acceptance of God's Word.
"Consequently, faith comes from hearing the message, and the message is heard through the word of Christ" (Romans 10:17).

"And we also thank God continually because, when you received the word of God, which you heard from us, you accepted it not as the word of men, but as it actually is, the word of God, which is at work in you who believe" (1 Thessalonians 2:13).

Pray that Satan would not blind them.
"When anyone hears the message about the kingdom and does not understand it, the evil one comes and snatches away what was sown in his heart" (Matthew 13:19).

"The god of this age has blinded the minds of unbelievers, so that they cannot see the light of the gospel of the glory of Christ, who is the image of God" (2 Corinthians 4:4).

Pray that the Holy Spirit would convict of sin.
"When he comes, he will convict the world of guilt in regard to sin and right-eousness and judgment" (Matthew 16:8).

Pray for someone to share Christ with them.
"Ask the Lord of the harvest, therefore, to send out workers into his harvest field" (Matthew 9:38).

Pray God provides His grace and repentance.
"Repent, then, and turn to God, so that your sins may be wiped out, that times of refreshing may come from the Lord" (Acts 3:19).

"For it is by grace you have been saved, through faith—and this not from your-selves, it is the gift of God—not by works, so that no one can boast" (Ephesians 2:8–9).

Pray that they believe in Jesus as Savior.
"Yet to all who received him, to those who believed in his name, he gave the right to become children of God" (John 1:12).

"I tell you the truth, whoever hears my word and believes him who sent me has eternal life and will not be condemned; he has crossed over from death to life" (John 5:24).

Pray they confess Jesus as Lord.
"That if you confess with your mouth, 'Jesus is Lord,' and believe in your heart that God raised him from the dead, you will be saved. For it is with your heart that you believe and are justified, and it is with your mouth that you confess and are saved" (Romans 10:9–10).

Pray they grow and surrender all to follow Jesus.
"Then Jesus said to his disciples, 'If anyone would come after me, he must deny himself and take up his cross and follow me' " (Matthew 16:24).

"But whatever was to my profit I now consider loss for the sake of Christ. What is more, I consider everything a loss compared to the surpassing greatness of know-ing Christ Jesus my Lord, for whose sake I have lost all things. I consider them rubbish, that I may gain Christ" (Philippians 3:7–8).

"So then, just as you received Christ Jesus as Lord, continue to live in him, root-ed and built up in him, strengthened in the faith as you were taught, and over-flowing with thankfulness" (Colossians 2:6–7).

Notes

1. Adapted from Andrew E. Hill, Baker's Handbook of Bible Lists (Grand Rapids, MI: Baker Books, 1981).

2. Norman Geisler and William Nix, *A General Introduction to the Bible* (Chicago, IL: Moody, 1978), 36.

3. Frederick Kenyon, *The Bible and Archaeology* (NY & London, 1940), 288–289.

4. Kurt Aland, *The Problem of the New Testament Canon* (London: Mowbray, 1962), 18.

5. Geisler and Nix, *A General Introduction to the Bible*, 134.

6. Geisler, *Baker Encyclopedia of Christian Apologetics* (Grand Rapids, MI: Baker, 1998), 93.

7. Cited in the article by John Ankerberg, "If Jesus Wasn't God, Then He Deserved An Oscar," Part 3. Accessed at http://www.johnankerberg.org/Articles/apologetics/AP0701W3.htm.

8. This chart was adapted from four sources: 1) *Christian Apologetics*, by Norman Geisler, (Grand Rapids, MI: Baker Academic, 1988), 307; the article "Archaeology and History Attest to the Reliability of the Bible," by Richard M. Fales, in *The Evidence Bible*, compiled by Ray Comfort (Gainesville, FL: Bridge-Logos Publishers, 2001), 163; 3) *A Ready Defense*, by Josh McDowell (Nashville, TN: Nelson Reference, 1992), 45; and 4) the online article "Manuscript Evidence for Superior New Testament Reliability," by the Christian Apologetics and Research Ministry. Accessed at http://www.carm.org/evidence/textualevidence.htm#2.

9. Paul Feinberg, in *Inerrancy*, edited by Norman Geisler (Grand Rapids, MI: Zondervan, 1980), 294.

10. James M. Boice, Does Inerrancy Matter? (Wheaton, IL; Tyndale House Publishers, 1980), 15.

11. This section on inerrancy is adapted from John Ankerberg and John Weldon, "Biblical Inerrancy—part 3," Ankerberg Theological Research Institute, July, 1999. Accessed at http://www.johnankerberg.org/Articles/_PDFArchives/theological-dictionary/TD3W0799.pdf.

12. From http://www.biblein90days.com/homepage.

13. Ibid.

14. Adapted from Norman Geisler, "The Need for Apologetics." Accessed at http://www.normgeisler.com/.

15. Matthew J. Slick, "God Cannot Be Tempted," *CARM Resources*. Accessed at http://www.carm.org/doctrine/obj_Jesus_sin.htm.

16. C. S. Lewis, *Mere Christianity*, quoted at the C.S. Lewis website http://cslewis.drzeus.net/papers/mere.html.

17. Darrell Bock, in an interview on "A Response to ABC's the Search for Jesus," on *The John Ankerberg Show*, 2001.

18. Claire Pfann, in an interview on "A Response to ABC's the Search for Jesus," on *The John Ankerberg Show*, 2001.

19. Craig Evans, in an interview on "A Response to ABC's the Search for Jesus," on *The John Ankerberg Show*, 2001.

20. Ben Witherington, in an interview on "A Response to ABC's the Search for Jesus," on *The John Ankerberg Show*, 2001.

21. Much of this outline is adapted from Norman Geisler, *Systematic Theology, Volume Two: God, Creation* (Minneapolis, MN: Bethany House, 2003), 468–73. Used by permission.

22. For more on this issue, see Gleason Archer, *Encyclopedia of Bible Difficulties* (Grand Rapids, MI: Zondervan, 1982), 49.

23. Ron Rhodes, *Christianity According to the Bible* (Eugene, OR: Harvest House, 2006), 98–99.

24. For more on this issue, see Ken Ham, "Dinosaurs in the Bible." Accessed at http://www.answersingenesis.org/docs/2.asp.

25. Hugh Ross, "Why Shorter Life Spans?" *Facts for Faith*, Issue 5. Accessed at http://www.reasons.org/resources/fff/2001issue05/index.shtml#why_shorter_life_spans.

26. Matthew 26:17—27:61; Mark 14:12—5:47; Luke 22:7—23:56; John 13:1—19:42.

27. M. Hengel, Crucifixion in the Ancient World and the Folly of the Message of the Cross, J. Bowden, translator (Philadelphia, PA: Fortress Press, 1977), 22–45, 86–90.

28. R. Bucklin, "The Legal and Medical Aspects of the Trial and Death of Christ," *Science Law,* 1970; 10:14–26.

29. P. Barbet, A Doctor at Calvary: The Passion of Our Lord Jesus Christ as Described by a Surgeon, Earl of Wicklow, translator (Garden City, NY: Doubleday Image Books, 1953), 12–18, 37–147, 159–175, 187–208.

30. Ibid.

31. Thanks to the article "Crucifixion" for many of the concepts utilized in this section. Accessed at http://www.frugalsites.net/jesus/crucifixion.htm.

32. See the image at from http://www.pbs.org/wgbh/pages/frontline/shows/religion/jesus/crucifixion.html.

33. J. H. Charlesworth, "Jesus and Jehohanon: Archaeological Notes on Crucifixion," *The Expository Times*, February 1973, volume IXXXIV, No. 6. Accessed at http://www.pbs.org/wgbh/pages/frontline/shows/religion/jesus/crucifixion.html

34. C. Truman Davis, "A Physician Analyzes the Crucifixion," *New Wine Magazine*, April 1982. Accessed online at http://the-crucifixion.org/jesus/physician.html.

35. Geisler, *Baker Dictionary of Christian Apologetics* (Grand Rapids, MI: Baker Books, 1998), 128.

36. Mark 16:4.

37. All interview quotes in this chapter, unless otherwise noted, are adapted from interview transcripts on "Are Christians Intolerant to Claim Jesus Is the Only Way?" on *The John Ankerberg Show*, 2001.

38. "Empty Tomb," at http://en.wikipedia.org/wiki/Empty_tomb.

39. All interview quotes in this chapter, unless otherwise noted, are from interviews on "A Response to ABC's the Search for Jesus," on *The John Ankerberg Show*, 2001.

40. N. T. Wright, in an interview on "A Response to ABC's the Search for Jesus," on *The John Ankerberg Show*, 2001.

41. Edwin Yamauchi, in an interview on "Are Christians Intolerant to Claim Jesus Is the Only Way?," on *The John Ankerberg Show*, 2001.

42. Erwin Lutzer, *Where Was God? Answers to Tough Questions About God and Natural Disasters* (Wheaton, IL: Tyndale, 2006), 6.

43 Ibid, 83.

44. Geisler, *When Skeptics Ask* (Wheaton, IL: Victor Books, 1990), 62.

45. C. S. Lewis, in *The Problem of Pain*.

46. J. Hampton Keathley, III., "The Doctrine of Suffering," *Biblical Studies Foundation*. Accessed at http://www.bible.org/page.php?page_id=771.

47. Adapted from Rick Rood, "The Problem of Evil," LeadershipU. Accessed at http://www.leaderu.com/orgs/probe/docs/evil.html.

48. Lieghton Ford, *Good News is for Sharing* (Colorado Springs, CO: David C. Cook Publishing Co., 1977), 34.

49. David L. Hocking, "What We Believe," *The Biola Hour Guidelines* (La Mirada, CA: Biola University, 1982), 11–14. Accessed at http://www.bible.org/illus.php?topic_id=715.

50. Adapted from Ron Rhodes, *Christianity According to the Bible* (Eugene, OR: Harvest House, 2006), 272.

51. George Sweeting, *Today in the Word* (Chicago, IL: Moody Publishing, 1989), p. 52. Cited at http://www.bible.org/illus.asp?topic_id=1190.

52. Luke 24:25–27

53. J. Hampton Keathley, III., "Foundations for the Study of Prophecy (Revelation)," *Biblical Studies Foundation*. Accessed at http://www.bible.org/page.asp?page_id=1747.

54. Cited in Lehman Strauss, "Bible Prophecy," *Biblical Studies Foundation*. Accessed at http://www.bible.org/page.asp?page_id=412.

55. Renald E. Showers, *Maranatha Our Lord, Come!* (Bellmawr, NJ: The Friends of Israel Gospel Ministry, Inc., 1995), 17.

56. Tim LaHaye, *Revelation Unveiled* (Grand Rapids, MI: Zondervan, 1999), 10.

57. Showers, 256.

58. LaHaye, *Are We Living in the End Times?* (Downer's Grove, IL: Tyndale House Publishers, 2001), 6–7. Cited at http://www.leftbehind.com/channel endtimes.asp?pageid=510&channelID=71.

59. Ross, "Fulfilled Prophecy." Accessed at http://www.reasons.org/resources/apologetics/prophecy.shtml.

60. Alfred Edersheim, *The Life and Times of Jesus the Messiah*, one volume edition (Grand Rapids, MI: Eerdmans, 1972), 163. You can also view the electronic format of all 456 of these prophecies at http://www.levendwater.org/books/life_times_edersheim_appendix.pdf, 59ff.

61. Emil Borel, *Probabilities and Life*, M. Baudin, translation (New York: Dover, 1962), 28.

62. Thomas Huxley, *The Works of Thomas Huxley* (New York: Appleton, 1896), 153.

63. "Some Well-Known Miracles of Jesus," *Bible Resource Center*. Accessed online at http://www.bibleresourcecenter.org/vsItemDisplay.dsp&objectID=F38BB037-BFF6-47FE-A828BEA35B562AE8&method=display.

64. Benedict de Spinoza, *Tracctus Theologico-Politicus*, in *The Chief Works of Benedict de Spinoza*, trans. By R.H.M. Elwes, (London: George Bell & Sons, 1883), 1:83.

65. Interview quotes in this chapter are all from "A Response to ABC's the Search for Jesus," on *The John Ankerberg Show*, 2001.

66. Allan Bloom, *The Closing of the American Mind*, (New York: Simon & Schuster, 1987), 182.

67. Cited at http://www.christiantrumpetsounding.com/heavens_declare.htm.

68. Norman Geisler, "Questions About Miracles—Part Five," *ATRI*. Accessed at http://www.johnankerberg.org/Articles/_PDFArchives/theological-dictionary/TD3W0300.pdf.

69. Erwin Lutzer, *How You Can Be Sure That You Will Spend Eternity with God* (Chicago, IL: Moody Publishers, 1996), 45, 113.

70. M. Cocoris, *Evangelism: A Biblical Approach* (Chicago, IL: Moody, 1984), 77.

Notes

Notes

Notes

Notes

Notes

Notes